A JUST MEASURE OF PAIN

A JUST MEASURE OF PAIN

The Penitentiary in the Industrial Revolution, 1750-1850

MICHAEL IGNATIEFF

COLUMBIA UNIVERSITY PRESS / NEW YORK

Library of Congress Cataloging in Publication Data

Ignatieff, Michael.
   A just measure of pain.

   Reprint of the ed. published by Pantheon Books, New
York.
   Originally presented as the author's thesis, Harvard.
   "Bibliography of manuscript sources": p.
   Includes bibliographical references and index.
   1. Prisons—Great Britain—History.   I. Title.
[HV9644.I36   1980]   365'.941   80-12076
   ISBN 0-231-05057-7

Columbia University Press

New York   Guildford, Surrey

Columbia University Press Morningside Edition 1980

This edition reprinted by arrangement with Pantheon Books,
a division of Random House, Inc., New York

Printed in the United States of America

Acknowledgments for the use of illustrations appear on pages vii–ix.

Contents

Illustrations

Acknowledgments

•

I wish to express my gratitude to the Canada Council and the Central Mortgage and Housing Corporation Fellowship Program in Urban History for supporting my research and writing. To Professor David Landes, who directed my work when it was taking shape as a dissertation at Harvard University, I want to express my appreciation for his hard lessons and shrewd criticism. My thanks also to Professor John Clive, who saw this work through two earlier incarnations.

The following scholars and friends have offered detailed criticism of the manuscript: John Beattie, Douglas Hay, Edward Thompson, Peter Linebaugh, Tom Laqueur, Raphael Samuel, Margaret Eisenstein, Johanna Innes, Michael Donnelly, Jim Clifford, Kate Lynch, Frederika Randall, Ted Rosengarten, Jon Prude, Alex Keyssar, Eric Olson, Susan Barrowclough, Harvey Mitchell, and Ed Hundert. Their criticisms led me to rewrite the dissertation entirely and rethink the dimensions of the problem. They have done their best to point out errors of judgment and fact and should not be held responsible for those that remain.

Preface

It is easy to take prisons for granted. For those who manage to stay out of trouble with the law, prisons and punishment occupy the marginal place in the social awareness reserved for facts of life. Recurrently in history, however, prisons have forced themselves into the center of public attention. At such moments they cease to be taken for granted and become problematic.

Within the last decade the question of punishment has returned once again to the forefront of public debate. At such close range, it is difficult to account for the sudden "visibility" of incarceration, yet some reasons can be suggested. The rise of crime rates in most Western countries since 1960 has renewed the ever-recurring doubts about the effectiveness of incarceration as a deterrent. At the same time, the increasing pressure of numbers has acted to aggravate living conditions in often outmoded and decrepit institutions. Into overcrowded facilities have been cast a new generation of prisoners, more insistent on their rights than any in recent memory. In response to these pressures, reform-minded administrators have liberalized the security and custody of many institutions, arousing intense antagonism and overt opposition among guards. This combination of population pressure, public disillusionment, fumbling reform, prisoner militancy, and guard intransigence has broken the fragile order inside the prison. From this breakdown there has followed nearly a decade of hostage-takings, demonstrations, and full-scale uprisings. At first an American phenomenon, the prison revolt has spread to prisons in Spain, France, Canada, Britain, and Italy. It is still not clear whether such revolts have wrested anything more than token concessions. Yet undoubtedly, for the watching public, they have at least jolted prisons out of the realm of the taken-for-granted.

The uprisings and their suppression have also brought home the central role that coercion plays in the maintenance of the social order. This has come as a shock to many. When the American journalist Tom Wicker went to Attica and crossed the no-man's-land dividing the state troopers from the insurgent inmates holding D yard, he was

> acutely conscious . . . that he was leaving behind the arrangements and instruments by which his civilization undertook to guarantee him order and safety—the law with its regulations, officers and guns. At the moment he stepped from under their protection, he realized not only how much he ordinarily assumed their presence, without acknowledging or even recognizing it, but also how much, even in a civilization, law seemed to assume in the same unspoken manner, its dependence, at bottom, upon guns.[1]

As Wicker realized, prisons raise the issue of the morality of state power in its starkest form. Force being necessary to the maintenance of any social order, what degree of coercion can the state legitimately exert over those who disobey? Every debate about prison conditions and prison abuses is ultimately about such questions. Attica raised these old questions in new and urgent form.

At a time when the morality and tactics of punishment are under renewed scrutiny, it makes sense to return to the moment in eighteenth century Europe when John Howard, Jeremy Bentham, and Cesare Beccaria first placed prisons on the agenda of social concerns of their class. Out of their rethinking of the legitimate rights of the state over the confined came the reformative and utilitarian justifications of punishment that order our thinking to this day. Out of their attack on the abuses of the old institutions came the ambiguous legacy of the modern penitentiary.

These late eighteenth century reformers continue to define the terms with which we encounter the dilemma of punishment. In current debates, for example, there are influential voices urging us to return to the classical Beccarian verities of certainty and economy in punishment, while others seek to discredit the classical heritage by pointing to its major institutional legacy, the penitentiary.

This book describes the new philosophy of punishment as it emerged in England between 1775 and 1840. It is a social history of these new ideas, focusing upon the fight to embody them in the penitentiary, the resistence they aroused among prisoners and political radicals, and the ironies of intended and unintended consequences that followed their triumph in the 1840s. The book concerns itself with the emergence of the modern norms governing the exercise of power within prisons. It tries to establish why it came to be considered just, reasonable, and humane to immure prisoners in solitary cells, clothe them in uniforms, regiment their day to the cadence of the clock, and "improve" their minds with dosages of scripture and hard labor. Between 1770 and 1840 this form of carceral discipline "directed at the mind" replaced a cluster of punishments "directed at the body"—whipping, branding, the stocks, and public hanging. What new exigencies, what new conceptions of pain explain this decisive transformation in the strategy of punishment? The appearance of a new style of authority within the walls obviously must be linked to changes in class relations and social tactics outside the walls. Hence a study of prison discipline necessarily becomes a study, not simply of prisons, but of the moral boundaries of social authority in a society undergoing capitalist transformation. Ultimately, therefore, the book is an effort to define where the rich and powerful of English life placed the outer limits of their power over the poor, and how these limits were redrawn during the making of an industrial society.

London, 1977 M.I.

A JUST MEASURE OF PAIN

CHAPTER ONE

Pentonville

I

As soon as it was opened in 1842, Pentonville penitentiary on the Caledonian Road in north London became one of the controversial symbols of the age, extolled by some as the solution for the problem of crime, satirized by others, notably Thomas Carlyle and Charles Dickens, as a "palace for felons."[1] In a way that no prison today could ever be, it was both a focal point of public debate and one of the monuments of its day. Dukes and princes, foreign officials and county magistrates, politicians and preachers toured its vaulted galleries to see the new discipline of solitude and silence in operation.[2] Pentonville quickly became a model for prison architecture and discipline not only in England but in most of Europe. It represented the culmination of three generations of thinking and experimentation with penitentiary routine. Standing on a huge six-acre site, behind twenty-five-foot-high walls, it loomed over the workers' quarters around it, a massive, three-pronged fortress of the law.

In the 1840s a convict's day at Pentonville began at 5:45 A.M. with the clanging of a bell in the vaulted corridors.[3] The day then followed the cadence hammered out by that bell: wake-up, work, meals, chapel, exercise, inspection, lights out. Now, in the fifteen minutes before inspection, the convict pulled on his uniform, stowed his hammock, slapped water on his face, swabbed down the slate floor, and pulled out his cobbler's bench ready for work.

His cell was thirteen and a half feet from barred window to bolted door, seven and a half feet from wall to wall, and nine feet from floor to ceiling. Its contents were spare: a table, a chair, a cobbler's bench, hammock, broom, bucket, and a corner shelf. On the shelf stood a pewter mug and dish, a bar of soap, a towel, and a Bible. Except for exercise and chapel, every minute of his day was spent in this space among these objects. When the prison was opened in 1842, convicts spent eighteen months in solitude. As the authorities became familiar with its effects, the period in solitude was reduced, first to twelve and then to nine months.[4]

There were 450 prisoners at Pentonville, in identical cells ranged along the tiers of three blocks. The man in the next cell was only two feet away through the walls, and at night convicts tapped messages to each other like miners in a shaft. They risked punishment by doing this, since contact of any sort between prisoners was forbidden. Silence was the rule of the place, and a convict could be sent to the dark cells in the basement for a gesture, a sign, a smile, or a whisper.

At 6:00 A.M. the convict heard footsteps pause outside his cell door, and, without looking up, he knew that the warders' eyes were sweeping over him from the inspection hole, checking the order of his cell and making sure that he was at work at the cobbler's bench. Some of the convicts spent their days at the bench making and repairing prison boots. Along the corridors they could hear the tapping of hammers, and from the tiers above, the whir and clatter of looms as other prisoners wove the brown convict broadcloth in their cells. The labor was long and incessant, an hour and a half before breakfast, three hours before lunch, four hours in the afternoon. Once a day the taskmasters passed along the tiers stopping in each cell to pick up finished work and hand out new materials.

At 7:30 A.M. the trapdoor in the cell dropped open and a hand pushed forward a mug of cocoa and a piece of bread. As he ate his breakfast, the convict could hear the wheels of the food carts rolling along the tiers and the echoing sound of trapdoors flipping open. The prison was run like a machine. Breakfasts for 450 men could be delivered in ten minutes.

At 8:00 A.M. the cell doors swung open with a crash of levers and a grinding of bolts. Muster for chapel. Before stepping out on the catwalk, the convict donned a brown, spade-shaped mask with holes for his eyes. It was worn so that he would not be able to recognize friends and accomplices confined with him. The convict stepped forward out of his cell and stood at attention, staring across the stairwell at the other men—motionless but for the darting of their eyes.[5] On command, the masked figures marched along the catwalk, down the spiral iron staircase, through the high corridors illuminated by the flickering of gas jets, to the chapel.

The chapel was the brain of the penitentiary machine. It was divided into hundreds of boxlike compartments big enough for a body, ranged underneath a pulpit. The file of men halted at the chapel door. A duty warder went to a number machine and began to crank. When the convict's number appeared on the board, he stepped out of file and moved along the rows until he reached his box and closed the door behind him. The chapel filled with the sound of the rumbling of convict boots and the slamming of box doors. Perched on high chairs sat warders who swept the chapel with their gaze, looking for gestures among the mass of heads below them.

The chaplain mounted the stairs to the pulpit and began reciting the collects and prayers for the day. Then he read from the Bible:

> Make a joyful noise unto the Lord, all ye lands. Serve the Lord with gladness; come before his presence with singing.
> Know ye that the Lord he is God; it is he that hath made us, and not we ourselves; we are his people, and the sheep of his pasture.
> Enter into his gates with thanksgiving, and into his courts with praise; be thankful unto him and bless his name.
> For the Lord is good; his mercy is everlasting and his truth endureth to all generations.[6]

The chaplain followed the Bible reading with a sermon:

> Prisoners, were it in my power, I would touch your feelings and consciences to the quick—I would lay your hearts open to your own eyes—so that, by contemplating the desperate wickedness which lies there, you might be struck with horror at its appearance; so that before the gates of mercy are closed upon you for-

ever, you might turn to the Lord your God, and humbling yourselves before Him, in deep and sincere sorrow for your past lives, devoutly and unceasingly pray for the assistance of his blessed spirit in guiding you through the narrow way which leads to eternal life.[7]

After the last prayer, the convicts shouted an Amen. It crashed out in the silence like a volley.

After chapel, the convicts were marched to the yards for exercise. The yards were walled slivers of ground built around an inspection post. Each man stepped alone into one of the yards and began marching around in quick time. From the inspection post, a warder shouted commands to keep the prisoners moving:

> Left! Right! Left! Right!
> Move on, will you, come on, move!
> Step out there, man, step out!
> Halt!

At 9:00 A.M. the bell sounded for the infirmary call and prisoners with medical complaints mustered outside the doctor's office. The rest were marched back to their cells for labor, three hours of it before lunch and four after. While his hands worked, slicing boot soles off the upper, fitting the new soles, and stitching them down, a convict's mind was free to travel, back to the life he led outside, back perhaps to the day when he lost his freedom. . . .

On the day of his conviction, he was brought from the courtroom to the reception wards at Pentonville and made to strip naked. His clothes and possessions were taken from him, and the contents of his pockets—a lock of hair, a letter, loose change—were emptied into an envelope. His street clothes were bundled together and sent to the ovens for fumigation.

The naked convict was led into a wade-in bath and immersed in waist-high water smelling of carbolic acid. After drying himself, the convict marched to a desk behind which sat a prison officer with a large register open before him. While this officer copied down the information, another officer inspected the prisoner's body for scars, deformities, tattoos, and other "visible distinguishing marks." Most convicts were marked in some way. The members of London gangs like the Forty Thieves had black dots on each knuckle as a sign of their fraternity. Sailors usually were marked with tattoos of mermaids on their biceps. Miners could be identified by the black seams of coal dust worked into their chests

and backs, and dockers often wore trusses. All of these marks were
entered into the register:

George Withers, HF 4736

25, single, French polisher, reads and writes imperfectly. Larceny
from the person with a previous conviction for felony. Tried at
the Central Criminal Court, July 2, 1850. Sentenced to Seven
Years.

Address of Next of Kin: 7 Willmott's Buildings, Kent Street,
Boro'.

Height: 5'6". Weight: 132 lbs. Hair: Brown. Eyes: Grey. Build:
Middling.

Other Visible Distinguishing Marks: Small-pox scars left cheek;
scar above right eye. Anchor and Cross right bicep; G. W. and F.
R. tattoed on left bicep.[8]

After his identity had been fixed in the state record system, the
prisoner was led to the doctor for the medical inspection:

There now, place your feet on the mat. What's the use of your
going on the cold stones when there's a rug put out for you, eh?
Now open your mouth, and lift up your tongue. Did I say put out
your tongue, man? Lift it up, don't you hear?

Turn around, lift both arms. Lift the right leg, now the left. Hold
up the sole of the foot. Now, the other. Now stoop. Now stand
up. . . .[9]

Next, the prisoner's head was shaved and he was issued with his
prison uniform. The final act in the ritual of initiation was the issue
of his prison number. He was no longer George Withers, but HF
4736.

Once initiated, the convict was severed from the "outside." He
was allowed one visit every six months. A warder escorted him
down to a compartment divided in two by a screen and just big
enough for him and his visitor. The warder listened in on the
conversation, watched to see that nothing was passed between
them, and timed the visit with a sandglass. After fifteen minutes,
he led the convict back to his cell.

A convict was allowed to write and receive one letter every six
months. On the top of the prison stationery was a notice that read:

All letters of an improper or idle tendency either to or from
convicts or containing slang or objectionable expressions will be
suppressed. The permission to write and receive letters is given to
the convicts for the purpose of enabling them to keep up a connec-

tion with their respectable friends and not that they may hear the news of the day.[10]

At Pentonville there was a rule for everything, from what was allowed in a letter to the place of the mugs on the shelf of the cell:

ARRANGEMENTS OF PRISONERS' CELLS

Rules to be invariably suspended over the bedding. Pot-cover and pot under the table. Cell broom on the middle rail of the table. Soap, comb, brush on the rail in front of pot-cover. Drinking mugs, one at each corner of the table. . . . Books behind the salt box. Slate against the wall, behind books. Signal board in front of slate. Towel neatly folded on the clothes' pegs.[11]

The workday at Pentonville ended with dinner at six o'clock. The food carts whirred down the corridors, the trapdoors flipped down, and a tin plate slopping over with stew was thrust into the cell. The diet was an unvarying round of cocoa and bread for breakfast, gruel for lunch, stew for dinner, with occasionally some cheese or an onion.

After dinner, the prisoner had two hours to himself to pace the cell, to write a letter, to think, or to read from the Bible:

Hear my prayer, O Lord, and let my cry come unto thee.
Hide not thy face from me in the day when I am in
trouble;
incline thine ear to me: in the day when I call
answer me speedily.
For my days are consumed like smoke, and my bones
are burned as an hearth.
My heart is smitten and withered like grass so that
I forget to eat my bread.
By reason of the voice of my groaning my bones
cleave to my skin.
I am like a pelican of the wilderness; I am like an
owl of the desert.
I watch and am as a sparrow alone upon the house top.
Mine enemies reproach me all the day; and they that
are mad against me are sworn against me.
For I have eaten ashes like bread and mingled my
drink with weeping.[12]

At 9:00 P.M. the gas guttered and dropped, levers were pulled, and the double bolts crashed down across the cell door. Lights out. Lying on his hammock, in the blackness of the cell, a convict would hear the muffled tread of the warders, the click of their sabres against their leggings, and the clang as they punched in at the clocks posted around the galleries.

Sometimes, beneath all the other sounds, he would hear the patter of the prison telegraph through the walls and drainpipes. All night the men struggled through the stone to reach each other with laborious messages as faint as heartbeats.

The night was the hardest time of all. Sleep was likely to be fitful and restless. A convict waited out the night watching the stars or the clouds scudding across the moon through the cell window, and listening to the catacomb silence.

Sometimes there were screams. Men came apart in the loneliness and the silence. One prisoner kept dreaming that his sister was on the footpaths outside the wall, searching for his cell and calling his name. One midnight, he leapt from his hammock, ran to the window, clutched the bars with his fists, and began crying her name.[13] Another man saw burning lights in his cell and began screaming out in fear. Another saw snakes coiled around the bars of his window and rising out of the basin. One man became convinced that the hand that pushed the food through the trapdoor was trying to poison him. He began moaning about the hand at night. The warders came for the ones who cried out and took them down to the infirmary. There the doctor made out his report:

> Convict DF 4920: Five and a half months after admission, he was observed to be depressed in spirit and strange in his manner and conversation. He seemed to be oppressed by vague fears and apprehensions of impending evil which increased towards night. He stated that he was in constant dread of punishment for breaking the prison rules and was impressed with the idea that he had in some way incurred the penalties due to the commission of a serious offense. The prisoner's account was sufficiently confirmed by his haggard appearance.[14]

Every year at Pentonville between five and fifteen men were taken away to the asylum.[15] If they remained insane, they were confined in the asylum for the rest of their lives; if they recovered, they were brought back to finish their time. The authorities made sure that shamming madness offered no escape from the penitentiary.

If the solitude and silence drove some to madness, it drove a few others to suicide:

Convict RL 1412 was found dead in his cell at the unlocking at 6:00 A.M. on the 5th of June. The body was suspended from the iron window-frame of the cell by a rope of "waxed ends" as used by the prisoner at his trade of shoemaker.... On the prisoner's slate was found a letter addressed by him to his parent, in which he expressed a deliberate intention of suicide, assigning as the reason the difficulty of obtaining honest employment when liberated from prison, and the consequent probability of being driven to the commission of other crimes and in the end, murder.[16]

Some prisoners were broken by Pentonville, but others were not. A few fought its discipline openly. From the punishment reports there appears a picture of continuous struggle between the "incorrigibles" and the prison staff:

... for highly insubordinate conduct at all times, and on the 28 of September for using most violent and threatening language to his officer by saying, "You had better not begin with me or I'll be the death of some of you buggers." A hardened and most incorrigible prisoner.

... Twenty lashes of the birch to P. G. for placing his shirt and vest over his clothes and setting them on fire; also for declaring that, if kept in separate confinement, he would destroy the prison property till he gained his end....

... 5451, WR, aged 20, 24 lashes with the cat for destroying two blankets, two sheets, 1 mug, 1 mattress, 1 bowl. Further for threatening language saying, "I will do for some of you buggers," also for conduct of a most filthy and disgusting nature after eight previous reports....[17]

The birch and the cat were used on prisoners who assaulted or swore at warders. For lesser breaches of discipline, the usual punishment was a term in the dark cells, black holes in the basement of the building. While the normal punishment was three days in one of those cells, some convicts were locked in for as long as three weeks at a time. Some of the younger convicts endured almost continuous punishment in the cells before being broken by the cold and the dark. One told the warders he would never come out and vowed to kill the man who came in to get him. The warders pumped a mixture of smoke and cayenne pepper into the cell and within a minute the prisoner was pounding at the cell door, begging to be let out.[18]

Most convicts gave up trying to fight Pentonville. They settled into the routine, kept out of trouble, and waited out their time.

Some showed no apparent signs of being damaged by the silence and the solitude. But most prisoners bore its marks in some way.

Upon release, convicts were set off by the visible signs of confinement—the liberty clothing, the shaven head, and the pallor of their skin.[19] Then there were the marks inside. Those who observed prisoners upon their release noticed that many suffered from bouts of hysteria and crying. Others found the sounds of the street deafening and asked for cotton wool to stop up their ears. Still others frightened their families by a listless torpor that took weeks to shake off. Even those who thought they had got used to solitude found themselves dreaming about the prison long after. They would hear the bolts crashing shut in their sleep—and the screams.[20]

I I

Pentonville represents the culmination of a history of efforts to devise a perfectly rational and reformative mode of imprisonment, a history that stretches back to John Howard's first formulation of the ideal of penitentiary discipline in 1779. The point of departure for a social history of the penitentiary, therefore, is not the 1840s, but the 1770s, when the vision of the "total institution" first began to take shape out of two centuries of accumulated experience with workhouses, houses of correction, and jails.

The 1770s, our starting point, was not the first period to witness a wave of experimentation with modes of total discipline. Four earlier waves can be discerned, each providing precedents and examples for the 1770s. The earliest forerunner of the penitentiary was the Elizabethan bridewell or house of correction.[21] Jails for the confinement of prisoners awaiting trial had existed in the Middle Ages and limited use had been made of imprisonment as a punishment. But the house of correction was the first European institution in which men were both confined and set to labor in order to learn "the habits of industry." It is to this first use of confinement as a coercive education that we should trace the germ of the idea of recasting the character of the deviant by means of discipline.

In England, the bridewells were established for the confinement and deterrence of the host of "masterless" men thrown onto the highways by the dissolution of Catholic monastic charity, the breakup of feudal retinues, enclosure and eviction of cottagers, and the steady pressure of population growth on a small and over-stocked free labor market.[22] Similar institutions were built in Europe, the most famous being the Amsterdam Rasp House, established by the city fathers in the 1550s for the confinement of a horde of vagrants and camp followers uprooted by the Spanish War in the Low Countries.[23]

By later standards, there was nothing "total" about these early houses of correction. They were loose and disorderly places. An etching of the courtyard in the Amsterdam Rasp House, for example, shows a random miscellany of activity—a man being birched in one corner, two men rasping logs in another, a group of women being led on a tour, and a man beating a little boy. No one is shown to be clearly in command. The activity swirls around a statue of Justice, who looks down on this miscellany, fierce but impotent.[24]

The buildings were not designed to facilitate the exercise of control. The first house of correction was established in London in a reconverted royal palace, Bridewell, and later ones were set up in barns, alehouses, and outbuildings. A specifically institutional architecture was still two hundred years away.

The later history of the house of correction in the seventeenth and eighteenth centuries is unclear and awaits its historian. It appears, however, that confinement fell into desuetude during the Restoration and other punishments like whipping, branding, and the stocks assumed their place as the penalties of first resort. Historians have speculated that confinement had its greatest vogue in times of high unemployment, expanding population, rising prices, and falling wages. Such periods occurred between 1590 and 1640 and again between 1690 and 1720.[25] In such periods, confinement had the effect of withdrawing labor from the already overstocked market and putting it to the use of the state. In times of reduced unemployment and higher wages, on the other hand, noninstitutional punishments came back into vogue. Labor shortage conditions made it advantageous to keep the deviant circulating within the labor market as much as possible.

Obviously, labor market conditions are only one of the factors determining punishment strategy. Other factors such as fluctuations in cultural estimations of the proper social distance between "normality" and "deviance" were not determined by labor market conditions. Hence, until we have a more complete history of the seventeenth century house of correction than existing accounts have been able to provide, we will be unable to account for the ebb and flow of punishment in the period.

However, the acute distress and institutional overcrowding of the 1690s appears to have triggered a second wave of thinking about the "total institution." This was the period of John Bellers's Colledge of Industry, the Quaker businessman's scheme for a communitarian industrial colony within the walls of a disciplinary institution; the Bristol "Mint," a huge workhouse established in 1701 by the merchants of the city for the confinement of the vagabond poor; and John Locke's proposals for penal workhouses as a means of reducing the parishes' burden of maintaining the poor on outdoor relief. The efforts of Thomas Bray and the Society for the Reformation of Manners to reform Newgate and introduce solitary confinement for the untried also date from this period.[26]

In the 1720s, a crime wave in London and a sharp increase in the costs of poor relief in the countryside provoked another spate of institutional construction. Legislation was passed authorizing the construction of Houses of Maintenance and enforcement of the workhouse test as a means of stemming the rise in the rates. These houses would oblige the poor to "keep good hours; to refrain from spending their little Gains in Brandy Shops and alehouses to the destruction of their health; to be mutually assisting to each other in sickness or under the infirmities of age; and to avoid the temptations of pilfering and housebreaking to supply their wants."[27] Matthew Marryott, a Buckinghamshire overseer of the poor, managed thirty of these houses on a contract basis in the 1730s and served as a sort of traveling consultant on 150 more.[28] While about a dozen were built new, most were old poorhouses in which the poor were set to work spinning and weaving under conditions of tighter discipline. Marryott's heady dreams of fortune from the exploitation of his contracts foundered on the difficulties of enforcing labor among confined, and frequently aged paupers. By the 1750s workhouses had become once more somnolent shelters for the aged, the lunatic, and the orphaned.

The fourth wave of experimentation with the "total institution" was initiated by the landlords and clothiers of east Suffolk.[29] Between 1753 and 1771 nine huge workhouses called Houses of Industry were erected at a cost of between £10,000 and £15,000 each. Built at a time of local disquiet about the rising cost of poor relief, they were the most ambitious eighteenth century attempt to

exploit the labor of the workhouse poor and to deter the able-
bodied from "imposing" on the parish. Outdoor relief was cut
back, and as many as five hundred poor at a time were confined
in these huge barracks and set to work in the workhouse gardens
or picking and preparing wool for the Norwich clothiers. The
organization of these workhouses anticipates the compulsive regimens of isolation, and hard labor to be pursued far more thoroughly in the penitentiary. Upon entry the poor were stripped,
bathed, and clothed in uniforms. The institutional day marched to
a fixed cadence of activity. The doors were kept locked, and
paupers were allowed out only with the permission of the governor. In one house, special apartments or cells were reserved for the
punishment of the refractory. The agricultural laborers and artisans of east Suffolk fought back against retrenchment of their right
to outdoor relief. In 1768, they marched on Bulcamp House of
Industry and burned it to the ground.[30] To the tough-minded
advocates of the houses, however, this attack only vindicated their
deterrent value. In 1775, the Houses of Industry were at the height
of their reputation, living precedents for the makers of the penitentiary.[31]

Thus the 1770s were not, in an absolute sense, the starting point
for the history of the total institution. Yet the sheer quantity of
institutional construction in the following two decades entitles us
to look on that period as a moment of decisive acceleration. For
the first time, ideas of reformative discipline that had been experi-
mented with were put into practice on a large scale, in a dozen
country institutions. The vision of the total institution caught the
imagination of a reform constituency of politicians, philanthropists, and magistrates already engaged in the reform of Parliament
and public administration, the creation of the modern hospital, the
rationalization of the criminal code, and the tempering of its sanguinary penalties. The penitentiary was caught up in and borne
along by this much more widespread campaign for economic,
political, and social reform. It is this crescendo of reform activity
that marks the 1770s off from what had gone before.

In order to appreciate the nature of this reform campaign, it
is necessary to look closely at its major target, the structure of
eighteenth century criminal justice. To understand the new paradigm of assumptions about punishment that emerged in the 1770s,
we ought to investigate the paradigm it attacked.

Eighteenth Century Punishment

I

Before 1775, imprisonment was rarely used as a punishment for felony. At the Old Bailey, the major criminal court for London and Middlesex, imprisonments accounted for no more than 2.3 percent of the judges' sentences in the years between 1770 and 1774.[1] These terms of imprisonment were short—never longer than three years and usually a year or less—and they were inflicted on a narrow range of offenders—those convicted of manslaughter, commercial frauds, perjury, combining against employers, or rioting. The Wilkes and Liberty rioters and the London tailors, coalheavers, hatters, and sailors who demonstrated for higher wages during the 1760s were all punished with prison terms.[2] Only minor offenders of this sort received imprisonment. Those convicted for their part in the violent frame-cutting war in the Spitalfields silk trade in 1769 and 1770 were either executed or transported to America.

The rationale behind the judges' use of imprisonment in these cases is far from clear. In cases arising from conflicts between masters and workers, however, some of their criteria are revealed in the correspondence between the Lord Chief Justice and the Secretary of State in 1773 about the fate of seven journeymen weavers in Paisley convicted of rioting and combining against their employers.[3] The judge sensed that the execution of these men might so inflame the weavers that they would riot again or else emigrate to America en masse. The situation in the town was, as he put it, "very delicate." Deciding that a show of mercy was more likely to succeed in restoring order than a display of force, he ordered their punishments mitigated to imprisonment.[4] In Paisley, therefore, imprisonment figured in the tactics of concession as an "intermediate" and therefore "merciful" compromise between transportation and hanging. Apart from such special occasions, however, judges rarely used the prison as a place of punishment for major felonies.

For these crimes—the most frequent being highway robbery, housebreaking, beast stealing of various kinds, grand larceny, murder, and arson—the nominal penalty was death. The number of crimes bearing the punishment of death increased from about 50 in 1688 to about 160 by 1765 and reached something like 225 (no one was quite sure of the number) by the end of the Napoleonic Wars.[5] Some of these new statutes, the Riot Act for example, made offenses capital that had long been subject to lesser penalties. Others like the Black Act penalized activities that had not been criminal before, such as stealing hedges, underwood, fruit from trees, and timber; damaging orchards, hop-bines, or woodland; and taking fish from ponds or breaking the ponds to let fish escape.[6] The Black Act was enacted to make possible the conviction of the small farmers and tenants who were waging a guerilla-style resistance to the encroachment upon their customary forest rights by *nouveaux riches* estate holders and royal foresters in the woodlands of Hampshire and Berkshire. While passed as an emergency measure, the Black Act became a permanent addition to the armory of the game laws.[7]

Since other new statutes of the time have not yet received historical attention, it is not clear why this gradual and inchoate extension of the definition of crime took place over the course of the century. In very general terms it appears that the new acts reflected the commercialization of eighteenth century agriculture and the desire of landlords to make a profit from woodlands, ponds, and wastes on their estates, which they had previously ignored or allowed the poor to use without hindrance. The new criminal penalties were required as a legitimizing sanction for this assertion of property right because laborers, cottagers, and small farmers had customary use rights over game, wood, deadfall, peat, and other bounty of nature, rights which the gentry had formerly accepted as part of the binding order of custom in the countryside. Thus the extension of the definition of crime, brought about in the Black Act and in other new capital penalties, appears to represent the aggrandizement of the property rights of the gentry at the expense of common right and custom.[8]

In other cases, the criminalization of popular activity served the needs of commerce, the best example being the proliferation of new forgery and counterfeiting statutes in the first forty years of the century. The judge and jurist William Blackstone explained the growth of law in this field as an attempt by banking and commercial interests to secure protection for the new systems of paper credit and exchange created in response to the rise of a national market.[9] These interests apparently succeeded in convincing both the Crown and the judiciary that a rigorous enforcement of these new laws was of critical importance to commerce. Throughout the century, two-thirds of those convicted of forgery were actually executed.[10] With the exception of murder, no offense was more relentlessly punished.

In theory, the Bloody Code, as the criminal law was popularly known, appeared rigid and inflexible, prescribing death alike for murder and for the forgery of a petty deed of sale. In practice, the application of penalties was flexible indeed, allowing a large measure of play for judicial discretion, executive clemency in response to appeals for mercy, or exemplary displays of terror. The Paisley example already cited illustrates how judges could use their powers to temper the code in the direction of mercy. The same power, of course, could be used in the opposite direction. In 1775, two Halifax justices secured the approval of the Secretary of State to hang the body of Matthew Normanton, convicted for the murder of the supervisor of excise in Halifax, in chains on the top of Beacon Hill. It was unusual to hang a man in chains, the justices admitted, but they had been urged to do so by "very many respectable Gentlemen and Merchants in and about Halifax and Rochdale," who felt that "such a notorious and public example" would deter others from making counterfeit coin, the crime that Normanton had been engaged in when discovered by the luckless exciseman.[11] A legal system that allowed the judges to heighten the symbolic impact of the hanging ritual in response to the pressures of "respectable" citizens (or to forego it entirely in response to rebellious weavers) was obviously more flexible than its unvaryingly bloody penalties gave it the appearance of being.

There were of course more merciful uses of judicial and executive discretion. Judges in the Home Circuit during the 1750s, for example, pardoned a third of the offenders they had sentenced to death and sent them to transportation instead.[12] Their pardon power enabled them to mitigate capital penalties in "special" or "deserving" cases, to save "respectable" offenders who could enlist a patron to plead for their lives, and in general to temper the severest criminal code in Europe with an elastic measure of mercy.

The code was also modified in practice by the traditional privilege of benefit of clergy. At first a privilege enjoyed by clerics who came before the royal courts of the Middle Ages, a privilege that was then extended gradually to other groups until 1705 when it was made available to men and women universally, benefit of clergy was a plea that offenders convicted of a range of minor capital crimes could enter to save themselves from the gallows. After claiming their "clergy" (until 1705 giving proof of literacy by reciting a passage of scripture, the "neck verse," and after 1705 granted without requirement of proof), they were whipped or branded on the thumb and then discharged.[13] It is not clear which offenses were covered by benefit of clergy. Blackstone indicates that while the privilege was extended to everyone in 1705, the range of crimes for which it could be claimed was reduced considerably thereafter because branding on the thumb came to be regarded, in his words, as "next to no punishment." Thus in 1717 an act was passed disallowing the privilege of clergy in housebreaking cases. Blackstone observed that housebreaking was made capital because of "improvements in trade and opulence"—in other words, because of the increasing number of commercial properties and places of business requiring protection.[14] In practice, those convicted of capital offenses newly withdrawn from benefit of clergy or for those new offenses rendered capital for the first time since 1688 tended to be transported rather than executed. As J. M. Beattie's study of sentencing decisions in Sussex and Surrey has shown, those convicted of new capital offenses were much less likely to be "left for execution" by the judges than those convicted for the traditional capital offenses such as murder, burglary, or highway robbery.[15] By means of this differential enforcement of new and old penalties, therefore, Blackstone believed that the expansion of the capital statutes had proceeded without compromising their moral legitimacy.

The judicial habit of pardoning capital offenders, especially those convicted for newly criminalized activities, contributed to the rapid growth of transportation as a punishment. So did the act passed in 1717 changing the punishment for petty larceny from whipping to transportation. Other acts likewise substituted transportation for whipping as a penalty for robbery, minor kinds of coining, and the receipt of stolen goods.[16] While the substitution of transportation for whipping and branding might be interpreted, like the expansion of the Bloody Code itself, as an attempt by Parliament to increase the rigors of traditional punishment, the rising rate of pardons in capital cases after 1750 appears to indicate the opposite tendency among judges—a growing doubt about the fairness of visiting minor infractions with the punishment of death.[17]

Likewise, certain practices of juries suggest their unease about sending petty offenders to the gallows. Juries, like judges, were allowed a measure of discretion in arriving at verdicts. It was common for them to commit the "pious perjury" of convicting those charged with grand larceny (a capital offense) with petty larceny (punishable by transportation) by valuing the goods stolen at less than a shilling regardless of their real value.[18] Comments by legal authorities like Blackstone suggest that "pious perjury" became more common after 1750, indicating growing public dissatisfaction with the Bloody Code.[19]

Similarly, scattered evidence that victims of some crimes chose not to prosecute for fear of sending offenders to the gallows was cited by criminal law reformers of the time as proof that public opinion was no longer in sympathy with the Bloody Code.[20] But no study has yet shown that the incidence of dropped or abandoned prosecutions increased during the century. Even were such a study to exist, it would be risky to ascribe prosecutors' behavior to moral scruple alone. Besides moral anguish at sending a man to the gallows, the costs and delays of justice would have been enough to deter many from prosecuting.[21] Accordingly, some dropped prosecutions, gave "faint evidence" in court in order to spare the lives of those they prosecuted, or begged the justices to punish them "otherwise" than by hanging.[22] Obviously, a complex calculus ordered a prosecutor's, judge's, or juryman's conception of the proportionality of punishment to crime. We do not know enough about this calculus to explain why it changed during the eighteenth century. All we have is the clear fact that both Parliament, the judiciary, and the jury cooperated in extending the use of transportation as a punishment in place of both whipping and hanging. By the late 1760s, transportation to the American colonies for terms of seven years, fourteen years, or life accounted for 70 percent of all sentences at the Old Bailey, and a higher though indeterminable percentage if we include those convicts whose death sentences were later commuted.[23]

While the act of 1717 made petty thieves liable for transportation, many judges continued to sentence them to public whippings, occasionally accompanied by short imprisonments. It is difficult to discern the criteria, apart from personal whim, that guided the choices of the Old Bailey judges. A baker's apprentice is convicted in 1770 of running off with his master's breadbasket, value 18 pence, and is given a whipping. An agricultural laborer is whipped at the same sessions for stealing twelve shillings from a fellow lodger in rooms above a pub. Yet a ticket porter steals goods worth only 4 shillings from a tallow chandler and is transported.[24] Apparently, the value of goods stolen was only one of several criteria defining the "seriousness" of a crime. It seems that judges ordered whippings in lieu of transportation in cases that were a first offense or in which the theft was committed by a servant or apprentice against his master. While the criminal law looked on thefts by servants as more serious than simple larceny by strangers, since the trust implied by employment had been violated, in practice masters seemed to have pleaded with the judges for leniency, offering to take servants back into service after chastisement. Possibly the general conditions of labor shortage in the 1760s and '70s influenced the masters' desire to have their servants whipped rather than shipped beyond the seas.[25] Whatever the reasons for the judges' decisions, the Old Bailey Proceedings reveal that they ordered whippings, occasionally accompanied by imprisonment, in 14.2 percent of their sentences in the period between 1770 and 1774.[26]

Like hanging, whipping was a public ritual inflicted by a parish officer or court official for the edification of the populace. Hence it was considered important to stage the ritual at a time and a place sure of attracting attention. The Surrey justices seem keenly aware of this in a sentence recorded in their order books in 1775:

Robert Snowdon ... convicted of felony is committed to your custody for the space of three months and on Saturday the 15th instant between the hours of 12 and 2 of that day to be stripped from the middle upwards and tied to a cart's tail and publicly whipped from the stockhouse round thro' the Market Place at Kingston upon Thames and back again 'til his back is bloody and at the end of the said three months to be discharged without fees.[27]

Like their colleagues in Halifax who orchestrated the hanging of the coiner in chains, the Surrey justices displayed that shrewd sense of theater and timing on which the deterrent effect of ritual punishment relied.

Another punishment of public shame was the pillory. Offenders who aroused a high degree of public indignation, such as shopkeepers found using false weights, persons convicted of hoarding or speculating in the grain trade, or persons convicted of homosexual assault, were locked in head stocks in a marketplace or in front of a jail and sentenced to endure an hour of the crowd's abuse.[28] Such a punishment relied for its enforcement on the feeling of the populace. It could be a horror if the crowd pelted them with stones and offal, but if it sympathized with them there was little the magistrate could do to prevent the hour in the pillory from becoming a public triumph. Such was the case when Daniel Isaac Eaton, the aged and distinguished radical printer, was sentenced to an hour's pillory in Newgate in 1813. Much to the government's chagrin, Eaton's head was garlanded with flowers and he was brought refreshment during his ordeal, while the police and magistrates in attendance were reviled and abused.[29]

All such ritual punishments depended for their effectiveness as a ceremonial of deterrence on the crowd's tacit support of the authorities' sentence.[30] Hence, the magistrates' control of the ritual was limited. In theory, the processional to the gallows and the execution itself were supposed to be a carefully stage-managed theater of guilt in which the offender and the parson acted out a drama of exhortation, confession, and repentance before an awed and approving crowd. The parson's sermons were set pieces on social obligation, delivered at the gallows and subsequently hawked in the streets with an account of the offender's life and descent into crime. One sermon delivered at the Tyburn gallows in London in 1695 conveys the flavor of these set pieces. Addressing the condemned men, nooses already around their necks, the parson intoned:

Sad is the state, deplorable the condition you have brought yourselves to; adjudg'd by the laws of your country; and by them
accounted unworthy any longer to live, unworthy to tread this
earth, to breathe this air; and that no further good, nor further
benefit to mankind can be expected from you but only the example of your death; and to stand like marks on fatal rocks and sands
to warn others from the same ruin for the future.[31]

The trouble was that if the spectators did not approve of the
execution, the parson would find his worthy sentiments drowned
in the abuse welling up from the crowd. Moreover, the crowd had
a highly developed sense of the rights due the condemned, and if
any of these were abridged, they were quick to vent their wrath
on the authorities, especially if the condemned also happened to
contest the justice of the execution itself. This double sense of
outrage, at rights ignored and at offenders wrongfully sacrificed,
drove the Tyburn crowd attending the execution of the silk weavers who cut looms during the Spitalfields agitation of 1769 to
attack and destroy the sheriff's house after the execution. What
irked them particularly, one of them told a gentleman bystander,
was that the sheriff had not even had the decency to give the men
time to say their prayers. This was a courtesy that the poor of
London defined as one of the rights of the dying.[32]

How explicitly the authorities accepted the notion that the
condemned had rights is not entirely clear, though it is obvious
that they treated them with care. Their last wishes and dying
words were accorded a special degree of attention by prison officials, sheriffs, and parsons. These officials tried to maneuver offenders into using the influence of their dying words to exhort the
crowd to eschew crime and give obedience to the civil power. But
the authorities could not guarantee this happy outcome. The
offender had a choice of roles in the theater of death, either the one
of contrite repentance offered by the parson, or the defiant and
drunken one offered by the crowd. Such a choice necessarily
followed from the fact that the crowd and the state shared in the
making of the ritual. Not surprisingly, many offenders embraced
the role offered by the crowd and the chance of lingering on in
popular memory as a "game" death. Sometimes the dying man
would go so far as to contest the justice of his sentence, thus
turning the ritual from a vindication of the law into a public
disputation about its justice. This happened on the sixteenth of

June, 1693, when two printers condemned for high treason mounted the gallows at Tyburn:

> The ordinary [parson] exhorted Anderton and Dudly to beg of God they might be examples of true Repentance and to warn the people by their sad untimely end. They did not; and therefore the ordinary commanding silence spoke thus; be persuaded by the sight of these dying Persons, not to contrive any thing against the Government of this Kingdom, God will bring it to light and in Justice punish it. And he exhorted the people not to Prophane the Sabbath; which all bewail when they come to die publickly as that sin which brings on all other crimes. Anderton told the spectators that his sentence was very hard and severe. I [the parson] told him that he had endeavoured to overthrow the established government. He said that he forgave his judges. I replied that they needed not his forgiveness.[33]

Once the condemned or the crowd refused to play an accepting part, there was little the state could do to prevent the solemn ritual of processional and execution from being turned into a shambles. With only a small staff of constables at their disposal, and with resort to the army excluded except in situations of ultimate peril, the magistrates could only look on while the rabble surged beside the cart, taunting the parson and cheering the drunken and frequently insubordinate malefactor.[34]

This inversion of the ritual, from a solemn act of the state to a popular bacchanal, led some eighteenth century observers to doubt the efficacy of public hanging as a deterrent. Bernard Mandeville partly attributed the crime wave of the mid-1720s in London to the ribald and riotous defiance of the law at the Tyburn gallows. Such scenes, he concluded tartly, allowed the poor to believe that there was nothing to a hanging but "an awry neck and a wet pair of breeches."[35] Since Mandeville was not alone in doubting the efficacy of a ritual so easily perverted by the crowd, the question arises as to why English justice continued to rely on ritual punishment throughout the eighteenth century (and halfway through the nineteenth as well.) The philosopher and clergyman William Paley maintained that hanging persisted because occasional, highly public ceremonials of the sovereign's wrath were a more economical and more constitutional method of deterring crime than the "French" alternative, a centralized police patrolling the streets and deterring crime by intruding upon the lives and liberties of subjects.[36] The "English" conception of order implied a selective, highly visible dispatch of incorrigible malefactors, while the "French" method entailed a bureaucratized pursuit of even trivial offenders. From what we know of the French rural police under the *ancien régime*, this English account was a fanciful exaggeration of both their efficiency and their intrusiveness.[37] Nevertheless, the mythology of the "French police" helped to cast a libertarian glow over the English alternative of public execution.

Moreover, the public character of hanging was lauded as a guarantee of the victim's rights. The London magistrates John and Henry Fielding suggested in the 1750s that "private" executions be conducted within the gates of the prison so that the state could prevent the event from being perverted into a ritual of defiance.[38] Interestingly, the idea received no support, not even from those who were appalled by the bacchanal of Tyburn. If executions were conducted in prisons, who would ensure that the hangman actually executed the person condemned for the crime? There were fears, at least in popular myth, of rich malefactors bribing hangmen to substitute some poor wretch in their place. Only a public execution, played out in front of a crowd, could prevent such ghastly corruptions.

The crowd knew its role as witness in these matters. It knew, for instance, that it was there to ensure that the victim was not put to excessive suffering through the malice or incompetence of the hangman. An executioner who botched the job, who allowed the victim to twist and strangle, risked being torn apart by the mob.[39] The public character of punishment, therefore, had an obvious rationale as a protection of the liberties of the subject.

The rationale for these rituals must be emphasized, since nineteenth century reformers largely succeeded in convincing the public that these events were degrading and brutal spectacles. In this as in so many other matters, the historian's task is to recover the history of eighteenth century punishment from the version of it given us by the men and women who led the attack upon it.

II

Before 1775, major crimes were punished with banishment, whipping, hanging, or the pillory rather than confinement. Imprisonment, however, was used by local justices of the peace to punish summary offenses—those minor infractions that they had the power to adjudicate themselves without sending the offender to trial in the higher courts of assize or quarter sessions. The JPs' powers of summary justice increased so much during the eighteenth century that William Blackstone expressed concern that summary justice might eventually supplant jury trial altogether.[40] By 1755, it appears that the JPs had the authority to imprison for the following offenses: vagrancy, desertion of family, bastardy, disobedience and embezzlement in most trades, theft of turnips and other field produce, taking of firewood and deadfall from privately owned woods, and minor game law offenses.[41] Many of these offenses—vagrancy, for example—had always been punishable by imprisonment; now, in the eighteenth century, the scope of such punishable offenses was extended. The Vagrancy Act of 1744 assembled together categories of social condemnation that had been accumulating in various statutes since the days of Elizabeth and added new ones to bring it up to date with the labor discipline needs of eighteenth century masters. Besides giving magistrates the power to whip or imprison beggars, strolling actors or gamblers, gypsies, peddlers, and "all those who refused to work for the usual and common wages," it empowered magistrates to imprison wandering lunatics and "all persons wand'ring abroad and lodging in alehouses, barns and houses or in the open air, not giving a good account of themselves."[42]

In addition to their responsibilities under the Vagrancy Act, magistrates were empowered by the Statute of Artificers of 1604 to whip or imprison any servant or apprentice who left employ before his contract expired, who failed to give a quarter's notice, who struck his master, or who in any way disobeyed.[43] To back up these provisions a number of solitary cells were built in the London bridewell and the House of Correction, Clerkenwell, for the confinement of runaway or disorderly apprentices whose youth required their isolation from hardened offenders.[44]

The game laws also gave magistrates powers of imprisonment for the enforcement of wage discipline in the countryside. In the course of the century, many game law offenses were changed from indictable to summary crimes, because summary justice was cheaper and faster than jury trial and therefore more convenient to the squires who brought the prosecutions.[45] The trend toward summary adjudication of poaching meant a greater resort to imprisonments and whippings, since the justices in summary session were not empowered to sentence offenders to death or transportation. It is not clear, however, what guided the magistrates in choosing whipping or imprisonment.

The social functions of such punishment, nevertheless, were clear. The purpose behind penalizing the taking of rabbits, Blackstone said, was not only to reserve them as sport for the rich but also to prevent "low and indigent persons" from being lured away by the hunt from "their proper employments and callings."[46] Wage discipline required that alternative or supplementary sources of subsistence, like petty theft or the taking of game, should be sealed off as much as possible. Only in a labor market whose exits were effectively barred by the prohibitions of criminal law could the full dependence on wage income necessary for disciplined labor become possible. The preambles to certain game statutes made their labor discipline functions explicit:

> Whereas great mischief do ensue by inferior tradesmen, apprentices and other dissolute persons neglecting their trades and employments who follow hunting, fishing and other game to the ruin of themselves and their neighbours, therefore, if any such person shall presume to hunt, hawk, fish or fowl (unless in company with the master of such apprentice duly qualified) he shall ... be subject to the other penalties ... [i.e., varying terms in the house of correction].[47]

In the growth of the laws of embezzlement, most of which were subject to JPs' summary jurisdiction, one can detect the same attempt to "criminalize" the customs of the poor in the name of work discipline. Embezzlement statutes were used by masters in such outwork trades as textiles, toolmaking, iron and steel smelting, and tailoring to control the dispersed labor force who worked up the raw materials supplied by the master in their own cottages. In the woolen and cotton spinning and weaving trades, the statutes were used against cottage workers who oiled goods or stretched their length to increase the price the master had to pay for them.[48]

In the eighteenth century, outwork masters became more sensitive to such practices, which thwarted their efforts to monopolize the sale and disposition of both raw materials and finished goods. The workers, for their part, considered the scraps left over from the work process as theirs by right. It was their resistance that led the masters to resort to law to back up their assault on these prerogatives and customs.[49] In the woolen trade, for example, eleven new embezzlement statutes were passed from 1725 to 1800, more than in the whole previous history of the industry.[50] As time went by, the severity of these statutes increased. In 1749 the penalty for embezzlement was usually fourteen days in the house of correction; by 1777 it had risen to three months.[51] To back up their offensive, the masters banded together in associations for the prosecution of embezzlement, much as the rural gentry formed associations for the enforcement of the game laws and the pursuit of poachers.[52] These associations funded prosecutions and hired inspectors to search workers' homes for concealed and "embezzled" materials. Behind this offensive lay the employers' ultimate weapon, a term in the bridewell.[53]

Reviewing these game, vagrancy, and embezzlement statutes confirms Blackstone's impression that the magistrates' powers of summary justice increased during this period. It suggests, as well, that the new powers to whip and imprison were meant to support the attack of cost-conscious employers on the customs and work habits of the rural labor force. What is much less clear is how rigorously these new statutes were enforced. Masters had their own powers of chastisement; indeed the Statute of Artificers expressly sanctioned moderate use of the rod on the churlish or disobedient servant. In what situations would a master chose to punish workers himself, and in what circumstances would he drag them before the justice? Were large-scale employers more likely than smaller masters to enlist the agencies of the state in their support? Or was it the other way round? And when disobedient servants were brought before the justices, which ones were ordered whipped and which to prison? In the case of vagrancy, how energetically did beadles and constables pick up the wanderers, the fugitives, and the rogues? Answers to these questions would take us much closer to an understanding of the developing role of the law in labor discipline in this period.

Unfortunately, the study of summary justice does not provide us with a firm basis for conclusions. Scattered evidence, however, suggests that before 1775 enforcement of these statutes was selective indeed. From his experience as a Bow Street magistrate, the novelist Henry Fielding concluded in 1751 that the "business" of a JP had increased more rapidly than his powers of enforcement. He was unable to suppress vagrancy in London because corrupt and inefficient parish constables and beadles had little incentive to bring the ragged people before the bench.[54] At Fielding's urging, Parliament empowered magistrates in 1752 to reward constables for vagrancy arrests.[55] While some commentators believed that this effort to make a trade out of the harassment of destitution increased the rigor of enforcement, the poor law committee's inquiry into the vagrancy laws suggests that it was a more usual practice, at least between 1772 and 1775, to whip vagrants or return them to their parish than to confine them at county expense.[56]

As for other petty offenders subjected to summary justice, there is evidence, again of a fragmentary sort, to suggest that the strategy of English justice was still to ignore the small fry and concentrate instead on the highly publicized dispatch of major offenders. Certainly this is how the late eighteenth century reformers perceived the law's bent. Indeed, their most frequent criticism of the old law was that by failing to repress minor offenses it allowed petty criminals to proceed unimpeded to the commission of more dangerous offenses.[57]

John Howard's prison census of 1776 listed only 653 petty offenders in confinement in England and Wales at the time of his survey, and while his figures obviously do not include those who were whipped, fined, or discharged without confinement, they do seem to confirm Fielding's view that the JPs lacked the police necessary to enforce their new summary powers.[58] The figures might also be taken to mean that masters and squires preferred to inflict their own sanctions for petty disobedience rather than resorting to the justice of the peace.

These petty offenders accounted for only 15.9 percent of the total numbers confined at the time of Howard's visit. Of the rest, 59.7 percent (2,437 individuals) were debtors, and 24.3 percent (994 individuals) were felons, divided into three classes—those awaiting trial, those convicted and waiting for execution or transportation, and those few serving actual sentences of imprisonment. From these figures it is apparent that the prison before 1775 was more a place of confinement for debtors and those passing through the mills of justice than a place of punishment.

The restrained role of imprisonment as a punishment and the generally inefficient pursuit of minor, work-related offenses may indicate that the state, and the magistrates in particular, played less of a role in the regulation of labor market discipline in the eighteenth century than it had done either prior to 1640 or than it was to do after 1815. After 1660, the provisions of the Statute of Artificers requiring magistrates to regulate wages, fix prices, and bind out apprentices were allowed to lapse.[59] The memory of

Stuart "tyranny" acted to restrain the central state from intrusive interference in the local labor market.

Perhaps too, though this is highly speculative, the small size and familial character of many workshops and farms meant that employers were more likely to enforce discipline themselves than enlist the magistrate as enforcer or legitimizer of their sanctions. The father chastised the lazy son, the master chased and caught the runaway apprentice, the farmer reprimanded and dismissed his laborer. The face-to-face character of employment relations would seem to favor private enforcement of sanctions rather than recourse to the public remedies of the state, be they even so close as the local squire in his study. Perhaps too, masters were loath to go to law against their servants because of the notorious reputation of most local bridewells and the widespread conviction that a servant could only be debauched further by an incarceration. Undoubtedly, the low prestige of confinement acted to favor private as opposed to state disciplining. In order to explain why this should have been so, it is necessary to examine the experience of confinement before 1775 in closer detail.

III

Three major types of confinement need to be distinguished: the debtors' prisons, the jail, and the house of correction (or bridewell, as it was also known). The largest and most notorious debtors' prisons, Ludgate, King's Bench, the Fleet, and the Marshalsea were in London.[60] There debtors and their families were confined until they could give satisfaction to their creditors or until they were discharged as insolvents by act of Parliament. While inside, they were maintained at their creditors' expense. By right and custom, debtors could not be chained or forced to work: they were allowed to live with their wives and children inside; and they could not be debarred from visits or other contacts with the outside. The "better class" rented separate apartments from the keeper on what was called "the master's side." Once all the rooms were taken, newcomers were forced to "chum," that is, to sublet a part of the rooms from a prisoner, or even from someone unconnected to the prison who happened to rent accommodation there. At the Marshalsea, for example, the keeper let four rooms to a chandler: one in which he maintained his shop, two others in which he lived with his family, and the remaining room, which he sublet to prisoners. The "poorer sort" slept on the common side in crowded and often filthy wards. Here too newcomers purchased their "chum tickets" from old-timers, conferring the right to sleep in the ward.

The keeper derived his income from all those ingenious extortions practiced in many branches of eighteenth century institutional finance. Besides letting rooms to prisoners, he usually maintained a coffee shop and tap for prisoners and visitors. At the Fleet and at King's Bench, the keeper also sold the privilege of living outside the walls of the prison. For eight guineas the debtor could purchase the right to live "within the rules," that is, within two and a half miles of the prison. For a lesser sum, he could purchase the right to "day rules," that is, free exit from the prison during daylight hours. The turnkeys also sold the same privilege themselves, expressively called "a run on the key."[61]

Since the debtor enjoyed a privileged immunity from discipline, and since there were, for example, only three turnkeys and four watchmen at King's Bench for over four hundred inmates, the keeper left the debtors to police their own community. As a result, the social life of debtors' prison ran unchecked. John Howard saw butchers and other tradesmen from the outside freely mingling with Marshalsea debtors and joining them in games of skittles in the prison drinking room. The Fleet was reputed to be the biggest brothel in London. Howard discovered a beer and wine club in operation at King's Bench and a committee of inquiry in 1813 discovered a music society there.[62]

The second type of institution, the county and borough jail, was, like most eighteenth century institutions, heterogeneous in design and size. Some—for example, the county jails at Lancaster, Gloucester, and York—were the dungeons of medieval castles, while others, particularly those in small market towns, were little more than strong rooms above a shop or an inn. Newgate in London was very much the largest, with a capacity in 1750 of about two hundred inmates. Most of the other jails were considerably smaller. Of the fifty county jails listed in Howard's census, made during the extremely crowded year of 1787, only seven were holding a hundred or more prisoners at the time he visited; eleven were holding between fifty and a hundred, and the thirty-two remaining institutions held fifty or less.[63]

Confined in the jails were categories of individuals as heterogeneous as the buildings themselves, each accorded different status in law and each entitled to different privileges. Besides debtors, who were allowed to live with their families and who could not be subjected to coercive discipline, there were felons awaiting trial, usually in irons, but also allowed free run of the prison, unlimited visits, and exemption from labor; those awaiting trial for misdemeanors, rarely in irons, and allowed pretrial privileges; capital convicts awaiting execution or pardon, usually chained in the "condemned cells"; a few felons undergoing sentence of imprisonment; and finally, transports waiting to be shipped off.

In theory, these classes were supposed to be kept isolated from each other in separate wards. In practice, jailers usually lacked the manpower to enforce the separation. Prisoners mingled freely in the yards and shared in each other's privileges. For example, when debtors and felons shared the same wards, jailers usually gave up restricting the privilege of unlimited visits and outside food to debtors alone.

The reformers of the 1780s singled out this confusion of prisoner categories as a major obstacle to the imposition of rigorous discipline. Until all debtors were removed to distinct debtors' prisons, they argued, a jail could not become a place of punishment.[64] They also maintained that in the old jails the treatment due the innocent and the guilty was confounded. Those awaiting trial were ironed and plucked for fees no less than the guilty. To take but one example, a Bristol man put on trial for firebombing warehouses in 1730 told his jury that upon arrest he had been thrown into the "pit" at Bristol jail and there confined with condemned felons, "chained down to a staple and . . . kept fourteen weeks and three days in the winter weather without pen, ink, paper, fire, or candle, far distant from my relatives and destitute of money."[65] Eventual acquittal could not have softened this memory of punishment before trial. Howard also discovered that many prisoners were punished after acquittal. They languished in jail because they could not pay the discharge fees that the jailer required before he would knock off their fetters.[66]

The third institution, the house of correction or bridewell, was sometimes a section of the jail building itself, sometimes a separate though adjacent establishment, and sometimes too, entirely on its own. On the eve of the Howardian reforms, it was an institution in decline. Nominally, bridewells were supposed to put the poor to work and teach them the lessons of industry. Masters in a range of outwork trades, especially textiles and rope making, contracted with the county benches for the labor of the incarcerated. The Norwich clothiers, for example, depended heavily on workhouse and bridewell populations in rural Norfolk and Suffolk for the preparation and spinning of raw wool. Brickmakers used bridewell prisoners to beat bricks into dust; candlemakers set them to making candlewick; wood merchants employed them chipping logwood; masters in the iron trade set them to making butchers' skewers; and mattress makers contracted for their labor as feather pickers.[67] Many contractors in the outwork trades learned invaluable lessons in managing an extended division of labor from their experiences in the workrooms of bridewells and workhouses. In many respects, these state institutions were the earliest prototypes of the factory.[68] Yet most of the lessons learned were negative. The rapid turnover of prisoners and the proverbially low productivity of forced labor made it difficult to make a profit, and most contractors defaulted or gave up on their contracts. The failure of attempts to exploit the labor of the incarcerated by 1750 must have spurred outwork masters, desiring to profit from large-scale division of labor, to develop their own institution, the factory, for the exploitation of free labor. As a result, though, the factory was stained by its early associations with the bridewell and the workhouse, and the first generation of Lancashire workers refused, whenever possible, to send their children to work in the new institutions.

Because contractors rarely succeeded in making a profit on prisoners' labor, there were few bridewells in which work was steadily enforced.[69] When Jacob Ilive, a London bookseller, was sent to serve a term for libel in the Clerkenwell house of correction in London in 1757, he expected to find the vagrants, disorderlies, and prostitutes hard at work under the vigilant eye of the taskmaster. Instead he came upon this scene in the prison yard:

> I observed a great number of dirty young Wenches intermixed with some men, some felons who had fetters on, sitting on the ground against the wall, sunning and lousing themselves; others lying sound asleep; some sleeping with their faces in the men's laps, and some men doing the same by the women. I found on inquiry that these wenches, most of them, were sent hither by the justices as loose and disorderly persons.[70]

In a place ostensibly devoted to punishment, Ilive found men and women associating freely, drinking together in the prison taproom, and whiling away their hours in the prison yards playing at chuck farthing, tossing up, leapfrog, and a "very merry but abominably obscene" game called "rowly powly," which Ilive unfortunately was too delicate to describe.

To be sure, Clerkenwell was no merry idyll. Women who disobeyed the keeper were chained standing up for twenty-four hours at a stretch. The keeper himself told a Commons committee in 1779 that the magistrates allowed him to administer as many as twenty lashes for disobedience.[71] Moreover he and his turnkeys plucked everyone unmercifully for money while the ragged and exhausted vagrants brought in off the streets by the constables frequently died unattended and unfed on the cold boards of the cells. Ilive himself assisted at inquests on five of these deaths in prison, which he attributed to the failure of the keepers to provide adequate food, there being no statutory obligation requiring the county to feed bridewell prisoners. In theory, prisoners were supposed to earn their bread by hard labor, the county paying for bread from profits on the sale of prison goods. Because in practice many counties were unable to find contractors willing to put the prisoners to work, the justices were obliged to make some dietary provision for them, usually in the form of a penny loaf per day. Still, there were some bridewells in which no food was provided at all. John Fielding, the London magistrate, told an inquiry in 1770 that there was no dietary provision whatsoever for the six hundred to seven hundred prisoners annually committed to the Gate House in London. As he tartly observed, "when a magistrate commits a man to that gaol for an assault, he does not know that he commits him there to starve."[72]

In theory too, borough and county magistrates were required to provide a diet for persons awaiting trial at sessions or assize as well as those condemned, under sentence of imprisonment or awaiting transportation. In practice, the prisoners had to fend for themselves. Sometimes the keepers would pocket part of the sum allotted by the county for the maintenance of each prisoner. Even when keepers honestly distributed the country allowance it was rarely enough, by itself, to keep a person alive. Thus, at Newgate in 1760, the Corporation of London allotted a sum sufficient to purchase only 96 penny loaves per person per year (as compared to 432 loaves per person by 1813).[73] The keeper admitted in 1779 that most prisoners depended on "money and provisions brought by their friends," though for the "poor and friendless" he "provided at his own expense, coarse pieces of meat and made Broth."[74]

In some jails, poor prisoners were allowed to plead for food and money from begging grates. Prisoners at Rochester city jail seemed to have done well by the practice. The keeper told Howard that the "liberality of the public is so great that we cannot keep the prisoners sober. Persons have even desired to be confined to have the liberty of the begging grate."[75] The public is not likely to have been as generous elsewhere, but it appears that private charity did as much to feed and clothe prisoners as the state itself. It was a common philanthropic practice to leave bequests for poor prisoners and the discharge of penniless debtors. Sometimes members of the grand jury would donate the fees and expenses they received for jury duty to the maintenance of the confined.

Nevertheless, prisoners counted more on their family and friends than they did on the vagaries of private charity or the state. Since the county limited its obligations to the confined, it had to allow freedom of access to their friends and relatives. Thus, very little attempt was made to limit prisoners' visiting privileges. To have done so would have meant starvation for poor "common side" prisoners. It was common for wives to appear daily at the gates bearing meals for their jailed husbands. They were given the run of prison yards from dawn until locking up, and a judiciously placed bribe would make it possible to remain inside at night. The sexual commerce between the inside and outside was vigorous. As far back as the seventeenth century, one prisoner had observed that whores flocked to prison like "crowes to carrion."[76] In 1813, the keeper of Newgate said he turned a blind eye to illicit conjugality because it prevented the outbreak of "more atrocious vice,"[77] an apparent allusion to homosexuality or masturbation.

The easy commerce between the prison world and the street is also to be explained by the fact that the institution was so largely given over to the confinement of debtors and felons awaiting trial. By custom and statute, these prisoners had the right to unlimited access to lawyers and associates, since such access was deemed necessary for the preparation of a defense or the discharge of a debt. Debarred from subjecting them to discipline or in any way limiting their visiting privileges, the keeper was responsible only for guaranteeing the custody of these classes of prisoners and for delivering them to courts for trial. The cheapest and most effective way to guarantee the custody of felons was to chain them. This expedient did away with the need for a large custodial staff as well as high walls and secure buildings.[78] Paradoxically, the use of chains helped facilitate easy contact between inside and outside worlds. Because convicted offenders were chained, it was possible to give visitors free access to all parts of the prison. Because of chains many prisons also did away with walls altogether or allowed them to totter into disrepair. An example was the wall at the county jail in Southwark described in a justices' report in 1771:

> The brick walls which surround the yard where the prisoners are kept are so exceeding weak as to be dangerous to the safety of the prison that they are frequently shaken by the violence of the wind and that some part thereof was lately blown down and that the paling on top of the said walls is entirely rotting, broken and decayed that owing to the badness of the wall there is a large hole broke thro' that part of the wall which adjoins to Mr. Gordon's timber yard.... [79]

Such walls, often no more than eight feet high, could not prevent passersby from tossing food, notes, and letters over the other side, or stop prisoners from conversing with people in the street, or on occasion splashing them with dirty water.[80]

Yet if the physical distance between the two worlds was often maintained only by a low, rickety wall, the administrative distance was much greater. The authority of the keeper was exercised largely without supervision or scrutiny from the outside. While the two worlds were bound in symbiotic dependence over matters of diet and sexual commerce, the prison, in matters of power and finance, was a state within a state.

Nominally at least, the prison was supposed to be supervised by three outside authorities—the sheriff, the magistrate, and the grand jury. The assize judges also played a role in watching over the keepers charged with producing prisoners for trial. It is symptomatic of the informality of eighteenth century administration that reformers in the 1780s were unable to discover any act specifically setting out the duties of each of these parties. Nor were they able to find any act actually requiring the county and borough magistrates to supervise the keepers, review their expenditures, and conduct quarterly inspections. The first such statute was not enacted until 1791.[81] Until then, quarterly inspections, being an obligation of custom rather than a legal duty, were rare indeed. When Howard upbraided county JPs for neglect, they attributed their derelictions to fear of "gaol fever," or typhus. Howard found jailers who were not above hinting artfully that there was "fever about" to dampen the administrative ardor of the occasional eager beaver among the gentry.[82] Indeed, some of Howard's fame rests on the simple fact that he was one of the first county sheriffs to take seriously his customary obligation to inspect.

Nor did the magistracy bother to lay down rules defining keepers' authority and the type of discipline they were to enforce. The hours of rising and locking up, the program of work, the ironing and punishment of prisoners, as well as the cleansing of the prison were all left to the discretion of the keepers and their servants. Authority in prison thus varied according to the sobriety, dutifulness, and resolve of its enforcers. Unbounded by formal rule, it was by definition arbitrary, personal, and capricious. In their explanations of the causes of prison abuses, the reformers were to return again and again to the unfettered discretion of the keepers. Cruelty and leniency alike, they argued, were to be explained by the absence of rules and supervision from outside authority.

The keeper's fiscal independence of the state, made possible by their reliance on income from fees, all but emancipated them from the control of the magistracy. The keepers exacted fees for putting prisoners in irons, for taking them off, for "first locking up," for copies of all legal papers from court, for privileges such as a featherbed in place of boards or the cold stone floor, and finally for discharge upon acquittal or termination of sentence. Turnkeys also charged fees of their own, for example, for going out to buy the prisoners' food or for the privilege of remaining out of the cells after lockup.[83] Most prisoners, however, were too poor to pay the fees and would plead with the bench to be excused of the charges. In these cases, the magistrates would pay the keeper a sum in lieu of fees, but since the sum was usually a pittance compared to his other income it did not confer on the bench any leverage over his conduct.[84]

The keepers' fee income came largely from debtors and from wealthy persons confined for "respectable" offenses like libel, sedition, or embezzlement. These people were a bonanza for keepers. They rented them special apartments on the master's side, away from the frequently diseased common side offenders, and plucked them shamelessly for their bedding, food, and liquor. A system financed by fees thus institutionalized unequal treatment of rich and poor. Wealthy master's side offenders awaiting trial could purchase whatever money could buy—books, wine, a gourmet table, and the pleasures of sex. Common side offenders endured board beds, mouldy county loaves, and lice.

Another source of income for keepers was the prison "tap" or drinking place. Many keepers in fact were publicans by trade and carried on the keepership as a kind of sideline, leaving the day-to-day running of the institution to their turnkeys and spending most of their time away from the prison in their inns or taverns. The tap was a lucrative business. Besides their captive market of drinkers who could be made to pay whatever they had the effrontery to charge, keepers could also count on the patronage of the steady stream of visitors passing in and out of the gates.

Prisons were not the only institutions financed by fees and other extortions practiced on their users. Nurses in hospitals charged fees of patients to empty their chamber pots and change their beds; justices' clerks charged fees for every legal paper they copied and delivered to a prosecutor, defendant, or witness; constables were paid for the vagrants they arrested; the tiny government bureaucracy of clerks and copyists was financed largely by fees.[85] In every area of eighteenth century administration, those who used an institution paid for it, but no one was more helpless in the face of extortion than the prisoner, and no institution was more chronically underfinanced than the prison. This, however, suited the magistracy. The ruinous condition of so many of the prisons can be explained largely by the JPs' unwillingness to pump money into a system that lurched along mostly paying for itself. Moreover, since the state's fiscal commitment to the institutions was limited, magistrates could safely dispense with any close scrutiny of institutional governance. What reason was there to do it, so long as relatively little of the county's tax money was involved?

Unencumbered by state scrutiny or dependence on the state for their income, the keepers were in effect private contractors, rather than salaried officials. To be sure, they were required to tender their accounts to the bench for inspection and to deliver prisoners for trial, but only a mass escape or gross corruption made them liable for dismissal. Having secured the office through the patronage of some influential member of the bench, these petty tradesmen or former stewards and bailiffs of local gentry settled down to a lifetime of well-rewarded and undemanding extortion. They often handed on their appointments to their sons, even to their widows. At Bedford, for example, the keepership of the jail

passed through three generations of the Howard family (no relation to the reformer) from 1760 to 1814.[86] In Berkshire, the jailer
at Reading, John Wiseman, was succeeded in the 1770s by his
widow, Ann.[87] In fact, female jailers were sufficiently common to
require legislation in the 1780s outlawing the practice on the
grounds that a woman was unequal to the new tasks of discipline
that reformers sought to impose on institutional personnel.[88]

Regarded with condescension by the gentry on the county
benches, and at the same time largely outside their control, keepers
were left to run the prison world as they saw fit. They hired their
own turnkeys and enforced such discipline as they chose. And yet
their discretion was not unlimited. It appears that they had to share
power, or at least reach an accommodation, with various inmate
communities.

Contemporary sociologists have shown that it is not uncom-
mon for modern penitentiaries to be ruled according to an infor-
mal division of power between the guards and the prisoner elite.[89]
In the eighteenth century, inmate communities appear to have
been even more powerful. This was most obviously the case in the
large debtors' prisons in London, which were self-governing, self-
financing communities, subject only to the loose and occasional
tribute exacted by the keepers. Debtors' wards in jails also enjoyed
a large measure of self-government, since the keepers were forbidden to limit debtors' access to the outside world or infringe upon
their privileges.

Since felons awaiting trial likewise could not be forced to work
or be subjected to discipline, the keepers tended to allow them to
police themselves. It was in their interest to do so, since they paid
the wages of their turnkeys out of their own pocket. Most keepers
employed as few personnel as possible. At Clerkenwell bridewell
in 1779, there were only two turnkeys in charge of the 114 men
and women at work in the hemp-pounding wards.[90] In Newgate
in the 1760s there was roughly one turnkey, officer, or watchman
for every hundred prisoners.[91] This compares, incidentally, with
a ratio of one officer for every eighteen prisoners in Coldbath
Fields House of Correction in the 1830s.[92] Not only were there
few turnkeys, but their duties were limited to locking and unlocking at dawn and dusk, admitting visitors, guarding the gates, putting offenders in irons, and escorting them to and from court. They
did not patrol the corridors, supervise the day yards, inspect the
sleeping rooms, or march the felons about to prayers or exercise.

They did not enforce a "discipline" in the nineteenth century sense of the term. Internal order, such as it was, was enforced chiefly by the inmate subcultures themselves.

These subcultures flourished most vigorously in the big London prisons. Over 25 percent of the prison population of England and Wales in 1776 was to be found in the London institutions.[93] In the smaller borough and county institutions, where there was a long wait between arrest and trial and where the keepers were often nonresidents, an inmate subculture could develop. When keepers did live in the institution, their control was bound to be more direct and intimate than in the big London prisons.

The architecture of old Newgate, and even of the new Newgate opened in 1770, encouraged the flowering of inmate subcultures. While the design of Pentonville isolated and exposed the inmate before the gaze of authority, Newgate was a dark, damp warren of wards, yards, privies, and staircases nowhere affording authority a clear vantage point for inspection and control.[94]

In the communities established within this warren, the binding custom was the garnish, a fee levied on incoming prisoners by the established denizens of the wards. A prisoner who failed to pay was made to strip and run a gauntlet of kicks and blows. His clothes might be sold and the pennies earned would then be put in the ward fund for the purchase of wood, candles, drink, and extra food. By this brutal sharing out of resources the prisoners provided themselves with the necessities that the county or borough failed to supply. As a practice, garnish appears to have been tacitly sanctioned by the justices and to have survived three generations of tenacious attempts to root it out. Astonished prison inspectors came upon the practice in the common jail of Yarmouth in 1835. They found the following notice tacked up on the wall of one of the yards:

> The rules of this Room. for every man that come in to pay 3 d. for Cols sticks and candels. When you first Com in Tow, Men to Clen this Room and the Youngest Prisoner to do any thing that is arsk. The rules of this prison. Anyone that is cort pullin' this down will have 3 dowzan.[95]

These rules were enforced by the wardsman, a prisoner chosen by the keeper or by the prisoners themselves. He supervised the extraction of garnish, maintained a rough sort of order, and distributed the loaves and water provided by the' county. In 1813, a

Newgate misdemeanant named Davison complained to the aldermen about the wardsmen and described their corrupt division of
power with the keeper:

> Other felons and many of the misdemeanants will, whilst the
> keepers' power is without control and almost without responsibil-
> ity, acquiesce in his treatment whatever it may be and will even
> concur in drawing the cords that bind their fellow prisoners more
> closely provided they can by the favour and indulgencies of the
> keeper and his turnkeys, loosen a little their own.[96]

Occasionally the wardsman presided at mock trials for the
adjudication of disputes or infringements of the rules of the ward.
Given their intimate acquaintance with the courts, the prisoners'
trials were often savagely accurate burlesques of official ritual.
Reformers singled out these trials for especial condemnation, not
only because they mocked the solemnities of the law but also
because they attested to the vigor of a competing and countervail-
ing system of order within the prison. In 1725 Bernard Mandeville
took the keeper of Newgate to task for allowing the felons awaiting trial to spend "their most serious hours . . . in mock tryals and
instructing one another in cross questions to confound witnesses."[97] Since most poor prisoners had to conduct their own
defense and cross-examine witnesses, the "mock tryals" of the
prison subculture were the only form of "legal aid" they were
likely to get.[98]

The trials also represented a mocking symbolic inversion, a
standing-on-its-head of the official ritual that had condemned the
inmates to prison. As such, they are the institutional counterparts
of the charivari or rough justice tradition of English village culture, in which scolds, wife-beaters, and other offenders against
communal order were burnt in effigy or humiliated by cacopho-
nous processions.[99] Because of their symbolic satisfactions and
their utility, these trials proved difficult to stop. A shocked reformer encountered one in Newgate as late as 1817:

> When any prisoner commits an offence against the community or
> against an individual he is tried. Some one, generally the oldest and
> most dexterous thief is appointed judge; a towel tied in knots is
> hung on each side of his head in imitation of a cap. He takes his
> seat if he can find one, with all form and decorum; and to call him
> anything but "my Lord" is a high misdemeanour. A jury is then
> appointed and regularly sworn, and the culprit is brought up.
> Unhappily justice is not administered with quite the same integ-

rity within the prison as without it. The most trifling bribe of the judge will secure an acquittal, but the neglect of this formality is a sure prelude to condemnation. The punishments are various, standing in the pillory is the heaviest. The criminal's head is placed between the legs of a chair and his arms stretched out are attached to it; he then carries about this machine.[100]

Boxing matches between contending parties were another ritual used for the adjudication of disputes in the Newgate community. MPs investigating the prison in 1813 came upon a highly organized match, complete with ring, trainers, and referee, watched from a distance with apparent equanimity by the keeper and his turnkeys.[101] Prison officials also appeared to tolerate an especially uproarious ritual in the wards reserved for prisoners awaiting transportation. It was the custom on the night before the convicts were shipped out to the boats to smash up the wards, tear up the bedding, and break the furniture.[102]

When the reformers presented the keeper of Newgate with evidence of this robust subculture, he could only confess that he actually shared his power with the prisoner elite. Thus, for example, when asked by MPs in 1813 whether he could enforce cleanliness in the prison, he replied that it was the prisoners, not he, who had the power to force dirty men to wash. The whole exchange between the MPs and the keeper is worth citing:

Have you any means of enforcing cleanliness in the individual?
No, I do not know how to do it.
So that if one man is dirty the whole of the ward to which he belongs may be punished?
There is a vast deal of difficulty in that; sometimes the debtors, if a man is so filthy and lousy, for that is the chief complaint, if it is from his own want of cleanliness, will take his clothes from him, and put them under the pump and let him be naked.[103]

When asked at the same inquiry whether he outlawed gaming in the prison, he replied, "It is not allowed nor prevented." The MPs who had seen the dice in the ward rooms knew what to make of that answer. Similarly, when Howard visited in 1775 he found that the prison chaplain was unable to insist upon compulsory chapel attendance. He read prayers daily but few prisoners bothered to attend, and those who did found their devotions interrupted by the riotous noises coming from the courts and dayrooms below.[104]

Indeed, the keeper's control of Newgate was tenuous, especially when there was severe overcrowding. The radical tailor

Francis Place discovered this in 1795 when he attempted to escort the wives of two men confined for seditious libel across the crowded yards. At the entrance to the largest of these yards, they found their way blocked by a solid mass of nearly naked prisoners who "with loud vociferation, begged money . . . quarreled with one another and used the most revolting language." Upon appealing to a turnkey to assist him in driving away the crowd, Place was told that the crowd would only clear if he threw some half pence into a corner of the yard. Apparently the turnkey did not dare to appeal to the prisoners to move back. Place did as he was told and the prisoners all ran away to grovel for the money, "swearing at one another, their fetters clanking and altogether making a most hideous noise."[105] Recalling the scene from the vantage point of the 1830s, Place was surprised that such scenes of "grossness and violence" should have been tolerated in prison. It was almost as if the state had lost control of its own institutions.

To be sure, all of these examples of the weakness of internal authority and the autonomy of the prison subculture have been taken from one prison, albeit the biggest and most notorious. Yet this in itself is significant. Right through the 1830s, Newgate served as the *locus classicus* of unreformed abuse, first in Howard's *State of the Prisons* of 1777, then in the Commons inquiries of 1813, Thomas Fowell Buxton's pamphlet of 1818, and finally the first prison inspectors' report in 1836.[106] It was Newgate that defined and brought into focus the philanthropists' image of the old prison system. At the center of that conception was not only the idea of cruelty and unregulated discretion, but, more disturbing still, the image of an entrenched inmate netherworld, ruling an institution of the state with its own officers, its own customs, and its own rituals.

I V

With the eighteenth century system of punishment, heavily reliant as it was upon public ritual rather than confinement, ruling authorities expressed complacent content. In the sermons of the parsons at the gallows, in the judges' addresses to grand juries, and in the rotund periods of Blackstone's *Commentaries,* the law and its penalties received their justifications, and, at least until 1770, these justifications satisfied. Hanging was a just terror to the poor; yet its rigors could be mitigated in particular instances through the interventions of prosecutor, patron, judge, and jury. The rituals of pillory, whipping, and execution day carried the message of the law right into the market square, while their very visibility as deterrents did away with the need for a bureaucratic French-style police and an expensive system of confinement. Banishment rid the mother country of its incorrigibles and enriched the colonies with needed cheap labor. Self-satisfied variations were played on these themes.

Upon occasion dissenting voices could be heard. In Thomas Bray's report on the state of Newgate in 1702 for the Society for Promoting Christian Knowledge, in Mandeville's pamphlet of 1725, in the Commons inquiry into the death of two prisoners at the Fleet in 1728, and in John Wesley's journal accounts of his visits to prison, one encounters categories of denunciation similar to those later found in Howard's *State of the Prisons*.[107] Yet such voices had not yet swelled into a chorus. When told of the miseries of prisoners, magistrates were still able to say, "Let them care to keep out." Some even admitted that they considered "the close and squalid condition of a prison" to be "its necessary attributes." Until Howard was able to show them a medically sound program of deterrence, they were inclined to regard the "filth of the prison, the *squalor carceris*" as a proper and necessary instrument of terror.[108]

CHAPTER THREE

Cords of Love, Fetters of Iron:

The Ideological Origins

of the Penitentiary

I

The prison system first began to show signs of strain during the crime wave that followed the War of the Austrian Succession. Stephen Janssen, sheriff of London in 1750, attributed the increase of crime in the city to the thousands of young men turned adrift by demobilization and forced to fall to thieving as soon as their pockets were empty.[1] The London prisons were soon overwhelmed with the crush of destitute and ragged poor awaiting trial for petty property crime. In the wards of Newgate, typhus began making its deadly rounds. In April 1750, two diseased prisoners from Newgate infected the Old Bailey courtroom where they were standing trial. The "putrid streams from the bail dock" carried off at least fifty people, including the judge, the jury, the lawyers, and many spectators.[2] This disaster convinced the Corporation of London to set about negotiating with Whitehall for financial assistance in rebuilding what Sheriff Janssen had called "that abominable sink of Beastliness and Corruption." The negotiations dragged on until the early 1760s and the finished prison was not opened until 1770.[3] In the meantime, two London physicians,

John Pringle and Stephen Hales, devised ventilators for Newgate which drew off the "close, confined miasma" of the prison and helped to reduce mortality rates inside.[4]

While the crisis at Newgate passed with the easing of overcrowding, the Black Assize of 1750 was not forgotten. It had helped to focus medical attention upon the problems of hygiene in every sphere of institutional life. Hales's ventilators were soon introduced into hospitals and workhouses, and Pringle drew upon his Newgate experience when writing his treatise on hygiene in the army.[5] Jonas Hanway's campaign to lower infant mortality in London workhouses in the 1750s was based on the hygienic lessons learned as a result of the Black Assize.[6] Also affected was the navy doctor James Lind, chief proponent of the use of limes and other citrus fruit as a preventative for scurvy. Lind had become concerned with jail fever, which had been decimating the crews of transport ships in the Caribbean theater of the war. The disease, he realized, had been brought on board by prisoners pressed into naval service. By scrubbing the decks and hatchways, by bathing and delousing the men, and by forcing them to wear uniforms, Lind was able to reduce mortality among them. In the 1770s, when John Howard was developing his own ideas on prison hygiene, he acknowledged Lind's influence.[7]

Besides helping to stimulate improvements in institutional hygiene, the crisis of 1750 appears to have raised doubts about the effectiveness of the capital penalties for petty crime. A bill that passed the Commons substituted hard labor in the royal dockyards for the death penalty for a number of minor felonies.[8] Although it was thrown out by the Lords, its appearance suggests that some judges and MPs were beginning to see the need for a penalty somewhere between transportation and hanging.

At the same time, some prosecutors were apparently abandoning the prosecution of minor capital cases because the penalty of death seemed excessive. For the same reasons, Henry Fielding, then a Middlesex magistrate, raised doubts about the justice of sentencing persons to transportation for petty larceny. The penalty, he said, had "such an appearance of extreme severity" that judges ordered petty larcenists to be whipped instead.[9] Yet whipping, he also maintained, only forfeited the offender's public reputation and hardened him to the censure of the community. It was necessary to find an intermediate penalty, combining "correction of the body" with "correction of the mind." His suggestion was solitary confinement in new houses of correction built on a cellular plan:

> There can be no more effectual means of bringing the most Abandoned Profligates to Reason and Order than those of Solitude and Fasting; which latter is often as useful to a diseased mind as to a distempered body.[10]

To carry out this discipline, Fielding proposed the construction of a new house of correction for Middlesex. In this institution, prisoners would be roused by a bell and work from 6:00 AM. until 7:00 P.M.; their labors would be punctuated by a "short lecture or exhortation of morality." While nothing came of Fielding's idea, the words he used, especially the phrase "correction of the mind," foreshadowed Howard's language a generation later. Fielding was one of the few to perceive that the crisis of 1750 was more than a short-term scare that would pass away once the economy had returned to a peacetime equilibrium. Only he had asked the larger question: whether the "civil power" of the magistracy and the institutions of punishment had kept pace with urban growth in London.

In 1770, Fielding's prescient questions were taken up by his brother John, also a Bow Street magistrate. Demobilization, this time following the Seven Years' War, coupled with population growth, triggered an increase in Old Bailey committals. They were 35 percent higher in the five years following the peace than in the war years. In 1770, John Fielding told a Commons committee that he attributed the increase to the weakness of the watch and the vast numbers of "sons of unfortunate people of no trade" who could not find work in the London trades and were forced to thieve.[11] Once again, increases in the numbers committed for trial at the Old Bailey resulted in overcrowding at Newgate.[12] The passage of an act in 1774 requiring prisoners to be stripped of their street clothing and attired in carters' smocks for their court appearances attests to renewed anxiety in London of a repetition of the Black Assize of 1750.[13] Elsewhere in the London area, magistrates found themselves obliged to cope with the strain on the prison system caused by the growing pressure of population and crime. The houses of correction for Middlesex, Westminster, and Surrey were all rebuilt and enlarged between 1766 and 1776.[14]

The unsettled state of public order in London also revived doubts about transportation. In 1773 the Lord Chief Justice observed to the Earl of Suffolk that banishment to a settled and prosperous colony had lost all power to deter the poor. He also echoed Henry Fielding's call for a new intermediate penalty suitable for minor felonies. "It is much to be regretted," he said, "that the law as it stands does not admit of a greater diversity of punishments according to the different nature of crimes and circumstances of the offender."[15] William Eden's extremely influential treatise, *Principles of Penal Law*, published in 1771, reiterated doubts about the deterrent value of transportation and called for new intermediate penalties. Eden, however, rejected an increased resort to imprisonment on the grounds that confinement invariably made an offender worse.[16]

Only eight years later the same William Eden, now Lord Auckland, was assisting Blackstone in drafting the Penitentiary Act. It authorized the government to construct two penitentiaries in London and to experiment with terms of solitude and hard labor in place of transportation. The conversion of both of these men to the merits of confinement was largely the work of John Howard, a then obscure Bedfordshire squire whose exhaustive survey of prison abuses, *The State of the Prisons*, first appeared in 1777. Howard, who became the father of the penitentiary, provided them with the details of routine that they set out in the act.

II

John Howard never thought it necessary to explain why in 1773 at the age of 47 he forsook the quiet of his Bedfordshire estate and set out on a career of prison and hospital reform that was to take him to every institution for the poor in Europe, and which cost him his fortune and finally his life in a typhus ward of the Russian army at Cherson in 1791. While Howard never paused over the question of his own motives, his diaries and letters enable us to retrace the steps of that search for a spiritual vocation which he finally found on a visit to Bedford jail in 1773.

He was the son of a wealthy and pious Nonconformist warehouseman in Smithfield who, having acquired a "handsome fortune" in business, retired to a substantial house in Hackney, the center of London Dissent. Of Howard's mother we know little except that she died shortly after his birth, so that, as one of his biographers puts it, Howard was deprived of the "force of maternal endearment."[17] His father, by all accounts a strict disciplinarian and uncompromising zealot, apprenticed his young son to a wholesale grocer in order to "inure him to habits of method and industry." Howard hated his apprenticeship and upon his father's death bought himself out of his indentures. He married soon after and set himself up on an estate, first in Hampshire and then at Cardington in Bedfordshire, near his relatives the Whitbread brewing family.

From the beginning, Howard had a philanthropic bent. At Cardington he built a model village for his tenants, with a school, new cottages, and garden plots. Over these tenants he exercised what his friend and biographer John Aikin called "the superintendence of master and father combined." Besides guaranteeing their employment and providing schools and a free doctor, Howard exercised a moral surveillance, backed up by his powers as a landlord. He made it a condition of tenancy that they should regularly attend church and abstain from public houses as well as "such amusements as he thought pernicious," especially the cockfight.

Howard was twice widowed, his second wife dying in childbirth in 1765 leaving him an infant son to raise alone. He proved to be a strict father, even by the standards of his contemporaries. Aikin described his friend's conception of parental authority:

> Regarding children as creatures possessed of strong passions and desires without reason and experience to controul them, he thought that Nature seemed, as it were, to mark them out as the subjects of absolute authority, and that the first and fundamental principle to be inculcated upon them was implicit and unlimited obedience. This cannot be effected by any process of reasoning before reasoning has its commencement; and therefore must be the result of coercion.... The coercion he practiced was calm and gentle, but at the same time steady and resolute.[18]

Howard's coercion was of a "rational kind," as Aikin put it. When the child cried, Howard would sit silently waiting for it to stop, unwilling, as Aikin explained, to offer comfort lest the child learn to secure its wants through protest and complaint. On another occasion, Aikin reports, the child, now four or five, was confined for a short period in the root cellar at the bottom of the garden. Howard preferred this punishment to the use of the cane. Later, Howard prescribed for his child the same severe vegetarian diet he observed himself. When the child was five, Howard sent him off to a boarding school and thereafter saw him rarely, since he had already begun his almost continuous journeys on the Continent. Aikin admits that the relations between father and son were distant. A parent "whose presence was associated with . . . restraint and refusal" inspired "more awe than affection."

In 1786 his son became mad during one of his father's absences on the Continent and had to be forcibly removed from the estate to Dr. Arnold's asylum at Leicester. Howard's reaction to the news alternated between grief and detachment. In one letter to Samuel Whitbread, who served as the boy's guardian while Howard was away, he cried "Oh my son Absalom! my son! my son!" In another he observed frigidly: "I shall write to my son, but he is too ill to come abroad. Nothing but calm and solitary confinement can recover him."[19] Thus the father of solitary confinement prescribed it for his own son. Only one biographer goes so far as to claim that the boy's madness was a direct consequence of his father's "premature and excessive severity," but even his closest friends were awed and troubled by his uncompromising conception of the paternal role.[20]

While Howard's paternal severity may have represented a way of working out his grief at the loss of his wife in childbirth, it seems to have owed more to his formation in the ascetic traditions of Nonconformity. The splinter groups and sects of eighteenth century Nonconformity were the weakened remnants of the Puritan revolution of the previous century. Some of these sects—most Quakers, for example—had lost their sectarian fire and in the conduct of their outward life differed little from the members of the Established Church. Others remained fierce advocates of Calvinist predestinarian doctrines. Still other groups—the Unitarians and "rational dissenters"—subscribed to a highly rationalist creed emphasizing the intelligibility and regularity of divine behavior. All avowed Nonconformists, however, whatever their doctrinal differences, shared in common civil disabilities. Unless they were prepared to swear allegiance to the creed of the Established Church, they were debarred from public office.

Howard himself, according to his biographer Aikin, was an Independent, "a moderate Calvinist sect," though he also attended a Baptist congregation in London. While his own fervid and emotional piety gave him little in common with the "rational dissenters," one of his closest friends was the Unitarian radical, Richard Price, later to win fame as the target of Edmund Burke's indignant *Thoughts on the Revolution in France.*

Howard's personal asceticism was formed by his religion. Throughout life, he rose at dawn, took a cold bath every morning, and after prayers dressed himself "after the style of a plain Quaker." His diet for a whole day consisted of nothing more than "two penny rolls with some butter or sweetmeat, a pint of milk and five or six dishes of tea with a roasted apple before going to bed." He was a "lover of order and regularity" in all his affairs and was particularly noted for strict punctuality and for "the exact and methodical disposition of his time."

Such was the dour and composed visage that Howard presented to the world. While his austerity was exceptional for a county squire, it was entirely typical of the circle in which Howard found his friendships—the Quaker and Baptist professionals and businessmen of Bedford, Warrington, and London. Richard Price, the Unitarian divine and philosopher; John Aikin, the physician, writer, and tutor at Warrington Dissenting Academy; Samuel Whitbread, the Bedford brewer; and John Fothergill, Quaker physician and London philanthropist, would not have found their friend eccentric. Some of them submitted to the same regimens of self-denial. Fothergill, for example, is reputed to have confessed on his deathbed, with quavering pride, that he died a virgin.[21]

What needs to be explained is what caused such personal asceticism to be directed outward toward the disciplining of the poor, and, in Howard's case, toward the reformative regimentation of criminals. But before the question can really be asked of the class as a whole, it will be necessary to look more closely at those of his private compulsions that found an outlet in prison reform.

It appears that his wife's death in 1765 plunged Howard into a profound spiritual crisis. Seeking distraction from grief, he set out on the first of a series of restless tours of Europe. On these solitary journeys, his thoughts kept returning to the question of a spiritual vocation. What was he to do with his life? His traditions told him that he could only secure salvation through labor in a calling, but his father's success had freed him from the necessity of working. As the first member of his family to leave business and reject the path his father had laid out for him, he opened a void in his being that the life of a county squire failed to fill. What had he done with his talents? Dabbled in "improving" his tenants? Sauntered through Europe on desultory tours? Such tours might have suited a normal gentleman of established line, but Howard was the gentrified son of a Dissenting petit bourgeois family, and sightseeing only exacerbated his self-disgust. In Italy, the land of popery and saints' days, Howard's Nonconformist conscience bit deepest and caused him to feel his frivolity most painfully:

> Why should Vanity and Folly, Pictures and Baubles, gilded Churches and glittering Stones or even the Stupendous Mountains, beautiful Hills or rich Vallies which ere long will all be consumed, engross the thoughts of a candidate for an eternal, everlasting Kingdom, a worm ever to crawl on earth?[22]

The diaries written during these European journeys speak of a complex but veiled internal struggle, often exploding into flashes of self-laceration. In these diaries he describes himself as "a vile worm," a "fruitless, barren, cold, dead, vile creature," and "a worm ever to crawl on earth."[23] One diary entry, written in Holland in 1770, is entirely typical:

> When I consider and look into my Heart I doubt—I tremble! such a vile Creature Sin folly and imperfection in every action! oh dreadful thought a Body of sin and death I carry about me ever ready to depart from God and with all the dreadful Catalogue of Sins committed my Heart faints within me and almost despairs but yet oh my Soul why art thou cast down why art thus disquieted? hope in God! his free Grace in Jesus Christ! Lord I believe help my unbelief shall I limit the Grace of God! Can I fathom his Goodness! here on this Sacred Day I once more in the Dust before the Eternal God acknowledge my Sins heineous and agravated in his Sight I would have the deepest Sorrow and contrition on Heart and cast my guilty and poluted Soul on the Sovereign Mercy in the Redeemer—[24]

This, of course, is a language we find hard to understand, twentieth century canons of introspection being defined more by Sigmund Freud than by John Bunyan. Even those eighteenth century biographers still steeped in the Bunyanesque tradition found some of Howard's diary entries reading "like the ravings of a lunatic." Hence, it is particularly difficult to translate Howard's religious anxiety into social terms recognizable to us. The diaries disclose its intensity but conceal its source. Judgments must be made with caution.

Still such passages can perhaps be read in social terms as expressions of guilt at rapid ascent out of the ranks of those who must labor for a living as well as of futility at failing to find an acceptable alternative vocation. In Italy this guilt reached fever pitch and forced a moment of decision. After making a "compact" with himself to change his life, Howard cut short the tour and returned home to Bedfordshire.[25] He plunged into county politics, securing selection as county sheriff, and then standing unsuccesfully for Parliament as a Whig in the election of 1772.

It was as sheriff, however, that Howard finally discovered his vocation. Unlike most sheriffs, Howard took seriously his obligation to inspect the prisons. Discovering that acquitted prisoners were detained in prison for failure to pay discharge fees, he set out on a tour of neighboring prisons to investigate the extent of the practice. In 1774 he and his friend Fothergill appeared before a Commons committee to testify against the practice of fees and in support of a bill providing for the uniforming of persons taking their trials. Repelled but also fascinated by the prison netherworld he had uncovered, Howard then set out to visit every prison in England and Wales to document the evils he had first observed at Bedford.

Howard's denunciation of these abuses was not novel. It had almost attained the status of a proverb in the eighteenth century that prisons were "seminaries of vice and sewers of nastiness and disease," to use Henry Fielding's expressive phrase.[26] It was common knowledge long before Howard that prisoners were gouged for fees, cheated on their provisions, loaded with irons, exposed to disease, and liable for detention after acquittal. Nor did Howard denounce these abuses in a language that was foreign to his contemporaries' ears. The originality of Howard's indictment lies in its "scientific," not in its moral character. Elected a Fellow of the Royal Society in 1756 and author of several scientific papers on climatic variations in Bedfordshire, Howard was one of the first philanthropists to attempt a systematic statistical description of a social problem.

The State of the Prisons, when published in 1777, impressed the public as much by the awesome extent of its research as by its moral fervor. For every prison in the country, Howard had diligently recorded the dimensions of its building, the diet, the fee table, the inmate population on the day of his visit, the charitable bequests available for relief of the population, the weight of the chains used, and any other details that caught his eye. No wonder the "social statists" of the Royal Statistical Society in the 1870s were to laud him as a father of social science.[27]

The State of the Prisons gained further authority from the concreteness and detail of Howard's proposals for reform. These he seemed to have derived largely from his travels in Europe. The Rasp Houses of Amsterdam and Rotterdam, nearly two hundred years old when Howard visited them, showed him what the house of correction had been intended to be. These prisons were "so quiet and ... so clean," he remarked with amazement, "that a visitor can hardly believe he is in a gaol."[28] They provided Howard with most of the program of discipline set out in the Penitentiary Act of 1779—"fixed hours of rising, of reading a chapter in the Bible, of praying, of meals, of work etc."—as well as uniforms, cellular confinement, and constant inspection. The sober motto from Seneca carved in stone over the doorway of the Amsterdam Rasp House offered Howard a succinct definition of his developing conception of authority: My Hand is Severe but my Intention Benevolent.

In nearby Ghent, Howard discovered another suggestive model, the Maison de Force, built under the aegis of a local magistrate and urban reformer, J. P. Vilain. A combination of workhouse and house of correction, the Maison de Force was opened in 1771 as part of a new offensive by farmers and gentry in Flanders against the vagabondage and petty theft of the soldiers and camp followers disbanded after the Seven Years' War and set adrift to wander the roads.[29] Howard reproduced the architectural plans of the Maison de Force in his *State of the Prisons*.[30]

Vilain himself took the idea of solitary confinement from Clement XII's prison of San Michele, built in 1703 for the reformation of young juveniles in the Vatican. The prison, called the Silentium, applied the Catholic experience of monastic discipline to the purposes of punishment.[31] It still maintained the routine of solitary confinement and silent penance when Howard visited Rome in 1775, and he acknowledged its influence on his thought. An inscription in one of its courtyards became one of Howard's favorite mottos: "It is doing little to restrain the bad by punishment unless you render them good by discipline."[32]

Howard also acknowledged the influence of suggestions and ideas closer to home. Solitary confinement was not a new idea in the England of 1775. In 1701, the anonymous author of that charming pamphlet *Hanging Not Punishment Enough*, besides advocating that men be hanged in chains or whipped to death since ordinary execution had lost its terrors, also suggested that a prisoner awaiting trial be "immured in a box or cell to himself that they might not improve each other in wickedness."[33] A year later, Thomas

Bray of the Society for the Promotion of Christian Knowledge recommended the introduction of separate confinement of persons awaiting trial at Newgate.

In 1725 Bray's idea was repeated by Bernard Mandeville.[34] Convinced that the free association of hardened and novice offenders had turned Newgate into a "school of crime," Mandeville proposed the isolation of persons awaiting trial in "a hundred small rooms, perhaps of 12 foot square" strongly barred, and equipped with toilet and washing facilities. With these cells, he added, it would be possible to "secure prisoners without galling them with irons before we are sure that they deserve to be punished at all."[35] In the 1740s and '50s such diverse figures as Henry Fielding, Jacob Ilive, a publisher who served a term for publishing a religious libel, and the philosophical bishop Joseph Butler each suggested the idea of solitary confinement of prisoners before trial.[36] Two years before *The State of the Prisons* appeared, Jonas Hanway, an eccentric but influential London philanthropist, proposed the construction of a prison in London for the confinement in solitude of about two hundred offenders otherwise liable for transportation or execution. This was the first mention of the idea of using solitary on offenders under sentence. Hanway, as a member of the boards governing the Foundling Hospital, the Magdalen Hospital, and the Marine Society, as well as the leader of a campaign to reduce mortality in London workhouse wards, had had extensive experience in matters of institutional discipline and administration.[37] Just how completely he anticipated the discipline of the penitentiary can be seen in his description of the chapel in his model prison:

> The chapel should contain as many closets as there are cells, each closet communicating with its cell by a narrow passage under the corridor. The closets must have a double grate, that the prisoner may hear and see the clergyman yet not be able to distinguish the face of any prisoner.[38]

From all these sources—London philanthropy, the Catholic monastic tradition, and Dutch Protestant asceticism—Howard fashioned his vision of the penitentiary. The elements of that vision were available historically, awaiting authoritative expression by a man with the necessary aptitude for disciplinary thinking.

Yet there is more to Howard than the scientific technician of repression. His plodding empiricism was yoked to a pilgrim's sense of quest. He liked to compare his prison tours to Daniel's going alone into the lion's den, and in a letter to his friend Richard Price, he said the purpose of his work was to bear "the torch of philanthropy" into the netherworld of the dungeon.[39] He did not view the prison only with an administrative eye, as a cluster of inefficiencies and abuses demanding reform, but as the arena in which he would grapple with evil and demonstrate his worthiness before God. In his symbolic frame of reference, the prison represented a region of guilt, suffering, and remorse. Its dungeons were hell on earth to him, the earthly embodiment of eternal damnation, just as the assize day stood for the Final Judgment.

The man most responsible for imprinting this symbolic understanding of the machinery of justice on the minds of eighteenth century men and women was the Methodist leader John Wesley, himself a frequent preacher to the condemned prisoners at assize, the dungeon, or the gallows. It is just possible, though unlikely, that Howard himself was in the courtroom on March 10, 1758, when Wesley delivered the sermon that customarily opened Bedford assizes, before the assembled judges, jurymen, prisoners, and county gentry ranged in the spectators' benches. Wesley built up a crescendo of comparisons between the judgment of the assize day and the Final Judgment and then drew the eyes of his wealthy spectators to the prisoners in the dock:

> A few will stand at the judgment seat this day, to be judged touching what shall be laid to their charge; and they are now reserved in prisons, perhaps in chains till they are brought forth to be tried and sentenced. But we shall all, I that speak and you that hear, "Stand at the Judgment Seat of Christ." And we are now reserved on this earth which is not our home, in this prison of flesh and blood, perhaps many of us in chains of darkness too, till we are ordered to be brought forth. Here a man is questioned concerning one or two facts; there we are to give an account of all our works, from the cradle to the grave; of all our words, of all our works, of all our desires and tempers, all the thoughts and intents of our hearts.[40]

The burden of this symbolic system was that guilt transcended class and bound rich and poor, judge and prisoner alike in its chains. Wesley's own ministry to the condemned felons at Newgate attests to his sense of kinship with prisoners. Likewise, for Howard the chained wretches at the bottom of the dungeon steps appeared as a representation of his own sin. Had he not in a bitter and downcast moment called himself "a prisoner of the Lord" and on another occasion "an ill deserving, Hell deserving creature"?[41] He found his vocation in prisons because he was moved by a feeling of brotherhood with the confined. It was this kinship that gave Howard's work in prison reform its relentless quality. He gave everything to it, even his life, with a devotion that a man can only bring to a project when it serves his innermost compulsions.

His feeling that rich and poor, judge and prisoner were bound together under the common sentence of sin also constituted the emotional force behind his insistence that the state should extend its moral obligations to the prisoner.

"A felon," he said, "is a man and by men should be treated as a man."[42] He insisted that magistrates should take care to improve their prisons lest by the "necessary revolutions in human fortune" they find themselves suffering confinement themselves.[43] From his own internal battles, he knew how faint the line was between those on either side of the moral law. His proposals for the abolition of fees and fetters, the establishment of a regular diet, the provision of religious instruction, and protection against disease were moved by the belief that these were the due of all sinners, be they felons or judges.

Howard's sense of the universality of sin does much to explain his confidence that criminals were capable of reformation. His own discovery of a spiritual vocation in ministering to criminals gave him proof that God could enter a wasted life and give it meaning. It proved that no man, no matter how "vile a worm," was lost to God's mercy. As he exclaimed:

> And oh! How should I bless God such a worm is made the Instrument of alleviating the miseries of my fellow creatures and to connect more strongly the social bond by mutual exertions for mutual relief.[44]

His own conversion experience gave him confidence in the conversion of prisoners. If God could save a sinner like himself, could he not save the sinners in prison?

Wesley had felt the same keen affinity with prisoners, but he had confined his preaching mostly to the condemned, believing that only those about to meet their death could be successfully exhorted to repentance. Howard was more optimistic. He believed that it was possible to convert the living, and not merely the dying sinner. "Regular, steady discipline in a Penitentiary House" had the power to make "useful members of society" out of the "unhappy wretches" so wastefully dispatched on the gallows.[45] Salvation was not only God's work. It was the state's work too, and for the first time, Howard insisted, a technology of salvation existed for earthly use.

III

Howard was one of those rare men whose private compulsions seem to capture the imagination of their class. The attempt to raise a statue in his honor in 1786, as well as the hagiographies and elegies published after his death indicate how deeply his private quest appealed to his contemporaries. In ponderous but heartfelt stanzas, the poet Walter Lisle Bowles gave words to the public image of Howard as the emissary of divine mercy to the infernal regions:

> But who for thee, O CHARITY, will bear
> Hardship and cope with peril and with care?
> Who, for thy sake, will social sweets forego
> For scenes of sickness and the sights of woe?
> Who, for thy sake, will seek the prison's gloom
> Where ghastly guilt implores her ling'ring doom;
> Where penitence unpitied sits, and pale,
> That never told to human ears her tale;
> Where agony, half-famish'd cries in vain;
> Where dark despondence murmurs o'er her chain;
> Where sunk disease is wasted to the bone,
> And hollow-ey'd despair forgets to groan.
> Approving Mercy marks the vast design
> And proudly cries—HOWARD—the task be thine![46]

The veneration accorded Howard the man helps to explain the appeal of Howard the disciplinarian. He became the symbol of the philanthropic vocation, canonized by a middle class seeking representations of its best virtues. There is irony in Howard's reputation, since he was lauded by the very gentlemen whose neglect was set out in page after page of *The State of the Prisons.* Having demonstrated the emptiness of the magistracy's reputation for solicitude, he found his own crusade taken up as a vindication of that reputation. The irony is superficial though, since Howard had no intention of embarrassing his own class. While his censure angered individual magistrates, it did not antagonize them collectively because he cast his campaign in terms of a confrontation with Evil in the abstract, rather than with particular groups of men. Hence, he was able to gain a reputation for disinterested, apolitical philanthropy, which vested his disciplinary ideas with particular authority.

His ideas appealed, above all, to that sector of the middle class in which he himself had his roots, the Nonconformist businessmen, professionals, and small gentry. While Nonconformity was deeply fissured, he had friends in many camps. The Quakers, who were to be the most consistent advocates of prison reform, were much admired by Howard. He was drawn to Quaker asceticism and adopted the dress "of a plain Friend." His own brand of piety was strongly reminiscent of the Quaker traditions of silent prayer, "suffering" introspection, and faith in the illumining power of God's light. Quakers, for their part, were bound to be drawn to the idea of imprisonment as a purgatory, as a forced withdrawal from the distractions of the senses into silent and solitary confrontation with the self. Howard conceived of a convict's process of reformation in terms similar to the spiritual awakening of a believer at a Quaker meeting. From out of the silence of an ascetic vigil, the convict and believer alike would begin to hear the inner voice of conscience and feel the transforming power of God's love.

As the most rigorously self-disciplined of all the Nonconformist sects, the Quakers were naturally drawn to the idea of using regimens of discipline to reform the confined. For the Friends, discipline originally meant the rules of thought and action chosen by their sect to mark themselves off as a community from the sinful world: plain dress; "thee and thou" forms of address; and refusal to pay tithes, swear oaths, or doff hats before authority. By the end of the seventeenth century, the Quakers began to turn from discipline as a collective statement of apartness to discipline as an instrument of control over others. This change corresponded to their own social transformation from a persecuted, inward-looking sect of small craftsmen during the Civil War to a prosperous society of employers and merchants by the mid-eighteenth century.[47] Because of their experience with collective self-discipline, the Friends displayed a particular aptitude for devising institutional regimens for others. John Bellers's sketch for a Colledge of Industry in 1696, the Pennsylvania Quakers' reform of the Walnut Street jail in Philadelphia in 1786, and the Quaker asylum for the insane built at York in 1813 by Samuel Tuke are the most famous examples of this aptitude.[48]

The Quakers were also drawn to Howard's campaign because of their own bitter experience with imprisonment during the persecutions of the 1670s. Despite the increasing integration of the Friends into English society during the eighteenth century, they continued to be sent to prison for refusing to swear oaths, serve in wars, or pay tithes. As the sect with the strictest definition of what was due Caesar, they were in perennial conflict with Caesar's laws. Hence, of all sects, they asked the most searching questions about the right of the state to coerce citizens.

Having denied the right of the magistrate to compel men in matters of conscience, they were also led to deny his right to take human life in punishment. The abolition of the capital penalties in Pennsylvania and the reform of abuses in the Walnut Street jail followed from their doctrinal concern to set strict limits to the use of state force. When Howard set out to harmonize the imperatives of discipline and humanity, Quakers were among the first to enlist in his support.

Howard's closest friend and eventual co-adjutor on the penitentiary commission of 1779 was the Quaker physician John Fothergill.[49] By dint of relentless hard work and good connections with the Nonconformist establishment, Fothergill built up the most successful medical practice of his day, earning an estimated £10,000 a year taking care of the Wedgwoods, Gurneys, Darbys, Hanburys, Barclays, and other leading families in Nonconformist industry and banking. Like Howard, Fothergill was keenly interested in science. An amateur botanist himself, he subsidized Joseph Priestley's scientific research, besides treating him as a patient. Fothergill was also a mainstay of London philanthropy and a restless promoter of schemes for the "improvement" of hygiene in the metropolis. He wrote short treatises advocating hygienic burial practices for paupers and the construction of roads through the warrens of the city's criminal quarters to open them up to the beneficial circulation of air and commercial traffic. He was also the leading spirit behind the establishment of a boarding school for poor Quaker children at Ackworth in Yorkshire. At the school, the children's "active minds" were "put under a kind of restraint," Fothergill proudly asserted, and "habituated to silence, attention and due subordination." Howard, who toured the school in 1779, found that it accorded exactly with his conception of discipline.[50]

Fothergill was drawn to prison reform, not simply because he was a Quaker, but also because he formed part of a group of medical men who were revolutionizing the practice of institutional hygiene and management in hospitals, dispensaries, and workhouses. James Lind, the superintendent of Haslar naval hospital in Portsmouth; William Smith, the physician who wrote a scathing denunciation of the squalor in the jails of the London area in 1776; and Thomas Percival, the Manchester authority on hospital "police" and urban hygiene, were among those whose experience in hygiene in hospitals, foundling hospitals, dispensaries, troop transports, and men-o'-war provided Howard with the hygienic regimen he sought to introduce into prisons: uniforms, baths, delousing, whitewashing and liming of walls, regular diet, and medical inspections.[51] They in turn took up the campaign to publicize these techniques among magistrates and aldermen. For these medical men, therefore, prison reform was only one element of a general attack on the hygienic problems of all institutions dealing with the poor.

These doctors regarded the hygienic reform of institutions as a moral, no less than a medical crusade. The sicknesses of the poor were interpreted as the outward sign of their inward want of discipline, morality, and honor. As John Mason Good, physician of Cold Bath Fields prison, put it in 1795, "The poor are in general but little habituated to cleanliness"; they were therefore liable to disease, because "they feel not, from want of education, the same happy exertion of delicacy, honour and moral sentiment which everywhere else is to be met with."[52] This, of course, is the language of social and moral condemnation veiled as the language of medicine. The same tendency to slide from medical into moral and class categories is evident in Daniel Layard's pamphlet on jail fever, which appeared in 1773. Filth and disease were as natural to the poor, he asserted, as cleanliness and health were to the virtuous and industrious. The poor were "bound in the chains" of addiction to riotous living, sexual indulgence and intemperance.[53] They were susceptible to disease because they were susceptible to vice.

It was particularly easy for eighteenth century doctors to couch the language of class fear and moral opprobrium in the language of medicine. In their structure of assumptions, they drew a much less distinct demarcation between the body and the mind than nineteenth century medicine was to do. Their thought was imbued with the Hartleian materialism then in the ascendant at the medical school in Edinburgh.[54] According to David Hartley, the psyche was no less material than the body. Disturbance of the bodily system produced perceptual distortions and mental anguish, just as psychic disturbance could contribute to the break-down of physical functioning. Hence, it followed that physical diseases could have "moral" causes. John Coakley Lettsom, the wealthy London physician and protégé of Fothergill's, for example, had no trouble understanding that mental depression or remorse contributed to the mortality rates in prison, just as he attributed jail fever, not merely to improper hygiene, but also to improper discipline. Habits of intoxication, no less than bed lice, caused prisoners to succumb to typhus. Hartleian categories provided "scientific" legitimacy, therefore, for "medical" condemnations of the indiscipline of the poor.

Since disease in institutions had moral as well as physical causes, hygienic rituals were designed to fulfill disciplinary functions. To teach the poor to be clean, it was necessary to teach them to be godly, tractable, and self-disciplined. Hartleian assumptions led the doctors to be confident that once the bodies of the poor were subjected to regulation, their minds would acquire a taste for order.

Driven by this confidence, the Nonconformist doctors of the 1770s sought to transform the hospital from a warehouse for the dying into an institution for the moral reform of the poor through hygienic regimen. At the opening of the Liverpool Infirmary in 1791, Thomas Percival insisted that institutional confinement was the sole way to change the poor. The sick could not be cured in their homes; they had to be given moral therapy in the hygienic asceticism of an institutional quarantine.[55]

Early prison reformers owed much of their conceptual framework to these hospital reformers. Jonas Hanway, for example, was arguing within their categories when he described crime as a disease "which spreads destruction like a pestilence and immorality as an epidemical disorder which diffuses its morbid qualities."[56] Like the doctors, he saw crime issuing from the same source as disease, from the squalid, riotous, and undisciplined quarters of the poor. Prisons too were breeding grounds of pestilence and crime alike. In the fetid and riotous wards of Newgate, the "contagion" of criminal values was passed from hardened offender to novice, just as typhus spread from the "old lags" to the recent arrivals. Like the hospital, the penitentiary was created to enforce a quarantine both moral and medical. Behind its walls, the contagion of criminality would be isolated from the healthy, moral population outside. Within the prison itself the separate confinement of each offender in a cell would prevent the bacillus of vice from spreading from the hardened to the uninitiate.

Through the doctors and through his own friendships, Howard was able to draw upon another circle for support: the Nonconformist scientists and intellectuals of the dissenting academies and the scientific societies. Two members of the Manchester Literary and Philosophical Society, Thomas Butterworth Bayley and Thomas Percival, were to play leading roles in the construction of two new prisons in Lancashire, "built on Mr. Howard's plan." Erasmus Darwin, the key figure of the Lichfield Society, was to write one of his elephantine elegies in Howard's honor.[57]

The scientific societies provided the meeting ground for intellectuals and the leading manufacturers of the Midlands and the North, men like James Watt and Matthew Boulton, proprietors of the Soho Engineering works in Birmingham; Jedediah Strutt, the Derbyshire cotton factory dynast; Abraham Darby, founder of the iron and steel dynasty in Coalbrookdale; and Josiah Wedgwood, the pottery magnate from North Staffordshire.[58] These new industrialists were Quaker or Unitarian in religion, moderate or radical Whig in politics, scientific in their enthusiasms, and philanthropic in their avocations. These magnates financed a host of reform causes—the abolition of slavery, the construction of hospitals and dispensaries, the advancement of technical education, and the improvement of schools for the poor.

They are, however, best known as the fathers of the factory system and scientific management. Besides introducing mechanization, extended division of labor, and systematic routing of the work process, they also devised the new disciplines of industrial labor: punch clocks, bells, rules, and fines. In order to reduce turnover and stabilize the labor force in their early factories, they provided schools, chapels, and homes for their workers in model villages.[59]

Like the hospital and prison reformers these early industrialists rationalized their new discipline as an attempt to reform the morals and manners of their workers. In 1815, for example, the Strutts boasted that before the establishment of their works in Cromford and Belper, "the inhabitants were notorious for vice and immorality."[60] Regular work and wages, together with the stabilizing influence of a closely supervised village community, had transformed their behavior. Now, the Strutts said, "their industry, decorous behaviour, attendance on public worship and general good conduct," were "very conspicuous." Wedgwood, for his part, claimed that the drunkenness, sloppy workmanship, idleness, and violence of the potteries had been stamped out in his industrial fiefdom in Etruria. The punch clock, the fines, and his own intense and unremitting supervision had transformed the workers and "made machines of the men as cannot err."[61] In that first generation of industrialization, factories could still be justified not simply as technical achievements, but as moral ones as well.[62]

These Nonconformist industrialists, scientists, and doctors were also bound together by politics, most favoring one or another of the proposals for parliamentary reform which germinated in the 1770s. Fothergill, Howard, T. B. Bayley, and G. O. Paul lent their support to Christopher Wyvill's campaign for additions to the county representation in Parliament, retrenchment of expenditure, and reform in the administration of finance.[63] Wedgwood favored the more radical program of Major Cartwright and John Jebb, who advocated annual Parliaments and universal manhood suffrage.

Many figures who are better known as Whig radicals in the 1780s were involved in prison reform. John Jebb wrote a treatise on institutional discipline in 1785, based on his experience as a director of a House of Industry in Suffolk in the 1770s.[64] Other radicals—William Smith, Josiah Dornford, and William Blizard—wrote tracts denouncing the condition of London prisons and the state of the police.[65] The Duke of Richmond, who introduced the first reform bill into the Lords in 1780, was also responsible for directing the construction of the first penitentiary house in England, opened at Horsham in Sussex in 1778.[66]

These men integrated prison reform into a general attack on the administrative and political structure of the *ancien régime*. They took up Howard's indictment as further proof of the administrative incapacity of the Tory squirearchy. This is not to imply that prison reform became a "party matter." The cause enlisted support across the political spectrum. Nevertheless, it was among the Whig Nonconformist reformers that Howard found his most attentive hearing. The success of his crusade therefore was bound up with the whole resurgence of the Whig oppositional tradition.

This resurgence reflects the rise of the Nonconformist petty bourgeoisie into the ranks of the landowning and industrial middle class. The ascent of Howard's own family, from the carpet warehouse to the country estate in one generation, epitomizes the success of a whole segment of Nonconformity. Their struggle, launched in 1769 to repeal the Corporation and Test Acts debarring Dissenters from public office, was their first attempt to win political rights commensurate with their economic power.[67] Howard himself had felt the weight of these acts in 1773 when he found himself required upon taking office as sheriff of Bedford to submit to the humiliation of falsely swearing allegiance to the Thirty-Nine Articles of the Established Church.[68]

The long descent into the American War also helped to revive Nonconformist political radicalism. Ties of religion, politics, and commercial interest linked English Nonconformists closely to the American colonists. To take but one example, Howard's friend John Fothergill had relatives among the Quakers in Philadelphia, visited there in the 1750s, and established close friendships with Benjamin Franklin and Benjamin Rush. When in London in the 1770s, the Americans joined Fothergill to discuss politics with other "Honest Whigs" at fortnightly meetings in the London Tavern.[69] It was in circles such as this that the political philosophy of the Whigs was revived and recast in response to the colonial crisis, the struggle over the Test Acts, and the cause of parliamentary reform. Richard Price, Joseph Priestley, and James Burgh were the major voices of this new radicalism. It was to these writers that Rush, Franklin, and other American revolutionaries turned to justify their opposition to the British attempt to impose taxes and quarter standing armies on a people unrepresented in Parliament. From their writings too came the key principles of the American constitution, in particular the idea of checks and balances.[70] In England, the same writers provided Fothergill, Howard, Bayley, and other Whig reformers with the reasons for supporting the struggle of the colonists.

The actual outbreak of war in 1776 struck men like Fothergill, Howard, and Price with the force of a personal tragedy. For a decade they had struggled to mobilize opinion against it and had tried in vain to devise a compromise that would prevent a fatal estrangement with their American friends. When the government persisted in blundering into armed conflict, the Whig radicals interpreted the war as much more than a political error. Both Price and Fothergill saw it as nothing less than divine punishment for a nation that had lost its way morally. At the outbreak of the war, Price wrote:

In this hour of danger, it would become us to turn our thoughts to Heaven. This is what our brethren in the colonies are doing. From one end of North America to the other they are fasting and praying. But what are we doing?—shocking thought—we are running wild after pleasure and forgetting everything serious and decent in Masquerades—we are gambling in gaming houses; trafficking in boroughs; perjuring ourselves at elections; and selling ourselves for places—which side is Providence likely to favour?[71]

In their anguish over their country's fratricidal conflict with the colonies, they saw writ large the fatal consequence of the corruption of the political elite. Men who might have opposed the government's course allowed themselves to be bought off with offers of place or preferment; others who might have raised their voices against ministerial folly were too immersed in pleasure to devote themselves to public issues. The Whig opposition was in a frame of mind analogous to that of liberal opponents of the Vietnam War after 1968. The brutalities of policy abroad seemed to reveal deeper faults in the moral structure of society at home.[72]

The war vindicated the Whig opposition's appeals for political, administrative, and moral reform. It lent credibility to their argument that the imperial blunders of the ministry had occurred because a Parliament seeded with hirelings had lacked the independence to mount an effective opposition. In the strained and disillusioned wartime climate a host of proposals were put forward to restore the power of Parliament, right the balance of the constitution, and root out corruption in government departments. Appearing as it did in 1777, Howard's *The State of the Prisons* was swept up in the general clamor for reform.

At the center of this ferment was the circle of intellectuals who gathered at Bowood, the estate of the Whig politician Lord Shelburne. Jeremy Bentham, Samuel Romilly, Richard Price, and Joseph Priestley were the leading members of the group. Bowood could be described as the meeting ground of the materialist, scientific strain of Nonconformity represented by Priestley, and the continental Enlightenment, represented by Bentham and Romilly.[73] The relationship between these two traditions is exceedingly complex.

There was much about the *philosophes* that disturbed even those English reformers who admitted their influence. Romilly had family connections with the Rousseauian radicals of Geneva, and he visited most of the leading salons of Paris in the 1780s, paying calls on Diderot, d'Alembert, and Helvetius. He exchanged memoranda on hospitals and criminal law reform with Mirabeau. Until the September Massacres of 1792, Romilly remained a devoted supporter of the French Revolution and wrote two accounts of it for his increasingly apprehensive English audience.[74] His own legal thought owes much to Voltaire, Beccaria, and Montesquieu. Yet Romilly was also the son of a Huguenot watchmaker, and the Huguenot side of his nature was repelled by the atheism and libertinism openly espoused in Paris salons during the 1780s.[75] The same ambivalence is evident in Priestley. As Lord Shelburne's librarian and personal companion, he was required to accompany him on his visits to Paris. Yet he also disapproved of the religious and sexual opinions of the salons and preferred to stay in his hotel rooms as much as possible.[76]

Howard, for his part, called Paris a "dirty city" and took his ideas instead from good Protestant cities like Amsterdam and Rotterdam.[77] In *The State of the Prisons,* Howard makes little reference to Voltaire, Beccaria, or other key figures involved in the revolution in legal philosophy. In Europe, only the actual institutional practices of places like the Maison de Force seem to have influenced him deeply. In fact, Howard was by his own admission a "plodder." He had no taste for French theorizing.[78]

Hence, as Caroline Robbins has argued, the revival of Whig political ideology in the 1770s probably owed more to a rediscovery of the English radical tradition of the seventeenth century than to the influence of the European Enlightenment.[79] Yet the distinction between the English and European traditions must not be overdrawn. References to Montesquieu, Voltaire, and Beccaria recur in the writings of the Whig ideologues, and though Priestley's materialism drew on English sources, it was not substantially different from the continental version articulated by Offray de la Mettrie, Helvetius, or Cabanis.

English materialism derived largely from the work of David Hartley and John Locke. Since their doctrine denied the existence of innate ideas, it offered an immensely influential "scientific" rebuttal of the idea of original sin, and hence of the notion that criminals were incorrigible.[80] Materialism enabled prison reformers to ascribe criminality to incorrect socialization rather than to innate propensities. As Bentham put it, criminals were "froward children, persons of unsound mind," who lacked the self-discipline to control their passions according to the dictates of reason.[81]

They were not incorrigible monsters, merely defective creatures whose infantile desires drove them to ignore the long-term cost of short-term gratifications. Crime, therefore, was not sin but improper calculation.

Thus Howard and Bentham both denied criminal incorrigibility, but from diametrically opposed positions—one accepting the idea of original sin, the other denying it. One insisted on the universality of guilt, the other on the universality of reason. Materialists like Bentham and Priestley asserted that men could be improved by correctly socializing their instincts for pleasure. Howard believed men could be changed by awakening their consciousness of sin.

Howard's thought was cast not in the vernacular of mechanism, but in an older religious language, closer to Wesley's than to Hartley's. For him, criminals were not defective machines but lost souls estranged from God. Nevertheless, during the 1770s the Hartleian climate of belief in reformist circles did provide the context necessary for the acceptance of Howard's disciplinary ideas. Materialist psychology, by collapsing the mind-body distinction, seemed to offer a scientific explanation for Howard's claim that men's moral behavior could be altered by disciplining their bodies. Materialist psychology implied that a regimen applied to the body by the external force of authority would first become a habit and then gradually be transformed into a moral preference. Through routinization and repetition, the regimens of discipline would be internalized as moral duties.

The materialist conception of reformation also assumed that such programming could be aided by systematic moral reeducation directed at the mind. If all ideas, including moral ones, were derived from external sensation, it followed that people could be socialized by taking control over their sources of sensation. The attraction of the "total institution" then was that it afforded such a complete measure of control over the criminal's "associations." Materialist optimism of this sort also pervaded the Whig call for parliamentary and administrative reform in the 1770s. As James Burgh said, "An able statesman can change the manners of the people at pleasure." Is it not evident, he asserted, "that by management the human species may be moulded into any conceivable shape."[82]

The factory masters, doctors, and hospital reformers who took their politics from Burgh and Priestley also spoke of the human

species as machines to be tinkered with and improved. Josiah
Wedgwood boasted that he would "make machines of men as
cannot err." Bentham crowed that his Panopticon was a "machine
for grinding rogues honest." Robert Owen, who was strongly
influenced by the materialism of the 1780s, asserted that the "animate mechanisms" of New Lanark had been rendered as efficient
as the "inanimate mechanisms" under his management.[83]

Some of these disciplinarians, it should be said, saw themselves
in terms no less materialistic than they saw their workers. In 1782,
Josiah Wedgwood wrote to cheer up his friend James Watt, who
was tired and depressed from his labors at the Soho engineering
works in Birmingham:

> Your mind, my friend, is too active, too powerful for your body
> and harasses it beyond its bearing. If this was the case with any
> other machine under your direction. . . . you would soon find out
> a remedy. For the present permit me to advise a more ample use
> of the oil of delegation through your whole machinery. Seriously,
> I shall conclude in saying to you what Dr. Fothergill desired me
> to say to Brindley, "Spare your machine a little or like others
> under your direction, it will wear out the sooner by hard and
> constant usage."[84]

In the symbolic system that materialist assumptions made possible,
managing the self and managing other men became analogous to
the management of machines. Likewise, the reformation of men
could be seen, in Bentham's words, as a "species of manufacture,"
requiring "its particular capital or stock in trade," that is, a technology of its own.[85]

This materialist optimism was an international phenomenon. In
France, it inspired the movement for hospital and asylum reform
during the revolutionary decades. Materialist arguments legitimized the medical profession's struggle to establish a monopoly
over the management of asylums and the discipline of prisons by
casting criminality and insanity as medical pathologies rooted in
the lesions of the brain. P. J. G. Cabanis, the medical practitioner
and ideologist of the revolutionary period, was particularly influential in spreading the idea that "criminal habits and aberrations of
reason are always accompanied by certain organic peculiarities
manifested in the external form of the body, or in the features of
the physiognomy."[86] Such arguments were transparent claims to
medical hegemony in the ordering of the deviant. Cabanis was not
the first to advance such claims. In 1749, the author of *Man a
Machine*, Offray de la Mettrie, had predicted that there would be

a day when guilt and innocence would become matters for medical men alone to decide. As he said, "It is much to be wish'd that we had none for judges but the most skilful physicians." This prescient anticipation of the ascendancy that doctors and psychiatrists currently enjoy in the diagnostic stages of the criminal justice process followed naturally from a materialist model of crime that denied individual responsibility.[87]

In France, the most dramatic breakthrough for the medical profession in the field of institutional discipline was the appointment in 1792 of Philippe Pinel as superintendent of the asylum of Bicêtre in Paris. The act that made him famous, striking off the fetters of the insane, is so often regarded only as a humanitarian gesture that its connection to the disciplinary thought of the period has been obscured. As Pinel saw it, chains merely constrained the body. Discipline actually habituated the mind to order. Accordingly, he replaced chains with a disciplinary regimen of surveillance, hard labor, and submission to rules. Pinel's equation of discipline with therapy in turn assumed that madness, like crime, was a loss of self-control, a straying from the path of reason into the entangling thickets of passion. For the mind to regain the path of order, it was necessary first for it to relearn the habits of punctuality, obedience, and diligence.[88]

Pinel's conception of therapy reached England through a translation of his work that appeared in 1806. Like Howard, he found his most receptive and attentive audience among the Quakers. The asylum for the insane founded in 1813 by the York Friends, under the leadership of Samuel Tuke, was the first to replace chaining and blistering of patients with a "moral regime" supervised by doctors.[89]

In America, the materialist enthusiasm for discipline was articulated chiefly by Benjamin Rush, Philadelphia "mad doctor," physician, philanthropist, and politician. Like his friend Fothergill, Rush had imbibed Hartleian views during his student days at Edinburgh medical school.[90] In his *Enquiry into the Influence of Physical Causes Upon the Moral Faculty* he echoed Cabanis's belief that criminality and insanity were medical pathologies, and he stridently predicted that doctors would soon be able to prescribe cures for crime just as they prescribed "Peruvian bark for curing the intermittent fever."[91] Like Cabanis, he maintained that the "cultivation of the moral faculty" should become the work of the medical profession acting in the name of the state.

In his philanthropic avocations, Rush actually sought to vindicate his disciplinary faith. Along with a number of prominent Philadelphia Quakers, he served on the committee to introduce reformative discipline into the Walnut Street jail. When he visited the prison in 1792 he recorded his satisfaction with the experiment:

> All busy in working at: 1. sawing marble, 2. grinding plaster of Paris, 3. weaving, 4. shoemaking, 5. tayloring, 6. turning, 7. cutting or chipping logwood.
> Care of morals: Preaching, reading good books, cleanliness in dress, rooms etc., bathing, no loud speaking, no wine and as little tobacco as possible. No obscene or profane conversation. Constant work, familiarity with garden, a beautiful one, 1200 heads of cabbages, supplies the jail with vegetables, kept by the prisoners. . . .[92]

When the Duc de Rochefoucauld-Liancourt, the French institutional reformer, visited the new prison in 1795, he found that those condemned for crimes previously punishable by death were confined in cells 8' by 6' by 9' and were not allowed out even for exercise. There was a toilet in each cell and a small penned exercise yard attached so that prisoners remained in solitude even during recreation. The rest of the prisoners were confined in dormitories and worked together in workshops during the day. While the rule of silence was not prescribed, they were forbidden to "bawl after one another or to converse on the causes of their detention or to reproach each other on any account." General quiet was necessary, the duke was told, in order to eliminate the distractions of sense and to prepare the prisoner "to be converted, as it were, into a new being."[93]

The Philadelphia hospital for the insane offered Rush another opportunity to order men's minds through the regulation of their bodies. Rush was a consultant at the hospital as well as the author of a major treatise on insanity. His most notable contribution to the technology of therapeutic discipline was "the tranquilizer," a chair designed to subdue patients suffering from hysteria. They were strapped into the chair, and their heads were immobilized in a set of wooden blinkers. A toilet in the seat provided for their evacuations. They were to remain so confined until they became manageable. For patients suffering from "torpid madness," Rush devised a "gyrator," a rotating table. Lethargic or catatonic patients were strapped down on the table and rotated at high speed to force blood to the head and to shock the brain, so Rush argued, into rational activity. Both were discontinued, however, after patients were injured resisting Rush's benevolent therapies.[94]

IV

While the prison reformers often spoke of deviants as machines to be tinkered with, they were also able, quite contradictorily, to think of them, in Hanway's words, as "free agents, capable of chosing the good and repenting from evil."[95] Jeremy Bentham alternated, with no apparent sense of contradiction, between referring to criminals as defective mechanisms and calling them rational creatures entitled to the protection of the community.[96] Howard insisted not only that criminals were rational, but also that they were capable of shame. Criminals could be reformed, in other words, because they had a conscience like everyone else. As one reformer put it, there was in every person, criminals included, "a respect for law which he never violates by the first offense without a compunction that leaves his mind open to correction."[97] The moral law, another reformer wrote, was "engraved as it were upon the human mind."[98]

The reformers had some difficulty finding a place for the idea of conscience in their associationist assumptions. Materialist psychology explicitly denied the concept of an innate sense of right. Duty, Locke had insisted, was not inscribed on the human heart. It was an obligation learned through the rewards and punishments that a child received at the hands of authority. People were rational enough to discern the good, Locke believed, but if their moral socialization was faulty, there was no inner voice of conscience to call their ego back from its restless search for pleasure.[99]

By the 1740s, these unsettling implications had been glossed over in associationist theory. The third Earl of Shaftesbury insisted, for example, that people possessed a "natural moral sense which enabled them, if not prevented by adverse circumstance or environment to discover the laws of nature and attain to virtue."[100] Bishop Butler's sermons in the 1740s took up the same sunny theme: "Conscience and self love, if we understand our true happiness, lead us in the same way. Duty and interest are perfectly coincident."[101]

These glosses on the Lockian text spirited the idea of conscience back into associationist moral theory and offered validation for two distinct and contradictory approaches to the reformation of the deviant, one through the routinization of the body, the other through direct appeals to their conscience. In this second conception, the aim of punishment was to arouse guilt.

The reformers of the 1780s were not the first to discover the social utility of guilt. In his discussion of corporal punishment in *Thoughts on Education,* Locke had argued that tutors should make sparing use of the rod, lest children lose the shame of being beaten. "Shame of doing Amiss and deserving Punishment," he said, "is the only true Restraint belonging to Vertue." "The smart of the rod, if shame accompanies it not, soon ceases, and is forgotten, and will quickly by use, lose its terror."[102] When applied beyond the master-pupil relationship to the society at large, this idea implied that a social order ruled by terror could never be as stable as one bound together by voluntary obligation to the law. As Archbishop Tillotson was to put it in a sermon that Henry Fielding liked to quote in the 1750s, "fear of the Magistrates' power" was but a "weak and loose principle of obedience." It would cease "whenever men can rebel with safety and advantage." Rulers must make their subjects ashamed to disobey, the archbishop argued. "Conscience will hold a man fast when all other obligations break."[103]

If social order depended on making citizens feel ashamed at the prospect of punishment, then it was essential that the actual infliction of punishment conserve its moral legitimacy in the eyes of the public. The key problem for social order, therefore, was to represent the suffering of punishment in such a way that those who endured it and those who watched its infliction conserved their moral respect for those who inflicted it. The efficacy of punishment depended on its legitimacy. Hence a paradox: the most painful punishments, those that aroused the greatest guilt, were those that observed the strictest standards of justice and morality. From such punishment there could be no psychological escape into contempt for the punisher, assertions of innocence, or protests against its cruelty. Nothing in the penalty's infliction would divert offenders from contemplating their own guilt. Once convinced of the justice of their sentence and the benevolent intentions of their captors, they could only surrender to the horrors of remorse.

Certainly the reformers of the 1780s were not the first to see that punishment could only arouse guilt if it did not alienate the offender or the public. But they were the first to argue that criminals actually had a capacity for remorse, which could be awakened by carefully legitimated and scientifically inflicted pain. Locke, for example, had been dubious about the reclamation of offenders. He doubted that they had a conscience to work upon. In the *Second Treatise of Government,* for example, criminals were dismissed as slaves, whose wrongdoings conferred on society the right to exploit them as it saw fit.[104]

Howard, by contrast, had little doubt that he could govern criminals by appealing to their better nature:

> The notion that convicts are ungoverneable is certainly erroneous. There is a mode of managing some of the most desperate with ease to yourself and advantage to them. Shew them that you have humanity, and that you aim to make them useful members of society; and let them see and hear the rules and orders of the prison that they may be convinced they are not defrauded in their provisions or clothes, by contractors or gaolers. Such conduct would prevent mutiny in prisons and attempts to escape; which I am fully persuaded are often owing to prisoners being made desperate by the profaneness, inhumanity and ill-usage of their keepers.[105]

If the criminal conscience could be won over by fair treatment, it could also be alienated by abuse. The reformers were insistent that physical punishments like whipping, as well as the squalor of prisons, were eroding respect for law among offenders and the general public at large. Since there does not seem to have been any very noticeable public outcry against prison abuses or physical punishments prior to the reform movement itself, it appears that the reformers took their own heightened sensitivity to physical cruelty as symptomatic of general social feeling.

They warned that "the capricious severity" of needlessly frequent executions and bloody public scourgings stigmatized offenders and "confirmed them in villainy instead of leading to a happy alteration in their conduct."[106] "Excessive correction," as one writer of the 1790s put it, "counteracts the very intention of the law by drawing from the multitude a greater degree of compassion for the sufferer than of indignation for the offense."[107]

The prison reformers' heightened sensitivity to institutional abuse and physical cruelty reflected a deep-seated anxiety about the legitimacy of the legal system in the eyes of the public, particularly the poor. In the Whig radical advocacy of parliamentary reform in the 1770s one can detect a similar anxiety and a desire to use reform to fortify public respect for law. The Whig political writers liked to dwell, for example, on the contrast between public order in republican and monarchical government. Richard Price observed that public hangings were rare in Massachussetts because the people had a hand in the making of the laws. In England, where the citizen's internal obligation was not fortified by democratic participation, executions were a daily occurrence.[108] Benjamin Rush echoed this theme in 1787 when he argued that capital punishments were "the natural offspring of monarchical governments." Since kings believe they possess their authority by divine right, they naturally assume "the divine power of taking away human life." Considering their subjects as their property, they shed their blood "with as little emotion as men shed the blood of sheep or cattle." Republican governments, he said, "speak a very different language. They appreciate human life and increase public and private obligations to preserve it."[109]

In their effort to devise a firmer basis for social order in an unequal society, the Whig reformers placed renewed emphasis on the need for government to conform to the wishes of the people. None of them, with the exception of Major Cartwright, could be called democrats, but they all insisted, as Price put it, that "civil government . . . is the creature of the people."[110] The propertyless might not be entitled to vote, Burgh said, but they needed to be convinced that their governors were seeking the public good and not simply lining their pockets.[111]

The revival of consensual conceptions of authority during the American War helps to explain the prison reformers' insistence on finding a way to inflict pain without alienating the offender. But how were they to put such theory into practice? Howard insisted that "gentle discipline [was] commonly more efficacious than severity."[112] In place of the "gothic mode of correction," he proposed "the more rational plan" of "softening the mind in order to aid its amendment."[113] As John Brewster, author of *On the Prevention of Crimes*, said in a chilling phrase, "There are cords of love as well as fetters of iron." Undaunted souls who would not bend before the "passion of fear" might be won over by "more tender impressions."[114] Cords of love bound minds in guilty remorse; fetters of iron bound only the body, leaving the mind free to fester in anger.

By cords of love, Brewster meant the reformative and utilitarian justifications of punishment that would persuade the offender to accept his sufferings and face his own guilt. It is important to see these new theories of punishment as arguments directed at the prisoner. Reformative theory presented punishment to offenders as being "in their best interests" while utilitarian theory cast it as an impartial act of social necessity. In rejecting retributive theory, the reformers sought, in effect, to take the anger out of punishment. As it was legitimized to the prisoner, punishment was no longer to be, in Bentham's words, "an act of wrath or vengeance," but an act of calculation, disciplined by considerations of the social good and the offenders' needs.[115]

It was the prison chaplain who would bind prisoners with the cords of love. He would persuade offenders to accept their sufferings as an impartial and benevolent condemnation. He would force them to accept their own guilt. It was he who would enclose them in the ideological prison. In the 1790s, prisoners began to hear words such as these from the pulpits of prison chapels:

> The laws of our country are not instruments of vengeance but of correction. The punishment inflicted by the magistrate is not to be considered as the resentment of a man subject to various passions, who might mistake or wilfully torture the object of his displeasures, but as a mutual benefit to the offender and that society against which the offence was committed. Harbour not then within your breast any seeds of malice or ill-will against those who have been instrumental in bringing you to punishment.[116]

Yet sermons alone could not convince prisoners to accept the justice of their sufferings. In addition, of course, it was necessary that the discipline of the institution itself give confirmation of the benevolence and impartiality of the legal system. The reformers' task, in other words, was to make punishment self-evidently rational. On this question, Jeremy Bentham proved to be the most influential mind.

His conception of punishment is most graphically illustrated by his discussion of whipping. The severity of a whipping depended on the strength of the person who inflicted it and the degree of indignation that the offender aroused in the crowd. It struck Bentham as unjust and irrational that punishment should vary according to the emotions of those who inflicted it and those who watched. In his view, its severity should depend only on the gravity of the offense. Accordingly, he envisaged a whipping machine, a rotary flail made of canes and whalebone, which could be made to lash the backs of each offender with the same unvarying force to the number of strokes chosen by the operator.[117]

In his conception of pain, therefore, what was rational was impersonal, and what was impersonal was humane. Punishment should not be scattered by a monarch's wrathful hand, but apportioned to each crime as precisely as the market allocated prices to commodities. Ideally, machines could be used to inflict the exact price for crime. Punishment would then become a science, an objective use of pain by the state for the regulation of the egoistic calculus of individuals.

Bentham's idea of a science of pain should be seen in the context of the widespread belief within the Scottish Enlightenment and the parliamentary reformers of the 1770s that government itself could become a science.[118] Bentham thus was not alone in believing that men would one day discover the laws governing finance, administration, and social order. In these theories of government, punishment occupied pride of place, as the chief instrument available to a state to canalize the egoistic pursuits of individuals to lawful ends.[119]

This idea of authority permeated conceptions of philanthropy in the 1770s. The benevolence of early factory masters and institutional reformers is often interpreted as an effort to introduce an idealized version of rural paternalism into an industrial and institutional context. Yet Wedgwood, Strutt, or Howard did not use the old language of deference to describe their philanthropy, but chose instead new phrases like "political humanity" and "scientific humanity."[120] They aspired, as Thomas Bernard of the Society for Bettering the Condition of the Poor put it in 1798, "to make the inquiry into all that concerns the poor and the promotion of their happiness a science."[121] In Bernard's mind, this meant replacing indiscriminate almsgiving with a systematic attempt to distinguish between the deserving and undeserving poor. In the factory, the notion of scientific authority implied an attempt to reconcile the profitable exploitation of labor and the protection of its moral well-being. In the case of prisons, it meant reconciling deterrence and rehabilitation, punishment and reform.

But how was a rational authority system to be established in prisons and factories? How were the imperatives of "humanity" and "terror," "profit" and "benevolence" to be reconciled in practice? As far as the reformers were concerned, these questions translated into another: how was the supervisory personnel of these institutions to be controlled?

The answer was by an authority of rules. The prison reformers believed that punishment had lost its moral authority among the poor because those who inflicted it had been allowed unlimited discretion. Prisons had degenerated into squalid nurseries of crime because magistrates had failed to enforce explicit rules regarding discipline, hygiene, and hard labor. Corruption, favoritism, and cruelty flowered in prisons because the keepers' authority was not kept in check by rules and inspections. In place of "unregulated discretion" the reformers proposed to substitute "mild government by rule."[122]

In Howard's mind, the rules were supposed to apply to the staff no less than to the prisoners. Half of the new rules that he proposed were directed against trafficking, verbal abuse, fee taking, or physical acts of cruelty by staff. They also laid out a sequence of custodial tasks, inspection tours, roll calls, bed checks, and night patrols. The guards no less than the inmates were to be routinized by formal regulations.[123]

The reformers' attack on the fee system was particularly designed to limit custodial discretion. By abolishing fees, the reformers hoped to convert the keeper from an independent contractor into a paid subordinate of the state. To ensure his accountability, the reformers proposed that quarterly inspections by magistrates become mandatory.

This attack on discretion implied that punishment was too central to the exercise of class rule to be left to private contractors. Instead, the state would now supervise its infliction directly.

The rules also applied to the prisoners and prescribed a minute grid of deprivations designed to standardize the institutional day, to add the burden of monotony to the terrors of solitude, and above all to silence the inmate subculture. That subculture, no less than the keepers' discretion, had frustrated attempts to inflict a just and unvarying quantum of pain. The rules were intended to win back the prison from both the criminals and their keepers. In place of the unwritten, customary, and corrupt division of power between criminals and custodians, the reformers proposed to subject both to the disciplines of a formal code enforced from the outside.

Inspection was to be the watchword of the new authority. In *Panopticon*, the sketch for a penitentiary that he published in 1791, Bentham placed both prisoner and guard alike under the constant surveillance of an inspector patrolling in the central inspection tower. From this vantage point, the inspectors had a clear view of the prisoners in their cells and the guards on their rounds. In this way, the custodial staff were kept "under the same irresistible control" as the prisoners.[124]

Such inspection was to be democratic. Members of the general public were given free admission to the inspection tower to keep the inspectors under surveillance. Omnipresent inspection, of everyone, by everyone, was Bentham's solution to the old question of who guards the guards.

Rules, therefore, had a double meaning for the reformers. They were an enumeration of the inmates' deprivations, but also a charter of their rights. They bound both sides of the institutional encounter in obedience to an impartial code enforced from outside. As such they reconciled the interests of the state, the custodians, and the prisoners alike.

Solitary confinement, likewise, reconciled terror and humanity. The reformers did not doubt that it was an instrument of suffering. John Brewster dwelt graphically on the anguish that solitude would induce:

> To be abstracted from a world where he has endeavoured to confound the order of society, to be buried in a solitude where he has no companion but reflection, no counsellor but thought, the offender will find the severest punishment he can receive. The sudden change of scene that he experiences, the window which admits but a few rays of light, the midnight silence which surround him, all inspire him with a degree of horror which he never felt before. The impression is greatly heightened by his being obliged to think. No intoxicating cup benumbs his senses, no tumultuous revel dissipates his mind. Left alone and feelingly alive to the strings of remorse, he revolves on his present situation and connects it with that train of events which has banished him from society and placed him there.[125]

Solitude, as Jonas Hanway did not hesitate to admit, was the "most terrible penalty," short of death, that a society could inflict. It was also, he insisted, "the most humane."[126] No rough or brutal hands were laid upon the offenders. The state, as it were, struck off their chains and withdrew, leaving them alone with their conscience. In the silence of their cells, superintended by an authority too systematic to be evaded, too rational to be resisted, prisoners would surrender to the lash of remorse. "He who torments mankind," said Offray de la Mettrie, "becomes his own tormentor."[127]

Such was the theory of the penitentiary as enunciated by the constituency of Nonconformist doctors, philanthropists, and magistrates in London and the manufacturing towns who arose to support Howard's crusades. They took up the idea of the penitentiary because, as a system of authority and as a machine for the remaking of men, it reflected some of their deepest political, psychological, and religious assumptions. It promised, above all, to restore the legitimacy of a legal system that they feared was jeopardized by the excessive severities and gratuitous abuses of the Bloody Code.

Yet the appeal of the penitentiary reached beyond this immediate milieu to figures like William Blackstone and to scores of rural justices who were later to launch the construction of new prisons. Their support for prison reform cannot be explained in terms of an intellectual affinity with Howard's conception of discipline, but in terms of the objective urgency of reform in the decade of the 1770s. Had Howard's *State of the Prisons* been published at any other time, figures outside the small circle of reforming Dissenters might have been disposed to dismiss it as a worthy but tedious tract. Instead, it appeared at a moment of acute crisis in the administration of criminal justice.

CHAPTER FOUR

Preaching Walls:

The Penitentiary in Practice

I

The outbreak of the American War and the sudden suspension of
transportation to the thirteen colonies in 1775 dealt a paralyzing
blow to the authorities in charge of criminal justice. Immediately,
they had to devise an alternative punishment for most forms of
property crime. Their first inclination was to temporize rather
than to make fundamental changes. As a "temporary expedient,"
the government refitted a number of superannuated warships as
floating prisons and moored them on the Thames near Woolwich.
Later, additional "hulks," as they were called, were stationed at the
entrance to the harbors of Plymouth, Gosport, and Portsmouth.
By 1787 about two thousand convicts were employed on the hulks
in chain gangs, raising sand for ships' ballast or constructing new
dockyard facilities.

The government turned the management of these convicts
over to Duncan Campbell, a merchant with twenty years' experience as a contractor for the transport of convicts. Since, in the past,
he had made his money selling the convicts to American employers, he was accustomed to regard them as commodities. Campbell,

by no means an exceptionally callous contractor, looked upon a mortality of one in seven as an acceptable "inventory shrinkage." In the first three years, however, the death rate on the hulks under his supervision was nearer to one in four.[1]

The prisoners brought typhus with them from the county jails, and because Campbell did not take any hygienic precautions, disease ravaged the ships. When Howard inspected the convicts on board the *Justitia* in October 1776, he saw "by their sickly looks" that there was "some mismanagement among them":

> Many had no shirts, some no waistcoats . . . some no stockings and some no shoes; many knew him [Howard], one of whom he saw very ill; he touched his Pulse and asked him how he did? He said, he was ready to sink into the earth.[2]

Respectable London was kept on edge for a decade by the repeated escapes, outbreaks of typhus, and insurrections on board the hulks on the Thames. Clearly the national government was proving no more competent in administering places of punishment than the county and borough justices had been.

While the hulks remained in existence long after the immediate crisis of the 1770s had passed, they were never intended as a long-term replacement for transportation. For one thing they could only absorb 60 percent of those under sentence of transportation when the American War broke out. The rest, several thousand of them, had to be kept in the county and borough prisons, along with those new transportees sentenced after 1775. As a result, almost overnight, imprisonment was transformed from an occasional punishment for felony into the sentence of first resort for all minor property crime. The table below illustrates the dramatic increase in sentences of imprisonment at the Old Bailey after 1775.[3]

Table 1:   Distribution of Punishments,
Old Bailey, 1760–94

YEAR	PERCENT DEATH SENTENCE	PERCENT TRANSPORTED/ HULKS	PERCENT WHIP/BRAND/ FINE	PERCENT IMPRISONED
1760–64	12.7	74.1	12.3	1.2
1765–69	15.8	70.2	13.4	0.8
1770–74	17.0	66.5	14.2	2.3
1775–79	20.7	33.4	17.6	28.6
1780–84	25.8	24.1	15.5	34.6
1785–89	18.5	50.1	13.2	13.3
1790–94	15.9	43.9	11.7	28.3

Most of these new sentences of imprisonment were inflicted on first-time offenders convicted of minor larcenies. "Atrocious and hardened" offenders were sent to the hulks. At first, the prison terms were long and were frequently accompanied by a whipping. Judges routinely handed out five- and seven-year terms until a Commons committee pointed out in 1779 that such sentences amounted to a death warrant, given the condition of most prisons.[4] Thereafter, sentence lengths declined. By the 1790s, most were for less than a year.

The sudden resort to imprisonment thrust an added burden on institutions that had showed signs of overcrowding even before 1775. Until 1783, however, the system managed to function without outbreaks of fever. Howard did not find a single case during his tour of 1779.[5] This was not, however, because magistrates took any precautionary measures. Most did not. They assumed that after an early victory against the Americans the transports crowding their jails would be shipped off once again to a defeated and pliant colony. Accordingly, they did little about prison conditions, assuming that the problem of numbers would go away. Moreover, the wartime demands for manpower acted to stabilize the crime rate and thus to reduce pressure on the jails.[6] Judges also helped to relieve overcrowding by sentencing offenders to service in the fleet or the army instead of prison.[7]

It was the return of peace in 1783 that brought on the real crisis. Demobilization, accompanied by a trade depression following the loss of the colonial market, resulted in the most serious increase in crime since the 1720s.[8] The number of offenders committed for trial at the Old Bailey from 1783 to 1786 was almost 40 percent higher than in the previous three years.

While some observers attributed the "rapid and alarming increase of crime and depredations" to such short-term causes as the temporary glutting of the labor market and the falling off of trade, the prison reformers interpreted the situation in apocalyptic terms as evidence of a breakdown in urban order, class harmony, and moral discipline among the poor.[9] The key term in their diagnosis of the pathology of the age was the concept of "luxury."

"Luxury," in their view, had eroded that strict sense of civic duty among the rich upon which public order depended.[10] The poor, under this baneful influence, had shaken off the trammels of deferred gratification and the measured asceticism of wage labor, embracing the sensual pleasures of crime. In such a climate of

1. Male convict at Pentonville Prison, wearing the mask, and female convict at Millbank Prison.

Pl. 22.

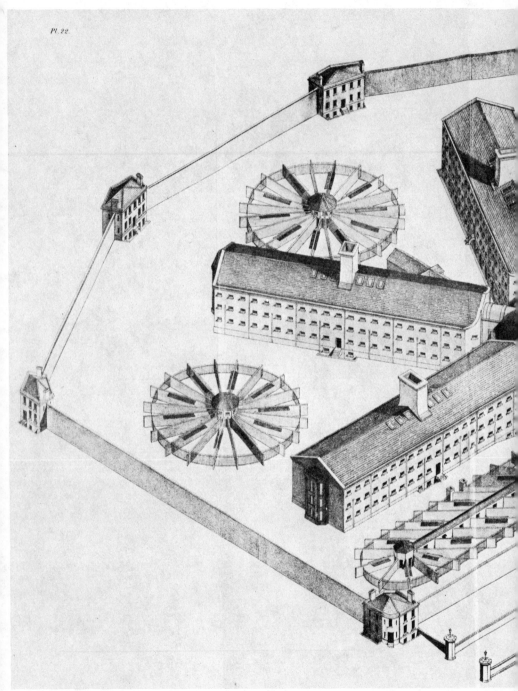

2. Isometrical view of Pentonville Prison, 1844.

ISOMETRICAL VIEW OF PENTONVILLE PRISON.

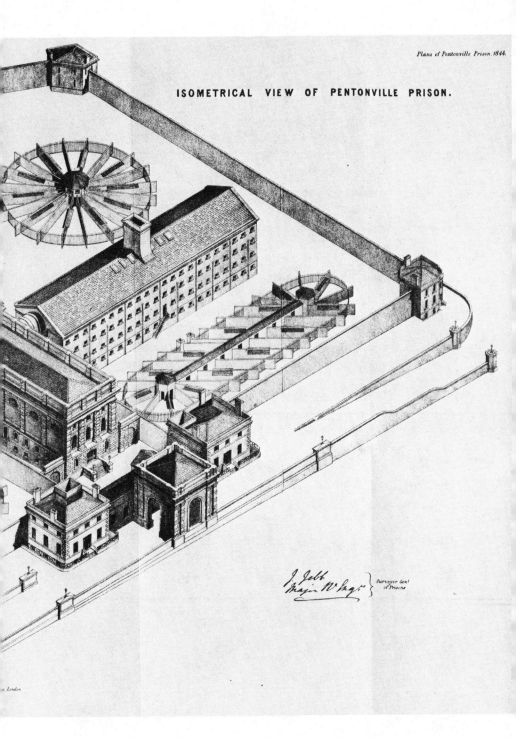

J. Jebb
Major W. Engr. } Surveyor Genl
of Prisons

London

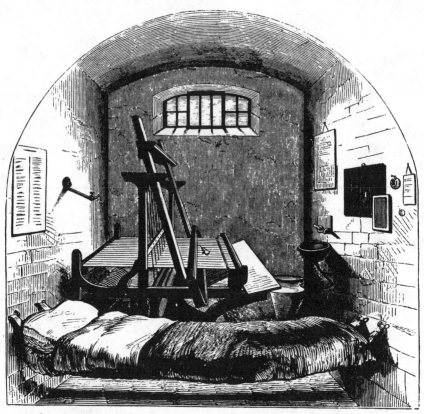

3. Separate cell in Pentonville Prison with hammock slung
   for sleeping and loom for day work.

4. Cell with prisoner at crank labor, Surrey House of Correction.

5. John Howard.

6. John Fothergill, Quaker physician and philanthropist.

7. The chapel at Pentonville, with guards on highchairs superintending prisoners in the boxes.

8. Gloucester Penitentiary, exterior view, 1795.

9. Gloucester Penitentiary, interior view, 1795, showing the
keeper conducting a lady and gentleman on a tour of the
second tier of cells and two prisoners exercising in the
palisaded yards.

10. Elizabeth Fry, 1780–1845.

11. Coldbath Fields Prison, Clerkenwell, London, 1795.

loosening moral authority, the increasingly hedonistic rich no longer exercised tutelage over the poor, children no longer obeyed their parents, and apprentices defied their masters.[11]

This catalogue of dissolution inspired Jonas Hanway to write a number of alarmist pamphlets on the state of the police in London and to urge the adoption of solitary confinement in prisons. "Everyday's experience proves the punishments we now inflict have lost their effect," he wrote. "Something new must be devised. . . . It is no exaggeration to say we live in a country where a man cannot retire to his home, not even in his chariot in a great city without danger of a pistol being clapped to his breast."[12] The authorities, he said, were "asleep on the verge of a precipice." They did not realize that "success in war, improvements in arts, prosperity in commerce," had lulled people into forgetting "the hand from whence these blessings flow." Hanway warned his class that their "dissipations" and "extravagance" were making the poor "desperate and rapacious" and driving them to "commit robbery and murder to obtain the means of gratifying themselves."[13]

Hanway's alarmism was echoed by the London police magistrate Patrick Colquhoun, the London physician William Blizard, and the Whig radical Josiah Dornford. It is not surprising that this alarmism should have been centered in London. For it was there that the temptations of luxury were greatest. Bales on the docks, hams in the window of cookshops, pots dangling from the awnings of ironmongers' stalls, parcels bumping invitingly on the flatbeds of carts offered incitements to criminal passion unavailable in the village.[14]

The city was also the mecca of the "masterless man," the escapee from village order. In the heart of the town congregated an ungovernable collectivity safe from supervision or intrusion. Blizard's description of one such "republic of thieves" in the neighborhood of Church Lane, Field Lane, and Black Boy Alley suggests that the area was a "sort of distinct town or district calculated for the reception of the darkest and most dangerous enemies of society."[15] When pursued by the constabulary, criminals could retreat into this safe warren of courts, alleyways, and underground passages, and from this refuge mock the law's impotence.

Every feature of this alarmist analysis—the corroding influence of luxury, the decaying moral authority of the rich, the defiance of the criminal underworld—can be found, long before the 1780s, in the writings of Joseph Butler, Henry Fielding, Thomas Bray, and Robert Nelson.[16] For nearly a century, discussions of "luxury" and its moral effects had provided the forum in which the middle class, particularly the Whig Nonconformist sector of it, had calculated the consequences of economic growth. But if the content was not new in the 1780s, the conditions of crisis, war, breakdown of punishment, prison overcrowding, and unprecedented levels of crime made the alarmism suddenly more credible. As a result, after the surge in criminal committals of 1783, the London-based analyses of the pathologies of the age began to have a receptive audience in the counties. To many, the times called for a reassertion of social authority, a vindication of the moral legitimacy of the state, and a renewed effort to reform the morals of the disobedient poor.

Since men like Hanway and Blizard defined crime as part of a wider pattern of insubordination among the poor, they were fascinated by the thought of an institution that would give them total control over the body, labor, and even the thought processes of a poor man. The penitentiary, in other words, was more than a functional response to a specific institutional crisis. It exerted a hold on men's imaginations because it represented in microcosm the hierarchical, obedient, and godly social order, which they felt was coming apart around them.

The reformers' sense of social crisis was soon reinforced. In 1786, the research of the Commons committee on the cost of poor relief was published. It revealed that since 1776 the numbers of people claiming assistance from the parish had risen as much as 30 percent in some areas.[17] In addition, the unprecedented overcrowding of jails and houses of correction panicked magistrates everywhere. Unlike the overcrowding of 1750 and 1770, which had chiefly been evident in London, the crisis of the 1780s was felt in every prison in the country. Howard estimated that the prison population increased 73 percent between 1776 and 1786.[18] As a result, prison conditions deteriorated sharply.

The Secretary of State in Whitehall was in a good position to grasp the gravity of the situation. Between 1783 and 1785, he received dispatches from magistrates in thirty-five localities reporting outbreaks of fever, escapes or riots, appeals for military guards around their institutions, and pleas for the speedy resumption of transportation. At Maidstone, for example, an outbreak of "putrid disorder" carried off twelve prisoners and left twenty-seven others dangerously ill.[19] From Ilchester came reports that a "malignant disorder" had claimed eleven lives.[20] A petition from the Somerset justices informed the Secretary that jail fever had killed the jailer, his wife, and the local doctor and had "occasioned great apprehension in both the judges and magistrates" who had to hear the cases of diseased prisoners when they came to trial.[21] The justices at the Lancashire quarter sessions wrote to express concern that "pestilential fever" in Lancaster jail threatened to spread beyond the walls of the institution.[22] At Gloucester, this actually happened. In 1784, fever from the wards of the castle jail jammed with transports awaiting dispatch broke out in the neighborhoods in the shadow of the institution. Half a dozen poor people succumbed.[23]

The prisoners did not suffer their immiseration quietly. A riot at the Wood Street Compter, a London jail, led by a prisoner as "ferocious as Beelzebub," became so serious that the keeper had to appeal for help to a private military club of middle-class citizens, the London Military Foot Association.[24] At Clerkenwell House of Correction, three prisoners were killed and three were wounded when a mass escape attempt was foiled by the turnkeys.[25] The Surrey justices became so alarmed at the threatening behavior of the convicts in Southwark jail that they petitioned the Secretary of State for a military guard around the walls and protested bitterly when it was withdrawn after six months.[26]

The prisoners themselves took their grievances to the Secretary of State. From their petitions it appears that the magistrates had not faced up to the implications of sentencing people to imprisonment. The institutions were still run as places of detention. In many houses of correction no food allowance was provided for prisoners, and they were forced to depend on the uncertain charity of their friends. One group of prisoners at Durham convicted for sheep stealing wrote to Whitehall complaining that they had been respited from transportation on condition of entering the army, but had never been sent out. So they languished in jail:

> By which we are deprived of all means of support from our honest industry and our crimes having robbed us of the assistance of our Freinds, we have nothing to assist us more than the generous Bounty of the county which barely supplies us with Food and our cloaths are quite worn out and our bodies are almost naked. We

therefore humbly pray that you would take this our Unhappy
Situation into Consideration and order such Necessary Apparel as
in our goodness and wisdom may be thought fit.[27]

A petition from convicts in Lancaster Castle pleaded that they too
had been abandoned by county and friends to slow starvation.[28]
On July 20, 1785, eleven convicts in Leicester jail addressed these
plaintive words to the Secretary of State in Whitehall:

The most humble petition of the unfortunate convicts eleven in
number. Most Humbly Sheweth that we are Real miserable objects of Compassion having been Confined thus going on 3 years
in this Unhappy Prison on the Bare Allowance of Two Penny-
worth of Bread per Day which is not half sufficient to satisfy the
Call of Nature, the most part of us being Young People. Neither
does our Misfortunes End here for in Winter many of us has been
forced to part with some part of our Little Subsistence of Bread
to Help Buy a Little Coal to Make a Fire to Warm our Benumbed
Limbs that was Frocen by the Inclemency of the Season and
Heavy Irons Together. So Most Honoured Gentlemen Let our
Crimes Have been ever so Henious our Sufferings has been Past
Description, and we must certainly Perish in this our Native Country. Especially if we are to Stay another Winter in this Cruel
Unhappy Place for had our Sentences been put in Execution as
soon as we was Cast our Punishment might be this Time been over
and we might by the Blessing of God Have Done Better Abroad
than ever We Did at Home. But Instead of any Hopes we have
nothing but Dispair before our Eyes Being Almost Starved to
death with Hunger and Some Barefooted and Bare Leg'd, Others
never a shirt on their Backs and almost Eaten up Alive with
Vermin and in Short Nothing to Hide some of our Nakedness.
Some being 100 miles from Home and not a Freind in the World
to relieve them with a farthing and them that had a few Freinds
at first has Tired them Long Ago. So Most Honoured Gentlemen
as we are Real Objects of Misery and as the Almighty has pleased
to bless you with Plenty we most Humbly Beg and Crave you will
hold out your Ever Bountiful Hands to relieve the most Unhappi-
est of Beings. . . .[29]

I I

As alarming as the condition of the prisons was the evidence that
the crime wave did not seem to be responding to the usual dosages
of terror. The government's initial reaction to the upward climb
of committals in 1782 had been to proclaim that the King's pardon

would be denied henceforth to burglars and housebreakers.[30] The new policy had an immediate impact on sentencing patterns. In 1785, for example, in London and the counties adjacent to it, only about one-third of the capital convicts received pardons, as compared to about two-thirds in the years before 1782.

In the courts, juries appear to have supported this campaign of severity by cutting back on their resort to "pious perjury," the legal maneuver that enabled them to save offenders charged with grand larceny from the gallows by convicting them of petty larceny instead. As a result, the percentage of those found guilty and sentenced to death at the Old Bailey jumped from 17 percent in 1770–74 to 25.8 percent in 1780–84.[31] The number of persons executed in London between 1783 and 1787 was 82 percent higher than in the previous five years. Altogether 348 persons died on the gallows in London in the five years after 1783, 97 in 1785 alone.[32]

While this carnage made a deep and sorrowful impression on reformers like Romilly, it did not seem to stem the tide of crime. During a session of court in 1783, as one judge at the Old Bailey passed sentence of death on thirty-three offenders ranged before him in the dock, he observed that their numbers served as melancholy proof of the impotence of traditional deterrence:

> It must give inexpressible concern to all who see or hear of so crowded a bar of criminals to reflect that laws written in blood and denouncing death against those who violate them should in so many instances have lost their terror and that after such frequent executions and more frequent pardons, the exertions of publick justice and of royal mercy should seem to be thrown away upon such bold offenders.[33]

Seeing that mass executions were failing to stem the "torrent of wretches" coming before the bar, the Quaker writer Martin Madan argued in 1785 that the only course left was still harsher and more inflexible punishment. In a widely read pamphlet, he claimed that it was the frequency of pardons that vitiated the terrors of the capital statutes and left them "little more than a scarecrow set in a field to frighten the birds from the corn."[34] In the future he proposed that no capital convicts should be reprieved from execution.

Samuel Romilly, one of the young lawyers in Lord Shelburne's circle at Bowood, rushed out a demolition of Madan's argument, but his counterattack was superfluous, since none of the defenders of the Bloody Code came to Madan's defense. At ninety-seven executions a year in London alone, the Bloody Code seems to have been enforced at the limit of acceptable terror. To proceed onward into further carnage, as Madan proposed, would have forfeited the precariously maintained myth of the law's mercy and humanity.

In a brief to the Secretary of State, the Corporation of London argued that increasing the number of executions might even encourage crime by accustoming the populace to acts of brutality and by cheapening the value placed on human life.[35] Even the philosopher William Paley, who usually figures in the histories as a complacent defender of the Bloody Code, professed to doubts in 1786 about the justice of executing pickpockets. He lent his formidable prestige to the idea of replacing hanging and transportation with imprisonment in a penitentiary as the punishment of first resort for petty crime.[36]

In 1783 disillusionment with the ritual of public execution itself finally resulted in the curtailment of the Tyburn processional in London. Condemned offenders were drawn from Newgate by cart through the thronged streets to the Tyburn gallows near Marble Arch. This ostensibly solemn procession was designed to advertise as widely as possible the fate that awaited transgression. In practice the ritual was taken over by the crowd and converted into a thieves' holiday and poor people's carnival.

While criticisms of the ritual and its debasement had already become commonplace, it was only in 1783, at the height of the general crisis in criminal justice, that action was taken. The sheriffs of London and Middlesex abolished the processional altogether and ordered that future executions should take place in front of Newgate. The reasons they gave for their actions are worth quoting at length:

> It has long been a subject of complaint that our processions to Tyburn are a mockery upon the aweful sentence of the law and that the final scene itself has lost its terrors and is so far from giving a lesson of morality to the beholders that it tends to the encouragement of vice. No man who has been an eye-witness of it can deny the justice of the censure. The day on which some of our fellow creatures are doomed to be Examples of Terror to evil Doers and to Expiate the Offences of an Ill-Spent Life by an Ignominious Death is too often considered by the vulgar of this city as a Holiday; and the Place of Execution is more frequently resorted to with the strange Expectation of satisfying an unaccountable

Curiosity than with a Sober Solicitude for Moral Improvement. If the only Defect were the want of Ceremony, the mind of beholders might be supposed to be left at least in a state of Indiffer-ence, but when they view the Meanness of the Apparatus, a dirty cart and ragged harness, surrounded by a sordid Assemblage of the lowest among the vulgar, their sentiments are More Inclined to Ridicule than Duty. The Whole Progress is attended with the same effect. Numbers soon thicken into a Crowd of followers and then an indecent levity is heard, the crowd gathers as it goes, and their levity increases till on their Approach to the Fatal Tree, the Ground becomes a Riotous Mass, and their Wantonness of Speech breaks forth in profane Jokes, Swearing and Blasphemy.[37]

Since this attack on public executions had often been made before, the question is why the authorities were finally convinced by it in 1783. Perhaps the sharp increase in hangings after 1782 had some-thing to do with it. The disturbances caused by the surging, bois-terous crowds may have become intolerable when they became almost weekly occurrences. Perhaps too, though this does not figure explicitly in their explanations, the Gordon Riots were still fresh in their memory.

Only three years before, as a protest against a bill removing the civil disabilities of Catholics, the London populace had attacked the houses of judges, stormed the London prisons, and liberated prisoners, as well as jeering and jostling peers and MPs on their way to Parliament. Unlike the London election riots of earlier times, which had always been at least informally stage-managed by radical politicians, the Gordon Riots quickly slipped beyond the control of their chief instigator, Lord George Gordon. As such, they were an alarming sign of a new cleavage between the elite and the poor. In their wake, therefore, the authorities could be ex-pected to be less tolerant of forms of popular disorder like the Tyburn processional.

At any rate, it is clear that the sheriffs withdrew the gallows from Tyburn to the portals of Newgate in order to regain control of a ritual that had slipped out of their hands into the clutches of the mob. Seen in this way, their action is analogous to the prison reformers' effort to gain control of the prison from an inmate subculture that had turned it into a seminary for thieves. In turn, both acts call to mind Patrick Colquhoun's proposals in the 1790s for a metropolitan police force that would destroy the autono-mous criminal underworlds of St. Giles and establish the uncontested sovereignty of the law throughout London.[38] Each of these cases can be interpreted as an attempt to establish state hegemony over collectivities of the poor whose defiance of public authority had long been tolerated or taken for granted.

The curtailment of the Tyburn processional is also related to the reaction against whipping and branding that set in during the 1770s. It became common to argue that public scourgings and brandings "served no better purpose than to mark with indelible infamy those who suffer it and to give offence to every decent inhabitant."[39] Persons bearing the stigmata of punishment would be shunned by employers, avoided by the respectable, and hence driven inexorably back onto criminal paths. Instead of deterring, such punishments hardened offenders and "confirmed them in villainy." William Eden and Jonas Hanway maintained that such spectacles had both lost the confidence of the general public and given the law an image of severity that compromised its authority in the eyes of the poor.[40]

This new current of opinion resulted in significant changes in sentencing practices. Branding was abolished in 1779, by the same act that authorized the construction of penitentiary houses.[41] Meanwhile, the practice of whipping declined from 17 to 11 percent of Old Bailey verdicts between 1775 and 1790. When the first national statistics on punishment became available in 1805, whipping accounted for no more than 4.5 percent of sentences at assize and sessions, though probably a higher percentage of summary punishments.[42] In addition, the frequency of hangings was reduced. From 1787 onward, the number of pardons began to increase again. By 1800, only a little over 10 percent of those sentenced to die in London were actually executed.[43]

All this indicates a loss of confidence in the morality and efficacy of ritual punishments, a growing resistance to the idea that the state should share the infliction of the punishment with the community assembled at the foot of the gallows or around the whipping post. Withdrawing the gallows under the shadow of Newgate and increasing the use of imprisonment denied the offender the opportunity for public defiance and the crowd the chance to turn the ritual to its own purposes. Compared to ritual punishment, imprisonment offered the state unparalleled control over the offender, enabling it to regulate the amount of suffering involved in any sentence, free of the jeers of the populace.

At the same time, the rise of imprisonment indicates a growing scruple about the morality of punishing men by abusing their bodies, as did the widespread support given Howard's campaign against the chaining and beating of offenders in confinement. The reformers sensed that the "public," by which they meant the prisoner, the prosecutor, and the onlookers alike, no longer tolerated or accepted physical abuse as a sentence of the law.

If further resort to physical penalties was unacceptable as a response to the rising crime rates, what about a return to transportation? This was the universal cry of magistrates, faced with institutions filled to bursting with convicts under sentence of banishment. The Secretary of State himself looked to the resumption of transportation as a way out of the crisis. After the disastrous failure of an attempt to establish a convict colony in West Africa, and after both Nova Scotia and the Cape of Good Hope objected to the use of their fledgling settlements as convict depots, Joseph Banks, the botanist on Cook's voyages of exploration, suggested Botany Bay in Australia. His artful insistence on the mercantile value of a colony "larger than the whole of Europe," appealed to a ministry still smarting from the cession of a continent to the victorious Americans.[44] Before the first ships could be sent out in 1786, however, it was necessary to alter the sentences of those who had received terms on the hulks or in prisons and were now to be sent out. In a letter to the Secretary of State, Sampson Wright, a Bow Street magistrate, admitted that it was illegal to tamper with sentences in this way, but he brushed aside his own scruples, remarking that "the public will be happy to get rid of them at any rate."[45]

After what they had suffered on the chain gangs and in the dungeons, the convicts, or at least a group of them in London, were in no mood to let this tampering pass quietly. Nine men and seven women who had already been serving terms on board the hulks protested when brought before the judges to have their sentences changed to transportation.

Sarah Mills got up in court and shouted, "I would rather die than go out of my own country to be devoured by savages." And Sarah Cowden told the astonished and indignant judge, "I will die by the laws of my country before ever I will go abroad for my life." Jane Tayler agreed: "I will die first; I think I have suffered hard enough to be in gaol three years for what I have done." They had been led to believe that their sentences would be commuted after four or five years of imprisonment. As Mary Burgess told the judge: "I am sorry for the trouble I gave the court but I expected to have my Liberty every session for sixteen months. Lord Sydney [the Secretary of State] was my friend and I understood I was not to be sent abroad." After the judge had ordered them down to the condemned cells to reflect, all but one relented and allowed themselves to be taken down to the ships. Sarah Cowden persisted. When brought back into court she began to bargain for the life of a fellow prisoner:

> I will tell you what; I am willing to accept of whatever sentence the King passes upon me, but Sarah Storer is innocent. I would not care whatever sentence I went through; I will accept it if that woman's sentence is mitigated.[46]

At this the judge lost his temper and ordered her confined to await execution. Her life was saved, however, by the intervention of a lawyer in the courtroom who went down to the cells in Newgate and persuaded her to go to the ships. Such was the resistance encountered at the Old Bailey. It would be interesting to know whether prisoners in other courts followed Sarah Cowden's example in that anguished moment when they learned that they were to be sent on a voyage to the end of the earth.

The convicts were not the only ones to resist the resumption of transportation. Howard himself inveighed against the "Botany Bay scheme," arguing that it forfeited an opportunity for the reform of the deviant. Even the committee of 1785, which argued for its resumption, did so with some misgivings:

> Transportation answers very imperfectly the purpose of example. . . . tho' a transported convict may suffer under his sentence, his sufferings are unseen . . . his Chasm is soon filled up and being as soon forgotten, it strikes no terror into the minds of those for whose correction it was intended to operate.[47]

Such disillusionment helps to explain why transportation began to lose its preeminence in the armory of punishment after 1787. By the 1790s, it was ordered in less than 50 percent of guilty cases, as compared with over 70 percent in the period before its suspension in 1775.[48] Imprisonment began to take its place as punishment of first resort for petty felonies. Transportation and hanging remained the major punishments for serious crimes of violence against the person and for the violent crimes against property, such as robbery, burglary, and housebreaking. Now, for the first time, however, there was an "intermediate" penalty for minor property offenses.

In the short space of a decade, the whole stategy of eighteenth century punishment had been thrown into question—by a crime wave that refused to respond to the old remedies, by the suspension of transportation, and by the arguments of reformers who contended that there was a more just and rational way for the state to inflict pain on its subjects.

III

The major document to embody this conception was the Penitentiary Act of 1779, drafted by Howard, Eden, and Blackstone. In their original proposal, they called for the creation of a whole network of "hard labor houses," either by reconverting existing facilities or by building new ones at national expense. This plan was scaled down considerably in the version that became law.[49] The act provided for the construction of two penitentiaries in the London area, one for six hundred males, the other for three hundred females. The prisoners were to be taken from the courts in and around London. Convicted of crimes that otherwise would have rendered them liable for transportation, the offenders were to be imprisoned for a maximum of two years. During the night they were to be confined in solitary cells, while laboring in association by day. The labor was to be "of the hardest and most servile kind, in which Drudgery is chiefly required and where the Work is little liable to be spoiled by Ignorance, Neglect or Obstinacy." As examples, the act recommended sawing stone, polishing marble, beating hemp, rasping wood, or chopping rags. Howard hoped that these clauses would inspire emulation in the counties and usher in a new era of severity in local institutions.

The same spirit is at work in the clauses of the bill dealing with diet and uniform. In place of the intermittent and inadequate dietaries provided by the counties, there was to be a regular provision for each offender. Lest any magistrate think that this might compromise deterrence, the act specified that the diet was to be "Bread and any coarse Meat or other inferior food and water or small beer." Likewise, the prisoners were to be provided with clothing for the first time, instead of being forced to remain in their frequently filthy and diseased rags. Once again, the imperatives of deterrence were harmonized with those of humanity. The clothing was to be a "coarse and uniform Apparel, with certain Obvious Marks or Badges affixed to the same, as well to Humiliate the wearer as to facilitate Discovery in Case of Escapes."

To those who feared that improvements in diet, hygiene, and clothing of prisoners would remove the "dread" of being confined and lead the "lower classes of people" to prefer prison to "their own houses," Howard replied that he wanted to make the pains of prison more just, not reduce their intensity. As he said:

> I have proposed nothing to give them an air of elegance or pleasantness. . . . With respect to the more humane treatment of the prisoners in the articles of food, lodging and the like, I venture to assert that if to it be joined such strict regulations in preventing all dissipation and riotous amusement . . . confinement in a prison, though it may cease to be destructive to health and morals, will not fail to be sufficiently irksome and disagreeable, especially to the idle and profligate.[50]

Howard took most of the "strict regulations" from his European models, the Maison de Force in Ghent, the Rasp House in Amsterdam, and the Silentium in Rome. None of these had been called a penitentiary. At some moment in 1778, however, Eden, Blackstone, and Howard discarded the phrase "hard labor house" in favor of "penitentiary." That word seemed to express the ideal of a place not merely of industry but also of contrition and penance. In the last edition of his *Commentaries* published before his death, Blackstone announced his conversion to the idea of penitentiary confinement:

> In framing the plan of these penitentiary houses, the principal objects were sobriety, cleanliness and medical assistance, by a regular series of labor, by solitary confinement during the intervals of work and by some religious instruction to preserve and amend the health of the unhappy offenders, to inure them to habits of industry, to guard them from pernicious company, to accustom them to serious reflection and to teach them both the principles and practice of every Christian and moral duty.[51]

Once the Penitentiary Act became law, a commission of three was appointed to chose a site for the two prisons, approve an architect, and begin construction. The three were Howard, his friend John Fothergill, and a man with whom they quickly began to quarrel, George Whateley, treasurer of the Foundling Hospital.

The death of Fothergill in 1780 and the resignation of Howard soon after forced the selection of a second commission, consisting of Thomas Bowdler, Whateley's colleague at the Foundling Hospital as well as Gilbert Eliot and Charles Bunbury, two MPs who had piloted the original act through the Commons.[52]

The four of them set to work adjudicating the architect's competition. That they intended something quite new in the history of prison design is clear from a letter Bowdler wrote to one of the competing architects: "Our undertaking is so different from anything that ever was built in this country that a person may be very fit for building a church or palace and very unfit for being architect to the penitentiary houses."[53]

William Blackburn, the architect who Howard said understood his aims better than anyone else, won the competition. He was to go on to build Gloucester and a number of other county penitentiaries. The commission, however, became deadlocked in fruitless negotiations to buy land on Battersea Rise for the prison site, and in 1785 plans for the penitentiary lapsed.

T. B. Bayley, the Lancashire magistrate who fathered the new Preston House of Correction, attributed the abandonment of the project to the "ill-judged parsimony of Ministers of State and of Nobility and Gentry of all Parties." He also inveighed against their "Aversion to any Scheme which requires *continued* attention, watchfulness and trouble."[54]

But there was more to the ministry's coolness than mere sloth. There were constitutional objections to its entry into the field of prison administration. Prisons were a county and borough matter, left to local justices. At most, those justices were prepared to tolerate the passage of nonbinding prison legislation. But they had influence enough in Parliament to prevent Whitehall from taking an activist role. As a result, while the government had established the hulks as a "temporary expedient," it decided not to proceed beyond this to the management of permanent institutions. Such constitutional objections also scuttled Howard's suggestion that Parliament establish two inspectors of prisons.

Another factor, harder to pinpoint but perhaps decisive, was the ministry's reluctance to abandon the banishment of notorious offenders for a system of imprisonment that would result in the eventual return of convicts to the community. The potential of confinement still remained to be demonstrated. For a society that had long accepted the incorrigibility of offenders, it was difficult to adjust to a punishment that presumed their eventual reintegration into the labor market.

IV

Despite the abandonment of the penitentiary plan, the act itself was not destined to end up as a dead letter. In 1783 and 1784, as magistrates decided, in the face of ever-worsening overcrowding and a steadily increasing use of imprisonment, to rebuild or enlarge their institutions, they turned to the Penitentiary Act as a model for discipline. This wave of institutional renewal had far-reaching results. In 1812, when James Neild, a London merchant and philanthropist, duplicated Howard's census of the prisons, he found that over half of them had been rebuilt or significantly enlarged since Howard's day.[55] In these institutions, fees and the sale of alcohol had been prohibited and the keepers placed on a salary. Prisoners were provided with "county clothing" and a regular though meager diet. In many cases, the use of chains was outlawed and the keepers were required to secure formal permission from the magistrates to inflict a whipping. It became a matter of rule that the walls be whitewashed regularly, the prisoners provided with washing facilities, and the toilets cleaned and disinfected on a regular basis.

A dozen counties went further and actually built small penitentiaries adjacent to, or in place of, their jails and houses of correction. The first of these, at Horsham and Petworth in Sussex, were begun in 1775, four years before the Penitentiary Act, at the instigation of the leading nobleman of the country, the Duke of Richmond.[56] While Howard praised the Horsham penitentiary as a true embodiment of his plans, he does not seem to have been consulted during its construction. It appears instead that the Duke of Richmond derived his concept of discipline directly from the Maison de Force in Ghent and the Rasp House in Amsterdam.

The old jail denounced by the Sussex grand jury in 1775 as "ruinous" and "insufficient both as to the security and health of the prisoners," was torn down and a new one was erected at a cost of £3560.[57] By nineteenth century standards, the new penitentiary was tiny, with only twenty-five cells. These were sparsely equipped with a "stone chamber pot, a mop, a broom, a leather buckett, a canvas straw bed and two blanketts." Offenders were stripped, bathed, reclothed in green and yellow uniforms, and then sealed away. They worked in the cells and were allowed out for only two hours of exercise a day, for "Divine Service," and for such visits as were sanctioned by order of the justices. Their diet consisted of nothing more than water and two pounds of bread per day. Fees were abolished, and the keeper, his turnkeys, a chaplain, and a part-time surgeon were placed on salary. Overseeing the institution was a justice appointed as "inspector" of the jail.

The penitentiary at Petworth, which was modeled on the same plan of discipline, replaced a tiny rural lockup that consisted, according to a justices' report in 1782, of "two miserable rooms . . . without a chimney, water, no yard nor any water, nor employment." The Duke of Richmond was apparently well pleased with this tightening up of the machinery of Sussex punishment. He boasted that the new institutions had become such a salutary terror to the poor that they were nearly always empty.[58]

After the publication of *The State of the Prisons* and the passing of the Penitentiary Act, the idea of the new discipline spread rapidly. By the late 1780s, Howard found that his work and the crisis in punishment had called into being a small constituency of reform-minded magistrates on the county benches. In Middlesex, William Mainwairing superintended the construction of a new house of correction on the Howard model in Coldbath Fields in Clerkenwell.[59] In Dorset, William Morton Pitt convinced the local bench to build a penitentiary house at Dorchester and put its denizens to work for the local hat manufacturer.[60] Thomas Beevor converted the Wymondham bridewell in Norfolk to the principles of penitentiary confinement in 1785.[61]

T. B. Bayley supervised the construction of New Bayley prison in Salford in 1787.[62] Its cornerstone declared that the prison was a "monument of the affection and gratitude of this county to that most excellent person, John Howard, who hath so fully proved the wisdom and humanity of separate and solitary confinement of offenders."[63] In 1792, Bayley presided over the opening of a "penitentiary house on Mr. Howard's plan" at Preston. Inside, two hundred inmates were confined in separate cells by night and set to work by day weaving and picking cotton in huge associated workshops for Mr. Horrocks, one of the giants of the local cotton trade. In Liverpool, John Aikin noted, a new jail, a new lunatic asylum, and a new bridewell had all been built since 1776.[64]

More new prisons might have been built had it not been for the high cost of reform. These costs included not only building expenses, but also salaries for institutional staff and the purchase of uniforms, bedding, and food for inmates. Under the old fee system, much of the cost of institutional upkeep had been borne by the prisoners themselves. When reform-minded magistrates sought to shift this burden to the county, they found their way blocked by indignant taxpayers. In Bristol, for example, the mayor proposed to build a new jail on the penitentiary model, only to find himself threatened with mob violence. He was also vilified in caricatures scattered throughout the city, showing him shouting to the Bristol aldermen, "I will have a Jail, I will have a Jail and Dam 'Em We'l Tax 'em from Generation to Generation"—while two card-playing prelates kissed his behind.[65] In the counties that did build penitentiaries, however, alarm at the crime wave of the 1780s and at the epidemic of jail fever was sufficiently strong to overcome these fiscal objections.

V

Of these new county institutions, the most influential and important were the ones in Gloucestershire. They were both the most complete embodiment of the penitentiary ideal at that time and a representative example of the difficulties encountered throughout the county in putting this ideal into practice.

The Gloucestershire prisons were the work of one man, Sir George Onesiphorus Paul.[66] His ancestors were Huguenot tradesmen who settled in the west country after 1685 and made their fortune in the woolen trade. Paul's father was a flamboyantly successful clothier, whose precipitous social ascent was capped by his elevation to a baronetcy in 1760. G. O. Paul was born in 1746. After a desultory period at Oxford and a year on the Grand Tour, he settled in London and led the life of a mildly dissipated young gentleman about town. On the death of his father in 1774 he inherited the baronetcy, leased the family woolen mill, and settled down on his father's estate. In 1780, Paul served as a steward for the meetings and banquets called in the county to support Christopher Wyvill's campaign for a moderate parliamentary reform and a retrenchment of public finance. Like Howard, Paul appears to have harbored political ambitions, but his attempt to stand for Parliament in the Whig interest was thwarted when his reputation as a radical incurred the displeasure of the county notables. Rebuffed, Paul settled down to making his reputation as a county justice.

Next to Howard, he was the most influential institutional reformer of his generation—a relentless, dictatorial administrator
who singlehandedly made Gloucester penitentiary the model for
prisons across the country. His disciplinary aptitude was not expended solely on prisons. He was frequently consulted on the
management of hospitals and dispensaries, and in 1807 initiated a
campaign in Parliament for the creation of a system of county
asylums for the pauper insane. This interest in the insane flowed
naturally from his interest in prison discipline. Many of the insane
were confined in jails for lack of alternative institutions. Because
their erratic and riotous behavior disrupted attempts to impose a
strict discipline in prisons, Paul was led to argue for institutions
specifically devoted to their confinement.[67] Paul's monument,
however, was the penitentiary house on the banks of the Severn
in Gloucester.

When Howard visited the castle jail at Gloucester in 1779, he
found a "close and dark" night room for felons with a floor "so
ruinous that it cannot be washed." Prisoners under sentence and
those awaiting trial were not kept separate, and men and women
were allowed a degree of "licentious intercourse" that Howard
found "shocking to decency and humanity." All attempts by the
chaplain to promote the reformation of prisoners were frustrated
"by the inattention of the magistrates and their neglect of framing
and enforcing good regulations."[68]

Like most other counties, Gloucester found itself overwhelmed by the suspension of transportation. In 1783, as foreman
of the grand jury, Paul appealed to the Home Secretary to remove
the transports in the jail, who "are so numerous and so desperate
that it is found impossible to ensure their safe custody."[69] Overcrowding was soon followed by an outbreak of typhus that spread
beyond the walls to the neighborhoods outside.[70] This catastrophe,
together with the continued inaction of Whitehall, convinced the
magistrates to rebuild all of their county institutions according to
the principles of the Penitentiary Act . William Blackburn, the
architect who had won the competition for the abortive national
penitentiary, was awarded the contract for the Gloucester prisons,
and Paul was given the direction of the project.

The five new houses of correction and the new county jail,
when opened in 1792, cost the county £46,000. They had a capacity for between four hundred and five hundred offenders, four
times the number the old institutions were capable of containing.
No other county went in for "reform" on this scale.[71]

The county prison at Gloucester consisted of three parts: a jail
for felons awaiting trial, a house of correction for minor offenders,
and a penitentiary house—a three-story honeycomb of cells built
around several penned exercise yards. There were fifty-two night
cells and fifty-two day ones, each 9' 10" by 8' 8". The corridors
and gates were made small and narrow (5' 6" by 2' 2") in order to
hamper sudden attempts at escape.[72]

Paul was at pains to reassure the Gloucestershire bench that
prison reform would not compromise the deterrent value of punishment:

> I am not of the Number of those who from a misplaced Tender-
> ness of heart would unbind the just terrors of the law. I am far
> from thinking that prisons should be places of comfort—they
> should be places of real terror.[73]

After a decade of rising crime rates and institutional overcrowding, Paul had to demonstrate to skeptical colleagues that reform
could reconcile "terror" with "humanity." Somehow he had to
increase the severity of the punishment without compromising its
legitimacy in the eyes of the offender and the public. Gloucester
penitentiary was an attempt to reconcile these opposites in practice.

The first source of routine at Gloucester was the hygienic
discourse of the medical profession. When the epidemic of jail
fever broke out in Gloucester Castle in 1784, Paul knew from his
close connection with hygiene experts like Thomas Percival that
the means for preventing its recurrence were at hand. The difficulty was to convince his fellow magistrates that the introduction
of baths, uniforms, infirmaries for the sick, regular medical attention, better diet, and whitewashed walls would not compromise
the pains of confinement. Paul's solution was to convince these
magistrates that hygienic rituals could be made to serve punitive
functions. Thus, for example, in a report to the justices in 1784, he
suggested the shaving of convicts' heads both as a measure of
hygiene and as a salutary humiliation:

> I consider shaving the head as an important regulation first, be-
> cause it infallibly cleanses the most filthy part of the person, and
> is the only means of preventing the introduction of vermin to the
> bedding. Secondly because it changes the ordinary appearance of
> the person, and goes far toward preventing prisoners from being
> recognized on their return to society, by those strangers who are
> daily admitted to a distant view of them when walking in the

yards. And thirdly, because so far as the shaving the head is a mortification to the offender, it becomes a punishment directed to the mind, and is (at least so I have conceived) an allowable alternative for inflicting corporal punishment intended to be excluded from this system.[74]

Thus, the medical rituals that accompanied admission to the penitentiary had a latent but explicit purpose of humiliation. On entry, convicts at Gloucester were stripped naked, probed and examined by a doctor, and then bathed, shaved, and uniformed. This purification rite cleansed them of vermin and filth, but it also stripped them of those marks of identity that defined them as persons. Offenders' individualities were recast in the ghostly sameness of cropped hair and institutional clothing. Latently, the admission ritual brought home to offenders the state's power to subject every outward feature of their identity to control. Similarly, the daily cleanups and hygienic inspections were intended not only to guard against disease, but also to express the state's power to order every feature of the institutional environment, no matter how minor.

At another level, the hygienic rituals were seen as reformative. Cleanliness was regarded as the outward manifestation of inner order; dirtiness, on the other hand, was seen as a sign of feckless indiscipline. Hence, as Paul said, "there was a moral as well as a physical purpose to be promoted" in hygienic routine.[75] If prisoners could be taught to be clean, they would learn the value of method and order in their lives.

Other measures for the protection of the inmates' health were made to serve disciplinary and reformative purposes. Paul insisted, on medical grounds, that the county should provide every inmate with a regular diet. In order to reassure his colleagues on the bench that this would not turn the prison into a haven for the starving poor, he pointed out the hidden disciplinary advantages of a county diet. In the old prisons, the inmates had depended on their family and friends for food, and, as a result, the county had been obliged to allow these people free access to the prison yards. If the county provided a diet, Paul argued, it would be possible to sever the prisoners' links with the outside world.

County diet, then, formed part of a set of practices designed to isolate the inmates from their previous social milieu. At Gloucester an eighteen-foot wall was constructed around the institution. Outsiders required written permission from the magistrates to get inside. For next of kin, visits were allowed only once every six months. No food, bedding, books, or furniture were allowed in from the outside.

The penitentiary enforced a new conception of the social distance between the "criminal" and the "law-abiding." Walled away inside Gloucester, "deviants" lost that precarious membership in the community implied by the free access once allowed between the old jail and the street.[76]

This quarantine was seen as the first precondition for moral reeducation. It severed prisoners from the peer group support of the criminal milieu outside the walls. The other precondition for reform was solitude. Solitary confinement was designed to wrest the governance of prisons out of the hands of the inmate subculture. It restored the state's control over the criminals' conscience. It divided convicts so that they could be more efficiently subjugated, so that they would lose the capacity to resist both in thought and action. Solitude was meant to remove the offender from the distractions and temptations of the senses. Only when such temptation had been shut out by walls of stone and doors of iron could the inner voice of conscience begin to assume its sway. Paul's enthusiasm for solitude was so great that he had the word itself inscribed in stone letters over the entrances to the new institutions. The penitentiary prisoners in Gloucester not only slept in solitary cells, but also worked in solitary day cells adjacent to their night quarters. They were allowed out for exercise once a day in yards in the prison courtyard, under the eye of an officer whose job it was "to see that they did not stand still and frustrate the purpose of exercise by loitering in parties of cabal and conversation."[77]

It is worth pointing out that Howard himself had been much more cautious about the uses of solitary than his admirers on the county benches were to be. He believed that solitude should be broken up by long periods of associated labor and communal exercise. He feared that unbroken solitude would break the spirit of inmates and lead them into either "insensibility or despair."[78] Yet in at least three counties—Gloucestershire, Sussex, and Berkshire—the criminals were confined all but two hours of the day in solitary cells. At Reading they even took their exercise alone, in walled pens attached to each cell. When Howard visited the prison, he expressed vigorous disapproval of the practice to the Berkshire justices and urged them to moderate their regimen with the addition of some communal exercise. His remonstrations do not appear to have been heeded. He had succeeded only too well in convincing magistrates of the dangers of "association" by criminals. They now invoked his principles to brush aside his expressions of alarm at their severities.[79]

Given the uncompromising mood of the magistracies in the 1790s, it was fortunate for the prisoners that it proved impossible to enforce a full measure of solitude. One reason for this was overcrowding. In the face of the precipitous rise in criminal committals during the starvation years of 1798–1801, many of the prisons on the cellular plan became so overcrowded that two and sometimes three prisoners were packed into each cell. At Gloucester, Paul managed to cope with the problem in 1801 by sending the overflow from the penitentiary to several of the county bridewells. In 1817, however, the huge increase in criminal committals after the Napoleonic Wars forced the abandonment of strict solitude in Gloucester. As in 1798–1801, two and three prisoners were lodged in cells built for one, and associated labor was instituted in place of work in the cells.[80] Even when the prison was not overcrowded, Paul found it impossible to prevent prisoners from communicating in the yards or through the walls.

No matter how insistently the solitary regime was legitimized to the prisoners as humane and reformative, at least some of them remained stubbornly unconvinced. It is always difficult, in the nature of things, to convince people that pain inflicted on them is in their "best interests." At Gloucester, the daily routine was frequently shattered by disturbances. Prisoners refused to work and called on others to put down their tools. One Benjamin Cattle was ordered to the dark cells "for saying last night at locking up that he would be damned if he ever done another days work in this Prison."[81] In 1815 there appears to have been a full-scale uprising, which Paul suppressed, despite his scruples about corporal punishment, by ordering the culprits to be given thirty-six lashes.[82]

Paul was frustrated not only by the resistance of prisoners, but also by the inefficiency of the custodial staff. He had hoped to replace the "unregulated discretion" of the old keepers with "mild government by rule."[83] However, this new style of authority required a new kind of personnel. As he said:

> It was a principal desideratum of our undertaking to make a change in the "race" or kind of men usually chosen for a gaoler or a keeper of a prison, with whose name and office ideas of cruelty and tyranny and oppression were so associated that it was

not one of the least difficult parts of the undertaking to convince
mankind that it was not a necessary association.[84]

The new disciplinarians, Paul realized, had to be capable of assuming a frigidly self-controlled institutional demeanor:

> The humanity of the gaoler should rather be the result of coldness
> of character than the effect of a quick sensibility. . . . He should
> be endowed with a patience which obstinacy the most pertina-
> cious could not overcome; a sense of order which is method, rather
> mechanical than reflective and which few men obtain but by long
> habits of subordination and obedience. Such men . . . would be
> found if sought for in a profession where the passions are habitu-
> ally subjugated to discipline.[85]

This insight that discipline is best exercised by those who already
bear its brand led Paul to search for institutional cadres among
NCOs and half-pay army officers, for it was above all in the army
that "passions are habitually subjugated to discipline."[86]

Paul had a rational, even humane purpose in insisting that custodians adopt a mask of glacial impersonality in their dealings with
prisoners. Their very coldness and detachment would prevent
them from being either cruel or corrupt. In his instructions to the
penitentiary governor, he warned him to "guard against every
impulse of personal resentment." It should never be necessary, Paul
asserted, to strike a prisoner or address him in a "violent or insolent
tone." The governor should "command with temper—enforce his
just authority with firmness and punish resistance without favor
or partiality."[87] Paul warned him that he would lose the respect of
prisoners if he allowed himself to be casual, familiar, or in any way
"personal" in his dealings:

> Authority must be founded either on the fear of punishment or
> on respect for superiors in whom the authority is lodged. . . . The
> question is how this force of opinion is to be imposed on the minds
> of these men? Is it by familiar conversation? Few men speak well
> enough to impose respect on their hearers—whilst every man has
> it in his powers to impose by silence and reserve.[88]

As Paul envisaged it, the encounter between captor and captive
would be highly ritualized: the governor standing at attention in
a uniform symbolizing both his authority and his subordination to
the state, issuing terse standardized commands; the prisoner in a
uniform symbolizing submission, locked in the pose of obedience,
tensely awaiting the word of command. In this encounter, the
inmate would have no rights of remonstrance or dispute:

Prisoners must understand that a quiet resignation to the rules and
orders ... and decent submission to the officers ... will be their
sole claim to any kind of protection from the magistrates.[89]

As a ritual of state power, penitentiary discipline contrasted
sharply with the ritual of public punishment. Whereas the public
execution afforded both the public and the offender a role that the
state was unable to control, the rites of discipline allowed no such
opportunity. They were played out in private, behind the walls of
the institution, according to the state's rules. The inmate could still
defy those rules, but that defiance could not call on the support
of a watching crowd. Discipline, therefore, was a new rite, one
from which the public was locked out. Unlike the condemned
man, the prisoner was bound to silence. Even if he or she did cry
out, there was no one to listen.

In practice, of course, this vision of a perfectly impersonal
disciplinary ritual could not be put into practice. Paul was consis-
tently frustrated by his failure to find personnel with the necessary
aptitude for his regimens. Half-pay officers continued to look on
prison work as beneath their dignity as gentlemen. During the war
years, NCOs and other subordinate officers were in short supply.
Paul was forced to make do with personnel who, in his words, "had
not conceived a clear idea of the rules" or "who had a doubt in
themselves," which made their orders "uncertain."[90]

Paul's early reports on the operation of the penitentiary were
a litany of failure:

> There still exists an unthinking and unrestrained mode of familiar
> conversation with the prisoners that precludes the idea of seclu-
> sion and silence and loosens the authority of opinion and respect,
> which if preserved would render modes of harsher severity en-
> tirely unnecessary....
> The prisoners in general have not behaved with due respect to
> rule....
> The prison is ... much wanting to fulfill the rules in point of
> cleanliness....[91]

He rebuked the first governor of the penitentiary for failing to
secure the respect of the prisoners or the obedience of his subordinates. The first governor resigned and Paul had to sack several of
the keepers of the houses of correction as well as several turnkeys
and taskmasters.

Other county reformers experienced similar difficulty in
finding men capable of executing the new discipline. The job

appears to have required attitudes and aptitudes alien to most of the NCOs, petty tradesmen, and publicans who applied for the work. Frequently, in fact, the personnel from the old prisons were simply appointed to the new. The magistrates in Staffordshire, for example, were forced to reappoint the keeper of Stafford jail, an illiterate and drunken incompetent, to the governorship of the new penitentiary. It was two years before they could find a more suitable replacement.[92]

When personnel from the old institutions were appointed to serve in the new, they either failed to adapt to the new discipline or actively sought to sabotage it. When the old jailer of Oxford, Solomon Wisdom, was put in charge of the new prison, he found the new hygienic regulations especially irksome. When the justices' clerk ordered him to remove a load of manure from the middle of the prison yard, he refused and commissioned a debtor in the prison to draw a caricature of the clerk. Wisdom affixed the unflattering portrait to the front gate of the prison. It showed the clerk standing on top of the controversial manure proclaiming, "I am Cock of this Dunghill, damme."[93] The magistrates were not amused. They ordered Solomon's dismissal and informed him that "his general conduct ... has been repugnant to every plan of reform lately introduced by the Magistrates into the said gaol."

The prison reformers' frustration with custodial staff recalls the difficulties of the early factory masters who were hampered by a chronic shortage of foremen and managers in their mills. Robert Owen's meteoric rise to the management of Drinkwater's mills while still in his twenties was possible, in large measure, because there were so few men with his aptitude for discipline.[94] Other masters, unable to find subordinates like Owen, were forced to supervise their work force themselves. Josiah Wedgwood, for instance, stalked through the potteries smashing bad work and watching his workers' every move. No matter how explicit his instructions, he found that only his constant attendance could keep production up to his standards.[95]

Like Wedgwood, Paul discovered that the enforcement of the rules flagged whenever he turned his back. Only by dint of his constant vigilance were the Gloucester staff kept up to the mark. He also discovered that he could only count on a few of his colleagues on the bench to join in the work of supervision and inspection. The justices, no less than the keepers, found that the new regime required an irksome degree of diligence. Paul did not hesitate to take his colleagues to task for their indifference:

> I cannot say the visits of the other justices are equal to my expectation. The Grand Jury of one assize and the Bench of two sessions have separated without visiting in a body, an omission which cannot fail to be of the utmost detriment to the hopes entertained by the public.[96]

From the opening of the penitentiary in 1792 until his retirement in 1818, Paul shouldered the administrative burdens of the county prison system himself, poring over the keepers' accounts, stalking the galleries, peering into drains, weighing the bread, constantly chiding and lecturing the institutional staff. When he became too old to continue, there was no one willing to take over the burden of maintaining his disciplinary regimen at its full pitch. Serious overcrowding forced the abandonment of strict solitude soon after Paul's retirement. At the same time, the increasing mechanization of the Gloucester woolen industry enabled the clothiers to do without prison labor in the preparation of raw wool. Hence the regime of hard labor fell into desuetude. By the 1820s, Paul's discipline lay in ruins.[97] Yet its influence was not entirely spent. In their 1838 report urging the construction of Pentonville, the prison inspectors, Crawford and Russell, cited the Gloucester experiment as a major anticipation of their proposals for "separate confinement."[98] There was indeed little of the Pentonville regimen that Paul had not foreseen fifty years before.

The construction of the new prisons also had an enduring impact on the sentencing practices of the Gloucestershire magistrates. The fourfold increase in prison capacity made it possible for magistrates to resort to imprisonment far more often. A comparison of Gloucester felony sentences in 1805 with those of the Middlesex justices in the same year indicates that the Gloucester magistrates handed down imprisonments for offenses that their Middlesex colleagues punished with transportation. This would appear to reflect both their confidence in the new prisons and their awareness of the enlarged prison capacity.

But it was the punishment of summary offenses that was most changed by the coming of these new prisons. Paul intended the new institutions to enforce a more systematic pursuit of minor offenders. It was a "mistaken lenity," he argued in 1784, to "consider great criminals as the only objects of attention." If the purpose of punishment was reformation, as it should be, then it was necessary to begin by correction of "early transgression." As he said, "Few men have been hanged for a felony who might not have been saved to the community for the correction of a former Misdemeanour."[99]

In place of the occasional and arbitrary sentences of whipping visited upon misdemeanants and petty offenders, Paul proposed to substitute short, sharp terms of solitary confinement. Paul's study of committals to the county institutions between 1792 and 1809 shows that petty offenders received the brunt of this new severity.[100] Over 70 percent of all committals were in the category of misdemeanors or summary offenses. Of these the most frequent were "breaches of contract in husbandry," a broad offense that comprised all the disobedience of the agricultural laborer against his employer, such as running away, breaking or violating contract, embezzling tools, using abusive language, or refusing to follow orders. The new prisons were also used for the punishment of "offenses in the woolen manufacture," the county's leading trade. These offenses included embezzlement of tools and raw materials by outworkers. Instead of being whipped, fined, or privately chastised, workers were now sent to prison.

The employers must have been pleased by the sharp new penalties for embezzlement, because the 1780s were, in the words of the industry's major historian, a time of "increasing bitterness in relations between workers and clothiers."[101] After 1750 many masters cut prices and hired people who had not been duly apprenticed to work in factory loom sheds. The weavers appealed in vain to Parliament and the magistrates to enforce the wage regulation and apprenticeship clauses of the Statute of Artificers. At the same time, the employers set up committees to fund embezzlement prosecutions and searches for embezzled goods. In this climate of deteriorating relations, the coming of the new prisons gave the employers an additional instrument in their struggle to eliminate the independence of their cottage workers.

Paul noticed that after the new prisons had been established, employers tended to bring disobedient servants to the bench instead of chastising them privately.[102] This is a straw in the wind, a portent of a shift in the locus of social control from the employers directly to the state as their "neutral" intermediary. At first only Paul seemed to detect the change, but by the 1820s magistrates in other counties noticed that they and their sanctions were being called in frequently to back up the discipline of local employers.

In Gloucester the new prison facilities enabled the magistrates to substitute imprisonment for whipping as the punishment for vagrancy, minor forms of poaching, and certain petty larcenies such as stealing turnips from fields or taking firewood from forests. Paul admitted that these thefts, which increased at every upturn in bread prices, were caused by "the pressure of destitute circumstances." The 1790s were the "worst period in the history of the Gloucestership laborer," with wheat prices rocketing from 75 shillings per quarter in 1795 to 119 shillings by 1801. The magistrates must have been glad of a new instrument of terror during these hard years.[103]

The new prisons also played a role in the enforcement of family discipline. Imprisonments for desertion of family and for bastardy increased markedly after the new prisons were opened, in large measure because parish officers decided that they offered a more severe punishment than confinement in the local workhouses. Paul thought the parish officers' zeal was excessive, and he quoted with approval what one indignant woman had told him when committed for bastardy. Why, she asked, "was the man who had seduced her not imprisoned as well as herself." Paul could only answer, "Because women were not legislators and men were parish officers."[104]

Women with illegitimate children, agricultural laborers who stole turnips, weavers who embezzled their masters' yarn, apprentices who absconded—these were the chief objects of the new strategy of summary justice that Gloucestershire's new prisons made possible. Whatever reformative purposes Paul had in mind for them, these prisons in fact continued to carry out the old functions of the law, but with a new rigor—penalizing the passage from labor into crime, and enforcing the authority of landlords, masters, and parish officials.

V I

Besides the penitentiary at Gloucester, the most haunting symbol of the disciplinary enthusiasms of the age was Jeremy Bentham's scheme for a penitentiary, called the *Panopticon*, or *Inspection House*. Following publication of his plan in 1791, Bentham set out on a twenty-year campaign of propaganda, cajolery, flattery, and harassment to persuade the King's ministers to back its construction and place him at its center—as Edmund Burke said, like a spider in the middle of a web.[105]

Bentham's fascination with the total institution had first been fired by reading early drafts of Howard's bill for "hard labour houses." The Panopticon project can be seen as his attempt to revive the abandoned idea of a national penitentiary. His design for the prison was modeled on a factory that his brother Samuel had constructed in Russia for Catherine the Great. It was a circular, tiered honeycomb of open cells ranged around a central inspection tower. From this tower, into which the prisoners could not see, but from which the keepers had a clear view of each cell, the untiring and subduing gaze of authority would be directed. Such unremitting supervision would effectively prevent clandestine communication among prisoners and would make chains and other physical restraints superfluous. The convicts were to be employed as much as sixteen hours a day in their cells, and all profits were to go to the private contractor—Bentham himself—who would supervise the house. Bentham gleefully anticipated his competitive advantage over manufacturers forced to rely on free labor:

> What hold can another manufacturer have upon his workmen, equal to what my manufacturer would have upon his? What other master is there that can reduce his workmen, if idle, to a situation next to starving, without suffering them to go elsewhere? What other master is there whose men can never get drunk unless he chooses they should do so? And who, so far from being able to raise their wages by combination, are obliged to take whatever pittance he thinks it most his interest to allow?[106]

At the same time, Bentham insisted on freedom from government interference. Government regulation of the Panopticon was unnecessary, Bentham argued, because it was in the contractor's own interest to maintain his labor force in a healthy and productive state, just as it was not in his interest to take away the terror of punishment by pampering them. The self-regulating mechanism of market interest, therefore, was to be left free to establish the level of terror and humanity within the Panopticon's walls. It was to be run as a capitalist enterprise.

Such a conception of institutional management may have been couched in the new language of political economy, but it was hardly novel. It was an adaptation of the contract system that had been practiced in many workhouses and houses of correction since the late seventeenth century. Under the system, manufacturers, often from the textile trades, would contract with the magistrates for the right to exploit the labor of their workhouse and bridewell populations. Usually the county would pay for the inmates' food. The deal rarely proved profitable for the contractors, either because they lacked the expertise to manage an extended division of labor or because of the low quality of work turned out by the incarcerated. Dishonest contractors took to pocketing part of the county allowance for food. The inmates, of course, bore the consequences of such chiseling. By 1782, opposition to the "farming" of the poor culminated in legislation outlawing the practice altogether.[107] The principle that institutions should not be run as capitalist enterprises was not established definitively, however, until the rejection of Bentham's scheme.

Bentham attempted to meet objections to the contract system by admitting two checks on the contractor's discretion. First, he allowed the public unlimited access to the central inspection tower, in order that the searchlight of public opinion would always be trained on the contractor and his staff. The second check was fiscal. To ensure that he would not work prisoners to death, Bentham offered to pay the state a forfeit of £5 for every death in prison that exceeded the average annual mortality rate in London. To admit the necessity of this check, however, was to admit that moral scruple had to be strengthened by economic interest.

Unlike other reformers, Bentham did not believe custodial discretion could be restrained by rules and inspection alone. He insisted that custodians would only observe rules if it was in their economic interest to do so.[108] He was also skeptical about appointing outside inspectors to watch over custodial behavior. He predicted that inspectors would be co-opted by the personnel they were supposed to supervise. Neither rules nor inspection were enough. It was necessary, in addition, to institute a system of economic penalties and rewards to make the self-interest of the custodial staff serve their professional duty.

Bentham was extravagantly optimistic about the Panopticon. Not merely prisons, but schools, asylums, factories, workhouses, and hospitals, he insisted, could be run on the "inspection principle." The design of the building would ensure that no matter who was in charge the inmates would be subjected to unvarying supervision, just as the contract system of management would guarantee, by means of its incentives and penalties, that the disciplining of the poor would be undertaken at no cost to the state. Bentham crowed:

> Morals reformed—health preserved—industry invigorated—instruction diffused—public burthens lightened—economy seated as it were upon a rock—the gordian knot of the Poor Laws not cut but untied—all by a simple Idea in Architecture![109]

The ministry remained doggedly unimpressed by his simple idea and after twenty years of tortuous negotiations, Bentham abandoned the project in disgust.

The definitive rejection came in 1810. The Commons committee that met to consider his proposals was much influenced by the objections of G. O. Paul, who argued that Bentham had placed too much emphasis on the exploitation of convict labor. Penitentiaries were not factories, Paul insisted, but places of religious reformation. "The employment of prisoners . . . is essential but subservient to the great purpose of reformation by seclusion."[110] In his conception, labor was a penance for sin rather than a commodity to be exploited for profit. It was more important, he insisted, to teach convicts the moral goodness of work than to make money from their labor. Paul warned that "the reformation of the offender" must necessarily be a "secondary concern" in any prison "where all the power and influence . . . are lodged in the hands of persons contracting for the manual labour of prisoners." Paul argued that Bentham had neglected the religious instruction of prisoners and was even prepared to sacrifice the regime of solitary confinement when the requirements of an extended division of labor made it necessary to do so. Moreover, the contract system of management opened up opportunities for corruption and unlawful discretion that would bring back the worst abuses of the old system. The Commons committee accepted Paul's arguments, much to Bentham's outrage and chagrin.

The rejection of the Panopticon was a major event in the history of imprisonment. In turning its back on the idea of running prisons like factories, ruling opinion also rejected the idea of modeling the authority relation between state and prisoner on the relation between employer and worker. This implied a further rejection of the use of market incentives and penalties for the regulation of dealings between state servants and the confined.

In place of a Benthamite conception of authority regulated by market incentives, reformers like Paul succeeded in vindicating a bureaucratic formalism that looked to inspection and rules as the means to protect inmates against cruelty and to guarantee the rigor of punishment. For opponents of the contract system, punishment was too delicate a social function to be left to private entrepreneurs. For state power to preserve its legitimacy, it was essential that it remain untainted with the stain of commerce.

While the management principles of the Panopticon were rejected, its design exerted a profound influence on the circular forms adopted for Millbank penitentiary; on Bevan's plans for a juvenile penitentiary in 1817; on the new prison at Bury in 1805; and on a number of other county prisons constructed after the Napoleonic Wars. Bentham's major contribution was to find the architectural form that most fully embodied the reformers' desire to subject men to the disciplines of surveillance.

While Bentham's own idiosyncrasies make it easy to interpret the Panopticon as the product of his personal obsessions, it was in fact a symbolic caricature of the characteristic features of disciplinary thinking in his age. To be sure, Bentham was dubious about the reformative value of solitary confinement, and his system of contract management was at odds with Paul's principles of institutional supervision. Moreover, he was out of sympathy with the reformers' conception of imprisonment as a religious penance. Yet, all the same, the affinities between the penitentiaries and the Panopticon are more important than their differences.

Both substituted the pain of intention for the pains of neglect, the authority of rules for the authority of custom, the regimens of hard labor for the disorder of idleness. In both, the criminal was separated from the outside world by a new conception of social distance epitomized by uniforms, walls, and bars. The ruling image in both was the idea of the the eye of the state—impartial, humane, and vigilant—holding the "deviant" in the thrall of its omniscient gaze.

CHAPTER FIVE

Whigs, Jacobins, and the Bastilles:

The Penitentiary Under Attack

I

By the mid-1790s, the reforming impetus that gave birth to the penitentiary had spent itself. The reform constituency was divided and disillusioned, increasingly given to second thoughts about its earlier enthusiasms. The Manchester hygienic reformer Thomas Percival's change of heart about factories epitomized the new mood. In the 1780s, like other members of the Manchester Literary and Philosophical Society, he had welcomed the new factories as benevolent instruments for the moral reform of the poor. By 1798, he had seen enough of the new industrialism to come to a different conclusion. In his reports on the moral and hygienic state of the Manchester population, he pointedly observed that factory masters overworked their parish apprentices and neglected their education.[1]

His critique was echoed by the most influential charitable organization of the 1790s, Thomas Bernard's Society for Bettering the Condition of the Poor. In its report for 1800, the Bettering Society denounced the factory no less vigorously than did the cottage weavers and spinners menaced by its competition. The society warned that the factory's reliance on child labor was dissolving the "family connection" in industrial employment. Children in the industrial cities like Manchester no longer worked under the "moral" authority of a parent or a small master. The mill overseers did not care whether the children swore or caroused after hours so long as they did the work. The new discipline was deficient, in other words, because its nature was merely economic. While lauding those industrialists, like Mr. Dale at New Lanark in Scotland, who continued to exert a paternal supervision over their workers, the Bettering Society observed that such employers were exceptions in the scrambling competitiveness of most English cotton towns. There, they warned, "the demon of gain" had betrayed the reformative promise of the factory. The society argued that without public regulation the factories "must be destructive to the moral and religious principles of the great mass of the people."[2] Pressure such as this, from the society and from the influential Thomas Percival, resulted in the passage of the first factory act in 1802.[3]

The Bettering Society's general disillusionment with the reformative promise of institutional confinement extended to the workhouse. The society argued that workhouses failed to deter the poor from applying for relief. Besides, they maintained, outdoor relief was a right of the poor that could not be abridged. The two leading authorities on poor relief in the 1780s and 1790s, Sir Frederic Morton Eden and Thomas Gilbert, took the same view.[4] More than anything else, it was the disappointing record of the Suffolk Houses of Industry that disillusioned Gilbert and Eden. Eleven of these huge workhouses had been constructed in east Suffolk in the late 1760s in an attempt to reduce the rising cost of poor relief. Outdoor relief was all but abolished, and claimants were required to submit to the deprivations of the house. These included separation of husbands from wives, hard labor, restricted visits, uniforms, and meager diet.

At first, the directors of the houses trumpeted their virtues, but by the 1790s they were obliged to admit failure. The institutions continued to be crowded with able-bodied laborers, the rates of east Suffolk had not been reduced, and some of the parishes were still paying off the costs of construction. Many of the houses, moreover, had become no less squalid than the parish poorhouses they replaced. The custodial staffs neglected hygiene, failed to enforce hard labor, and cheated the inmates on their food allowance. Using the workhouse for purposes of deterrence was all very well in theory, Eden concluded, but unworkable in practice, given the shortage of personnel capable of enforcing rigorous discipline.[5]

Within the reform camp itself, there were many who questioned the morality of forcing the poor to submit to confinement. John Howard approved of the internal regimen of the east Suffolk houses, but observed bluntly that the curtailment of outdoor relief was "repugnant to the feelings of an Englishman." Like Gilbert and Eden, he argued that workhouses should be used only for the confinement of those too sick or too old to be cared for at home.[6]

Howard's position can be contrasted to Bentham's, in whose disciplinary utopia the state would administer a whole network of panopticons for the confinement and reform of every dependent social category—including lunatics, paupers, criminals, and children. By the mid 1790s, however, the current of official thinking was running against Bentham's solutions. In criminal justice policy, the state abandoned the construction of a national penitentiary and rejected Bentham's plan for a Panopticon. In the field of poor relief, the parishes met the precipitous increase in pauperism after 1795, not by building more workhouses but by expanding outdoor relief, especially through the Speenhamland allowance in aid of wages.

The most popular schemes for the "reform" of the poor laws between 1795 and 1825 envisaged the outright abolition of a compulsory levy and its replacement by private charity. Private charity, it was argued, would re-create the face-to-face relationship of dependency and obligation between rich and poor that was sacrificed by a state stystem. Relief should become a gift of the rich rather than a right to which the poor could lay claim. Pamphleteers were fond of contrasting the poor's insolent clamor at the parish pay table and their "sparkling eyes, bursting tears and uplifted hands" when visited by Lady Bountiful.[7] In these fanciful and nostalgic elegies to private charity, there was an implicit hostility to the Benthamite conception of a society held together by a network of state institutions of control.

Within the reform camp itself, there were libertarian constitutionalists who did not share Bentham's vision of a disciplinary state that sacrificed liberty to security. Thus, while Joseph Priestley supported the education of the poor, he opposed the creation of a compulsory state system, arguing that it would give the state the same tyrannous power over secular opinion that the Established Church exercised over religious opinion. At the same time, he supported Howard's view that the state had the right to enforce a coercive moral education on the criminal. These two views were in tension, but not in contradiction, since Priestley could argue that criminals had forfeited those rights of freedom of conscience that law-abiding citizens were entitled to enjoy.[8] After all, hadn't Locke argued that a criminal had no more rights than a slave?[9]

While Priestley could resolve the tension between his libertarian position on compulsory education and his forthrightly coercive stance on punishment, others formed in the same traditions as Priestley could not. William Godwin was a lecturer at Hackney Dissenting Academy and a leader of a rationalist circle in London, which was to include his famous companion Mary Wollstonecraft. His *Enquiry Concerning Political Justice*, published in 1793, took Hartleian psychology and Whig constitutionalism to conclusions radically different from Priestley's. Godwin started from the Hartleian assumption that man was rational, predictable, and therefore improvable; his vices and moral weakness were not invincible. "Man is perfectible, or in other words, susceptible of perpetual improvement." Each person was "capable of perceiving what is eligible and right, of fixing indelibly certain principles upon his mind and adhering inflexibly to the resolutions he has made."[10] Godwin believed that most people had it within their power to improve themselves by education and introspection, unaided by any coercive tutelage. All "authoritarian" attempts to "improve" people only deadened their imagination and suspended "the elasticity and progress of the mind." Nor, Godwin argued, could people be punished into virtue:

> Let us consider the effect that coercion produces upon the mind of him against whom it is employed. It cannot begin with convincing; it is no argument; it begins with producing the sensation of pain, and the sentiment of distaste. It begins with violently alienating the mind from the truth with which we wish it to be impressed.[11]

Godwin thus opposed Howard's "scheme of solitary imprisonment." Solitude, he asserted, brutalized the feelings no less than physical punishment. Like any penalty, it inflicted pain, albeit of a psychological variety. Hence, it would never command the consent or respect of prisoners and would only succeed in arousing their resistance and resentment.

In essence, Godwin was denying Howard's most basic conten-
tion, that punishments directed to the mind were more legitimate,
and more acceptable to the offender, than punishments directed at
the body. Godwin went still further, arguing that no one could
ever be reformed in solitude. Reformation was a social process, a
matter of persuasion and example rather than force. It was hopeless
to expect that people would be changed by leaving them alone
with their conscience. At best, they would acquire a "gloomy and
morose disposition," and, at worst, they might be driven to madness. All punishment, he argued, should aim at the speediest possible return of the offender to the beneficial moral ambience of
society.[12]

Godwin's attack on Howard is important because it started
from the very premises of materialist optimism held by the supporters of the penitentiary system. The Hartleian text was apparently capable of sustaining contradictory glosses. If Bentham's
Panopticon proved that authoritarian implications could be drawn
from the materialist view of man, Godwin's *Political Justice*
showed that libertarian ones were just as consistent when sustained
by a suspicion of state power.

Opposition to the consolidation of state power also found expression in the campaign of the Whig leader, Charles James Fox,
against the establishment of salaried magistrates and a paid constabulary in London. Since the days of the Fielding brothers,
successive police reformers had pleaded with Parliament to replace
the corrupt, disorganized system of unpaid parish constables, beadles, and watchmen with a salaried constabulary supervised by
full-time magistrates. In 1770, the first London police force, the
Bow Street Runners, was established. In 1792, the government
appointed eight police magistrates with a small staff of paid constables under their command to improve the administration of justice
in the metropolis. At the same time, an amendment to the vagrancy
laws was passed, giving constables the power to arrest "suspected
persons" and "reputed thieves."[13] In Parliament, Fox and his Whigs
fought the new police offices and the new vagrancy law as inva-
sions of the rights of the subject. They claimed that giving salaries
to magistrates would compromise their independence and contra-
vene the English tradition of voluntary legal administration.[14]

One would have expected reforming Whigs like Samuel
Romilly, who supported the introduction of salaries for prison
personnel, to have favored the introduction of salaries for the

police. Yet in 1786 we find him denouncing a paid police as a "French" innovation:

> A system which betrays the greatest distrust of the people must never look for popular support; all that it can expect from the public is a constrained and reluctant obedience. Such is the case in France, where their *commissaires, lieutenants* and *intendants de police*, supported by all their train of subalterns, by all their avowed and disguised instruments . . . and aided by all the military power and by their *espions* of every description, prove that unhappy government to be under the miserable and disgraceful necessity of constantly making an open and insidious war upon the people.[15]

Because of the tension between authoritarian and libertarian strains in reformist ideology in the 1790s, we have the bewildering spectacle of some reformers like Romilly embracing the penitentiary, but rejecting a paid police, while their associates, Bentham and Patrick Colquhoun, endorsed both.

Such tensions within the reform camp were aggravated by the coming of the French Revolution. At the outset, most reformers welcomed the news of the fall of the Bastille, though some greeted the news with trepidation. Samuel Romilly, for example, visited Paris during the heady days of 1790 and watched from the galleries as the Convention struck down the legal superstructure of feudalism. On his return, he wrote two enthusiastic accounts of the revolution for English audiences. When the Terror was unleashed in the September Massacres of 1792, however, Romilly abruptly consigned a third laudatory pamphlet to the flames.[16] The excesses of the Terror convinced many free-thinking Nonconformist families who had flirted with the ideas of Voltaire and Rousseau in the 1780s that they had been "wandering in the thickets of error."[17]

The full retreat of English Nonconformity from their earlier enthusiasm for political reform did not begin until the upsurge of Jacobin radicalism among the common people in England after 1792. The artisans and journeymen of London who met under the leadership of Thomas Hardy, a shoemaker, in January 1792 to found the London Corresponding Society to initiate popular agitation for parliamentary reform said later that it was "the hardness of the times and the dearness of all the necessaries of life" that convinced them of the necessity of reform. Within months of the founding of the London society, branches had sprung up in Sheffield, Derby, Birmingham, and Manchester. These groups of "tradesmen, shopkeepers and mechanics" in effect forged the first workingmen's political organization with a national base and an appeal transcending craft and city. Their ideology was created partly from the inheritance of seventeenth century radical sects, partly from the tradition of the "rights of free-born Englishmen," and partly from the Jacobin tradition in France as articulated in Tom Paine's *Rights of Man.* Cheap penny editions of Paine were passed from hand to hand and read aloud to the illiterate in ale-houses and Corresponding Society meetings. The mushrooming of these societies, some of which had memberships two thousand strong, together with the avid response to Paine's doctrines, convinced the government of Prime Minister William Pitt that the common people at home were becoming infected with the leveling, atheistical doctrines that it was fighting abroad in its war with the French revolutionary armies.

The emergence of artisanal Jacobinism at home convinced many of the old reformers of the 1780s that they had been guilty of youthful indiscretion in advocating parliamentary reform. G. O. Paul told a correspondent in 1809 that he had abandoned politics in the 1790s "when reformation was urged in the language and stalked in the guise of revolution." Demagogues like Paine, he complained, had betrayed the cause of his youth. As a result, he had vowed, he said, to renounce politics for "apolitical philanthropy."[18]

The dissolution of the connection between philanthropy and political reform was confirmed, after 1793, when penitentiaries began to be used for the confinement of Jacobin political prisoners. Since the new institutions quickly were denounced as symbols of political repression, the reformers of the 1780s like Paul became implicated, by necessity and by conviction, in the defense of that repression. Soon the question of penitentiaries and prison reform had become enmeshed in the political and social conflict of the decade.

II

Gloucester penitentiary had been in operation less than six months when it was attacked by the Jacobin press in a pamphlet called *Gloucester Bastile,* describing the "pathetic particulars of a poor boy sentenced to suffer seven years' solitary confinement in Gloucester gaol." The pamphlet dwelt particularly on the effects of solitary confinement on the boy's mind:[19]

> What eloquence can express the horror of his mind. . . . The feelings of his mind may become depressed into a state of inanity, his eye-balls roll in wild horror upon a vast of emptiness, his features be wan and livid, his tongue forget the articulation of words and every faculty be stupified into dull insensibility.[19]

The Gloucester bench successfully prosecuted the printer, William Holland of London, for libel. *Gloucester Bastile* was one of the earliest attacks on the new disciplinary system; but other "scurrilous publications," as G. O. Paul called them, followed as soon as the penitentiaries began to be used for the confinement of Jacobins.[20] Solitary confinement came to be associated in radicals' minds with other instruments of their repression: the suspension of *habeas corpus*, the "gagging bills" curtailing free speech, and the paid informers and rigged juries of the state trials.

The campaign against Jacobinism began in earnest with the first roundup of the London Corresponding Society (LCS) and the suspension of *habeas corpus* in June 1794. Radicals were arrested on warrants from the Secretary of State and interrogated and confined without indictment or trial "at His Majesty's pleasure"—which meant anything from a few weeks to several years. State trials often proved an embarrassment, as for example when Thomas Hardy (the LCS secretary) and John Horne Tooke were triumphantly acquitted of high treason in 1794. Juries, even of middle-class citizens, turned out to be suspicious of political prosecutions, and defense lawyers like Samuel Romilly proved adept at demolishing the testimony of government witnesses.[21] As a result, Pitt and his ministers found it more convenient to confine political prisoners under the *habeas corpus* suspension acts than bring them to trial.

The suspension of *habeas corpus* was not, however, the only instrument available to the government. It used repeated libel prosecutions between 1794 and 1796 to drive the leading radical printer, Daniel Isaac Eaton, into temporary exile in America. Similar prosecutions succeeded in silencing Richard Phillips, the radical bookseller of Leicester. In addition, Pitt secured passage of the Treasonable Correspondence Bill of 1792, outlawing communications with France, and the Gagging Bills of 1795, which outlawed public meetings of more than fifty people and tightened up the laws of seditious utterance. These new acts, taken together with the suspension of *habeas corpus,* amounted to the severest curtailment of English liberties in the eighteenth century, and as such aroused intense opposition, not only from radical artisans but from "constitutional" sectors of the middle class and the gentry.

Several hundred political prisoners were confined during the decade. Some, like the members of the London Corresponding Society, were committed militants, but others were more marginal characters whose expressions of conviction were overheard by informers or vindictive neighbors. Richard Brinsley Sheridan, the radical Whig MP, told the Commons of a shopkeeper from Manchester called Patterson who objected to Pitt's income tax bill. As a protest he inscribed the names Pitt and Patterson on his shop cart. When asked what he meant by inscribing Pitt's name on the cart, he replied, "Ah, if he has no share in the business, he has a large share in the profit of it."[22] For this unguarded moment of levity, he was taken up and committed to Coldbath Fields prison. Pitt's repression could be savage, but it could be petty as well.

As Edward Thompson has observed, it was also strangely personal. Important political offenders were interrogated by the ministers themselves in the gilded chambers of the Privy Council in Whitehall. Sometimes even a certain element of sparring camaraderie can be detected in the ministers' dealings with their artisanal opponents. When John Binns of the LCS was confined in Gloucester penitentiary, Henry Dundas, the minister responsible for his confinement, stopped by the prison on the way to his estate to exchange pleasantries and barbed political banter.[23]

Though political radicals were confined in prisons of all types, particular use was made of the new penitentiaries. Most of those convicted at King's Bench or confined by warrant under the *habeas corpus* suspension acts were sent to the penitentiaries at Dorchester, Gloucester, or Coldbath Fields in London. From the government's point of view, penitentiaries had several advantages over ordinary prisons. With their cells, security rituals, and high walls, they were well equipped to deter escape or rescue. "Jail delivery riots" to free prisoners who the populace felt were unfairly imprisoned were an integral part of popular tradition, the most recent example being the Gordon Riots of 1780, during which the crowd had broken into the London jails and freed arrested rioters.[24] Such "outrages" were less likely to recur if the radicals were walled away in penitentiaries.

Penitentiaries also had the facilities for the isolation of political prisoners from ordinary criminals. Both the radicals themselves and the government insisted upon this; the former as a privilege of political confinement, the latter as a safeguard against the political contamination of the ordinary offender. The privileges of political detainees were justified on the grounds that political offenses were inherently more equivocal and subjective than criminal ones. The political heresy of one age, after all, frequently became the orthodoxy of the next. Moreover, the courtesy with which a government treated a jailed opponent was regarded as a test of its respect for civil liberties. Finally, though this was usually left unstated, most political offenders in the eighteenth century had been gentlemen. Arguments about civil liberties neatly dovetailed with feelings of class to reinforce the practice of isolating political offenders from the "low ruffians" in the rest of the prison. Thus the best-known political prisoner of the eighteenth century, John Wilkes, the radical MP and idol of the London crowd in the 1760s, and Lord George Gordon, the instigator of the Gordon Riots in 1780, were confined in special "apartments" and allowed books, furniture, personal wardrobe, as luxurious a table as they could afford, the ministrations of a servant, and unlimited visiting privileges.[25]

The artisanal radicals who demanded these privileges in the 1790s, however, were much more menacing than the gentlemanly dissidents of the past. The ministers felt bound to accord Jacobins the privilege of isolation from criminals, but they saw no reason why Thomas Hardy, shoemaker, should be allowed the "luxuries" granted to Lord George Gordon. They did exempt most Jacobins from hard labor and allowed them extra diet, books, and extended visits, but they insisted on their confinement in solitary cells and attempted to restrict their contact with each other. This led the Jacobins to protest that the "privilege" of being isolated from ordinary criminals had been perverted into a punishment. They were also to oppose solitary confinement as a violation of the rights of ordinary prisoners awaiting trial on criminal charges. Later they went still further, arguing that it was a cruel and unconstitutional punishment for those under sentence. On all these grounds, therefore, they brought the regime of solitary confinement under sustained attack.

III

The resistance of political prisoners to the penitentiary took many forms. At Gloucester, the unremitting solitude and the severity of the discipline made collective demonstrations impossible. Individual acts of defiance, however, did take place. The story of Kyd Wake is a case in point. Wake was a Gosport printer sentenced to five years hard labor in 1796 for hissing and booing the King as he drove in his carriage from St. James's Palace to an opening of Parliament. Wake's wife moved to Gloucester to support her husband in jail. In order to raise money to provide extra food for her husband, she sold an engraving of Wake standing downcast in his cell in his ill-fitting blue and yellow prison uniform. At the bottom of the engraving was Kyd Wake's anguished plea against solitary confinement addressed to the citizens of Gloucester:

> Five years confinement, even in common gaols, must surely be a very severe punishment; but if Judges or Juries would only reflect seriously on the horrors of solitary imprisonment under penitentiary discipline! If they would allow their minds to dwell a little on what it is to be locked up, winter after winter, for 16 hours out of the 24, in a small brick cell—without company—without fire —without light—without employment—and scarcely to see a face but those of criminals or turnkeys. No friend to converse with when well; or to consult with, or to complain to, when indisposed! Above all—to be subjected to a thousand insults and vexations, almost impossible to be described, and therefore scarcely to be remedied; but by which continual torment may be, and often is, inflicted. If they would but consider what an irreparable misfortune it is to have a considerable portion of life so wearisomely wasted; they would surely be more tender of dooming any man, for a long time, to such wretchedness. It is a calamity beyond description, more easily to be conceived than explained.[26]

Wake was in prison at the same time as John Binns, John Bone, and Robert Keir of the London Corresponding Society, but the strictness of the discipline made it impossible for them to develop more than a furtive acquaintance with each other. The three LCS men were confined in separate cells, but they were allowed to associate together in a dayroom and in the exercise yard. Their solidarity was less than perfect. The three fell into discord when Binns was invited to dine with the prison governor and his family. The other two, Bone and Keir, became jealous of Binns's privileges and complained to the magistrates. When Binns found out that his comrades had been complaining about him behind his back, he punched and assaulted them at the next opportunity in the prison yard. The turnkeys dragged them apart and took them off to their cells. They lost their privileges of association, and until their release did not see each other again. All three continued, however, to petition the Secretary of State demanding that they be brought to trial and protesting solitary confinement. The government remained deaf to their entreaties and did not release them until 1801.[27]

At Gloucester, the political prisoners did not make any contact with the criminals. At Dorchester penitentiary Gilbert Wakefield did. Wakefield had been a classical scholar and a lecturer at Hackney Dissenting Academy.[28] The academy was a center of Nonconformist radicalism until 1796 when a banquet held in honor of Tom Paine made it so notorious as a Jacobin hotbed that it was forced to close its doors. Like his friend Joseph Priestley, Wakefield was one of the old Nonconformist radicals who held firm to their convictions during the hard years of the 1790s. While not a member of the LCS itself, Wakefield visited them in prison at Newgate. From time to time he also left his classical studies to write fierce pamphlets attacking the war with France and the repression at home. The government, which had been considering an indictment against him for over a year, finally brought a prosecution for a pamphlet in which he said that the miseries of the English people were so great that they had nothing to lose from a French invasion. He was convicted of seditious utterance and sentenced in 1799 to two years in Dorchester penitentiary.

Dorchester was designed by Howard's favorite architect, William Blackburn, and administered according to the Gloucester model of discipline by William Morton Pitt, a relative of the Prime Minister and a magistrate with a philanthropic reputation. Pitt ran the prison as a factory. Prisoners were provided with a bread and water allowance and then purchased meat and vegetables with wages earned working in the prison hat manufactory.

With funds raised among Whig opposition circles, Wakefield was able to secure exemption from the worst aspects of penitentiary confinement. At a cost of £100 a year, he lodged in the jailer's apartments and ate at his table. The subscription also enabled him to move his family to Dorchester to support him in confinement.

In his apartments, Wakefield continued his classical studies and kept up a correspondence with the opposition leader, Charles

James Fox. At the same time, Wakefield took an interest in the plight of the ordinary prisoners. For the illiterate criminals he wrote petitions of clemency; for the destitute debtors he paid creditors and secured their discharge; for petty misdemeanants he paid their fines; for the hungry he purchased and distributed quantities of potatoes, mackerel, and bread. In return, some of the prisoners on their release sent him small presents of fish or "other trifling things" to show their gratitude.

In his letters to friends in the Whig opposition, Wakefield castigated the regime of the prison. "I wonder," he wrote, "that men can endure solitary confinement without distraction, melancholy and despair." During the winter months, he pointed out, the prisoners were kept in their cells for as much as sixteen hours a day. "Surely such an annihilation from active life is highly cruel."[29]

As in Gloucester, the building of the Dorchester penitentiary had made possible a more stringent enforcement of the laws against petty offenders. Wakefield questioned the justice of imprisoning those who "were impelled by distress and hunger to satisfy their own cravings or the irresistible demands of wife and children." Was it fair, he asked, for those "who enjoy all the comforts and affluences of life," to condemn the poor to "cold and gloomy seclusion from the world?" At a time when bread prices had escalated beyond the reach of all but the rich, it made a mockery of the law's reputation for mercy, he insisted, to clamp down on minor delinquency.[30]

When released in May 1801, Wakefield did not return immediately to London, but remained in Dorchester to bring up the issue of penitentiary discipline with the Dorset bench. He made a number of charges of neglect and cruelty against the governor, but was unable to prove them because prisoners still in confinement were unwilling to corroborate his allegations for fear of reprisals. Wakefield returned to London and died six months later of typhus at the age of forty-six.

IV

The first political prisoners who succeeded in mobilizing a popular campaign against solitary confinement were the LCS men and the Nore mutineers confined in Coldbath Fields House of Correction in London in 1798. Twenty-two sailors convicted in late 1797 for their part in mutinies protesting pay and conditions in the fleet moored at the Nore in the Thames estuary were confined in a section of the prison apart from the criminals. In April 1798 they were joined by sixteen men arrested at a London pub in the decisive roundup of the LCS. Soon after, about six men from the Manchester Corresponding Society were brought to Coldbath Fields and confined with their London friends. Arrested along with the LCS men was Colonel Despard, an Army officer of Anglo-Irish ancestry whose mistreatment in the service had driven him into plotting with a militant wing of the LCS and the United Irishmen to foment Irish and English uprisings which would prepare the way for a French invasion.[31]

The prison in which they were confined, Coldbath Fields, opened in 1794, had been built on the Blackburn plan, and its discipline was supposed to follow the Gloucester model. From the start it was suspected of being a place of cruelty. In his first sermon to the prisoners, Reverend Samuel Glasse alluded to attacks already made on the discipline in the radical press.[32] To counter these "prejudices" of "wretched individuals," Glasse did his best to convince the prisoners of the benevolent pedigree of Coldbath Fields. It had been constructed, he pointed out, according to the principles of "those great examples of goodness and humanity, Howard and Hanway." He concluded with an exhortation to obedience and contrition:

> Let me recommend to you an humble, peaceful, quiet behavior, such as is suited to the nature of your situation, and such as will entitle you to kindness from those that are set over you; resistance of that authority under which you are here placed will be as unwise as was the conduct which brought you to your wretched state. Above all, let me entreat you to frequently lift up your hearts to the God against whom you have been living in habits of disobedience and rebellion and implore those graces of patience and meekness which your situation particularly demands.[33]

The prisoners' reaction to these homilies is not recorded. Until 1798 we know that they were at least quiet, if not meek and contrite.

To enforce the new discipline, the Middlesex magistrates tried to recruit a former army officer, but finding them in short supply in wartime they gave the appointment to a former baker named Thomas Aris. By all acounts, he proved to be a corrupt, violent, and indolent administrator. The magistrates nonetheless gave him free rein. Judging from the prison committee's books, their inspections were occasional and perfunctory.

With no one to stop him, Aris reintroduced forms of extortion that the reformers had campaigned to abolish. He charged for beds and took fees from visitors. He also cut back on the prison diet, leaving prisoners to subsist on bread and water. Those with friends were able to get food from outside, but the friendless or destitute simply starved. The prison soon became overcrowded, and by 1797 solitary confinement had been abandoned, except for "politicals" and major felons. Petty offenders and persons awaiting trial slept two to a bed in the 8' by 6' cells. Because Aris ignored hygiene, overcrowding was accompanied by disease. In their petitions to the justices, the prisoners complained of the cold, the damp, the "swarms of mice rattling in their rooms," and underweight rations.[34]

The collapse of penitentiary discipline at Coldbath Fields may have been especially rapid because of the venal qualities of Aris, but it was not atypical. By 1806, for example, the hard labor regime had been abandoned at the new bridewell in Wymondham, Norfolk, and the prisoners were allowed to remain "in a torpid state of idleness."[35] The hat manufactory at Dorchester was also abandoned. In the new bridewell in Cornwall, James Neild found pigs and chickens owned by the keeper roaming around the yards. Even at Gloucester, as we have seen, overcrowding also forced the abandonment of the penitentiary routine.

The deterioration of discipline in these places indicates that the institutional revolution of the 1790s was unable to sustain itself. Howard and Paul were ahead of their times in the very real sense that they were unable to find reliable cadres of disciplinarians to carry their institutional vision into practice. Inevitably, therefore, traditional forms of corruption reemerged in ostensibly "modern" and rational institutions.

This was particularly the case at Coldbath Fields. However, the state of that prison did not become a matter of public controversy until the mutineers and the London Corresponding Society men were imprisoned there in 1798. The LCS men arrived already primed in their opposition to solitary confinement. In January 1797, an article against solitary had appeared in the LCS publication, the *Moral and Political Magazine*.[36] The article borrowed from William Godwin's strictures against "Mr. Howard's scheme" in *Political Justice*. The article described solitary confinement as "an ingenious mode of intellectual torture," and as a "mode of destroying the frame through the agonies of the intellect." It argued that solitude would never reform offenders. "Obdurate criminals" would "wallow in the luxury of revenge," while genuinely remorseful prisoners would be driven insane by the torture of guilt. "Remorse is to the intellect what the rack is to the body."

The LCS article insisted that reformation was a social process. The "consolation and sympathy" of the outside world were necessary to sustain an offender's sense of shame and his capacity for reintegration By severing his social ties, solitary confinement merely heightened a criminal's alienation. A later issue of the magazine returned to this theme, attacking the use of solitary confinement for "petty and inconsiderable offenders" such as vagrants. The Law Dictionary, one of the magazine's running features, had set the stage on the question of confining political prisoners by defining penitentiaries as "receptacles for persons who write or speak disagreeable truths." Thus, when the gates of Coldbath Fields swung shut behind the men of the LCS in April 1798, they knew what to think of the place.

Before they were brought in, agitation against Aris's regime had already been begun by the Nore mutineers. They had besieged the governor, the Middlesex magistrates, the Admiralty, and the Secretary of State for the Home Department, Lord Portland, with petitions protesting their confinement in solitude and their diet, which appears to have largely consisted of cat meat. After a riot in the chapel in April 1798, a group of them scaled the walls and succeeded in eluding pursuit. The remainder were chained in their cells. For a time this stifled further protest.[37]

The arrival of Colonel Despard and the LCS men triggered a new round of unrest. Colonel Despard's wife repeatedly petitioned the Duke of Portland to release her husband from solitary, and when these petitions failed, she released them to the opposition press. The LCS men's petitions to the Duke of Portland complained that Aris kept them ironed in their cells, gouged them for food and for the "privilege" of a mattress, and punished them on the slightest pretext. He had ordered one of their number down to the dark cells for five weeks for having drawn a cartoon on his cell wall depicting a decapitated Prime Minister Pitt sprawled beside a guillotine. The cartoon was captioned "This is a cure for the King's evil." Such defiant graffiti certainly suggested that the LCS men had not been broken by solitary confinement.[38]

When their petitions to Portland and the Middlesex magistrates failed to have effect, the LCS men decided to make contact with Sir Francis Burdett and the Foxite Whigs in Parliament, an obvious choice since they had fought passage of Pitt's measures of repression. During the debate on the *Habeas Corpus* Suspension Bill of 1794, Charles James Fox and Richard Brinsley Sheridan charged that the measure gave Pitt "absolute power over the personal liberty of every individual in the kingdom."[39] When the ministers used their warrants to lock up dissidents in penitentiaries, Fox and Sheridan charged, they were acting no less despotically than Louis XVI when he used *lettres de cachet* to consign objects of his displeasure to the Bastille. It was a particularly effective taunt to associate the Bastille and the penitentiary, since the ministry liked to compare the libertarian traditions of English constitutionalism with the tyranny of both monarchical and Jacobin France. It was ironic that the Whigs of the 1790s came to include the penitentiary in their catalogue of ministerial tyranny because, as we have seen, Whigs of the 1780s had championed the institution. Now the protests of the political prisoners were bringing home the darker side of Howard's philanthropy.

There is a tone of rueful awakening in the Whig's reevaluation of the Howardian program. In a Commons debate on solitary confinement in 1800, for example, one member of the Foxite group admitted that "the late Mr. Howard was certainly one of the worthiest men who had ever existed." But, he went on, "if he had been one of the worst, he could not have suggested a punishment of a more cruel and mischievous description." Solitary confinement inflicted a degree of mental torture on the subject that rendered it "inconsistent with the constitution of the country."[40] Samuel Romilly did not go so far. He joined the Foxite Whigs in opposing the solitary confinement of detainees awaiting trial while continuing to favor its use, in carefully regulated conditions, for prisoners convicted of major crimes. "Old-fashioned Whigs" like G. O. Paul remained unregenerate advocates of solitary confinement and found themselves at odds with the Foxite faction in Parliament. Thus, the repression of the 1790s had driven a wedge between the moderate and radical wings of the reformist middle class.

Even though Fox and the Whigs agreed to take up their grievances, the LCS men regarded them with suspicion. Before their arrest, they had already cautioned the rest of the LCS membership against letting cooperation with the Whigs on civil liberties issues lead them to forget their more fundamental differences. The London society, for example, gave the following instructions to a delegate sent to meet with the Birmingham branch of the society:

> As the Whig Club have called upon the people to associate for the repeal of the new Treason and Sedition Bills without making any explicit declaration of their principles, we recommend you to caution the Society you visit against every attempt to divert their thoughts from our ultimate object by such temporary and subordinate considerations.[41]

The Whigs for their part took pains to distance themselves from the ideology of artisanal Jacobinism, but they felt bound to support them against Pitt's repression. An alliance based on such "temporary and subordinate considerations" could not be anything but fragile, but it lasted long enough to sustain a vigorous campaign against Coldbath Fields.

The LCS men in the prison initiated the campaign in December 1798 with a letter to Sir Francis Burdett urging him to investigate the case of a vagrant who had recently died in the prison. The letter was accompanied by a petition to the Middlesex coroner protesting the verdict of "visitation of God," which the coroners' jury had handed down in the vagrant's case. The verdict, they charged, should have been murder by neglect:

> Were the Jury informed, Sir, that this man was barely cloathed? Did they inquire the quantity of food given him, did they know that he was put into a cold damp cell during a very severe frost without the use of a fire or anything to keep him from perishing? Did they hear that he complained 36 hours before his death that his legs would mortify if he was left in that state? Did they inquire what medical assistance he received after his complaints were known? Were any inquiries made of the prisoners near him of the circumstances of his death, and did the jury know that he was not a criminal?[42]

The petitioners said that they accepted that a prison should "not be a place of ease and convenience to felons," but they insisted that it should be nothing more than a place of security for vagrants waiting, as this man had been, to be passed to their parish:

> When our humane statutes made provision for passing the poor to their parishes they never intended that their lives sho'd be sported with like the worthless felon who is speculated upon to calculate what degree of hunger he can sustain!! What degree of cold he can bear!!

Upon receipt of the petition, Burdett visited the prison, until banned by the Duke of Portland, on the grounds that he was inciting resistance among the inmates.[43] Burdett confirmed the allegations of the LCS men about the vagrant as well as their complaints about the food, the cold of the cells, and the unremitting solitude. Armed with first-hand impressions, Burdett demanded the appointment of an independent commission of inquiry. In the Commons debate on his motion, the lineup of forces that supported the prison administration proved that, though some reformers like Romilly continued to support the idea of a penitentiary, it had increasingly become the property of the anti-Jacobin reaction.

Leading the defense of the prison was the Evangelical William Wilberforce. Using memoranda supplied by his friend on the Middlesex bench, Reverend Samuel Glasse, he denied allegations that prisoners had been starved. He even went so far as to say that some prisoners had roast beef and plum pudding for dinner.[44] The truth was, he insisted, that the prison was a monument to the benevolent spirit of John Howard.

Wilberforce's speech enraged the LCS men and the mutineers in prison. In a letter to Burdett, one mutineer commented, "How easy it is for people that know nothing about this place to think that it is one of the first reforming places in the country." Another mutineer referred to it as a "prison boasting of its benevolence but which in fact is guided by an organized system of cruelty."[45]

To the LCS men, Wilberforce's defense of the prison must have come as a bitter irony, for they had once looked to the Evangelicals for support. One of Thomas Hardy's first acts as secretary of the LCS in 1792 was to write a letter to Jacob Bryant, an Evangelical leader of the campaign to abolish the slave trade, appealing for support:

> Hearing that you are a zealous friend to the abolition of that accursed traffic, the Slave Trade, I infer from that circumstance that you are a zealous friend to freedom on the broad basis of the Rights of Man. I am fully persuaded that there is no man who from principle [is] an advocate for the liberty of the black man, but will zealously support the rights of the white man, and vice versa.[46]

Hardy could not have been more wrong. Jacob Bryant, to whom Hardy had written so hopefully, turned up in 1794 as the author of one of the spate of "loyal" pamphlets attacking Paine's *Rights of Man.*[47]

In February 1799, the Commons accepted Burdett's demand for a committee of inquiry into the state of Coldbath Fields, but insisted that Wilberforce serve on it. In April 1799 the committee issued a report praising the "very laudable vigilance and attention" of the Middlesex bench.[48] While admitting that Aris had assaulted certain prisoners and extorted money from them, the committee saw no grounds for his dismissal. Burdett denounced the report as a whitewash, but failed to secure the support necessary for the appointment of an independent commission of inquiry. For the rest of the year, the question of the prison lay dormant.

V

When the controversy over Coldbath Fields revived in May 1800, it was no longer the treatment of the political prisoners but the case of Mary Rich, a fourteen-year-old workingman's daughter, that aroused public indignation. Mary Rich alleged that she had been raped by a lawyer. Astonishing as it may seem, it was common in cases where the accusers were indigent to commit them to prison as material witnesses, while setting the defendants free on bail. This is what happened to Mary Rich. She was held in Coldbath Fields for over a month, while her assailant was allowed to post bail.

When the case came before the grand jury, Mary Rich showed signs of starvation and fainted on the witness stand. The jury immediately inspected the prison and discovered that material witnesses like Mary Rich were held in solitary confinement on a bread and water diet while waiting for their cases to come to trial. Sir Francis Burdett procured a copy of the grand jury's report and demanded another commission of inquiry.

William Mainwairing, chairman of the Middlesex justices and MP for Middlesex, replied to Burdett's charges of cruelty by claiming that Mary Rich was an untrustworthy whore. She had been discovered "with several boys on the stairs in a way not proper to mention and had received half pence from them." To the charge that she had been starved, Mainwairing replied that she was better fed in prison than at home:

> When at home she lived in extreme poverty; she was one of six children; the mother makes soldiers' buttons at a penny a dozen; the father earns about 12 s. a week; and they generally bought four or five pounds of meat to subsist their family. These and other circumstances formed the report of the magistrates who gave it as

their opinion that Mary Rich was treated better and lived more comfortably in gaol than ever she had done with her parents.[49]

To which Richard Brinsley Sheridan tartly replied, "It was a strange mode of arguing that because her parents were poor the wretched meagre diet of the gaol was excellent food."

The public learned of the Mary Rich case in July 1800, from an anonymous pamphlet entitled *An Impartial Statement of the Inhuman Cruelties Discovered in the Coldbath Fields Prison.* Popular anger grew in early August with the release of one of the mutineers in such a weakened condition that he died a month later.[50]

On August 13, at the evening lockup, the convicts at Coldbath Fields milled around, "murmured among themselves," and had to be forced into their cells. The next morning, they were seen gathering in groups in the exercise yard, apparently plotting a disturbance. At lockup on the fourteenth, they refused to enter their cells, and the turnkeys had to drive them in at gunpoint. Once inside, they began shouting from their cell windows, "Murder! Starving! Fever! We're Being Starved!" They began chanting and banging on their cell doors and bedsteads. The noise from the cells attracted a crowd of about five thousand from the working people's quarter of Clerkenwell. They milled around the walls, shouting encouragement to the prisoners who began to call down to the people to tear down the walls of the prison. Soon chants of "Pull down the Bastille!" began to rise from the crowd. Aris dashed out of the prison by a side entrance and went to Hatton Garden Police Office for help. A force of Bow Street Runners arrived. They were joined by a hastily mobilized group of local property owners, the Clerkenwell Volunteers. Together they began to disperse the crowd, with the help of a cannon positioned in front of the prison gate. After about four hours, the crowd was driven away and the prisoners were subdued.

Of twenty ringleaders who were chained and taken down to the punishment cells, none were political prisoners. This was perhaps the most significant aspect of the riot. Most of the mutineers had already been released. By a "very good piece of management," as *The Morning Chronicle* put it, they were seized by a press gang as they walked along Tower Hill on their first day of freedom and sent to sea again. As a result, they were not among the crowd outside the prison.[51] The LCS men do not figure in the authorities' accounts of the disturbance either, and appear to have remained in their cells throughout the riot, which seems to have represented the attempt of ordinary criminals to join in the agitation against the prison that had been initiated by the Jacobins.

The riot had an immediate effect. Within a month, the independent commission of inquiry that Burdett had demanded for two years was appointed. Its two leading members were William Morton Pitt of Dorchester and G. O. Paul of Gloucester. As expected, they defended the penitentiary system of imprisonment and vindicated the Middlesex magistracy's management of Coldbath Fields. But they also ventured some mild reproof. They condemned the confinement in the penitentiary of persons awaiting trial or persons like Mary Rich waiting to give evidence. They also confirmed that the prison was dangerously overcrowded, dirty, and badly ventilated. While admitting that Aris had allowed the discipline of solitary confinement to run down, they did not recommend his dismissal.[52]

Burdett bided his time after the commission's report and did not bring up the issue of Coldbath Fields again during 1801. In July 1802, however, he decided to resume his campaign against the prison by contesting the Middlesex seat held by its chief defender, William Mainwairing, the chairman of the Middlesex bench.

In its sneering way, the *Times* got the social alignments right when it described the election as a contest between "the respectable people" represented by Mainwairing, and the "refuse of St. Giles and Wapping" represented by Burdett.[53] From the outset, Burdett made it clear that a vote for Mainwairing was "a vote for that new and scandalous system of imprisonment." It was also a vote for "pensioned" magistrates created by the legislation of 1792. Burdett linked the penitentiary and police reform together as threats to the "good old constitution of England."[54] He also succeeded in making Coldbath Fields the symbol of the repression of the 1790s. The London crowd responded to his slogan "Burdett and No Bastille" with the most riotous show of support since the days of John Wilkes.

The election kept respectable London on edge for weeks. As the *Times* admitted, there was not a "jack ass driver from Kent Street" or "pot boy from Drury Lane" who did not sport Burdett's colors.[55] Burdett's managers worked on popular feeling against the prison, using all the symbolic techniques of the pre-1832 election. In addition to the processions and banners, there were tableaux vivants at the hustings depicting a man in sailor's dress, an obvious reference to the mutineers, being whipped by a sneering Aris-like figure with a cat-o'-nine-tails. Huge crowds gathered at the hustings every day to groan and hiss Mainwairing's supporters, some of whom were forced to disguise themselves with Burdett's colors in order to get to the poll unmolested. Mainwairing himself gave up speaking at the hustings after the first day because the crowds completely drowned out his speeches. When his carriage returned to London from Brentford that first day, it was pelted with dirt by "ruffians" standing on Kew Bridge.

Mainwairing was unable to muster comparable public support, but he did accept Burdett's challenge to make the election into a referendum on the repression of the Pitt years. Mainwairing's own politics were those of the organization that defended that repression most outspokenly, the Society for Preserving Liberty and Property Against Republicans and Levellers. The society's major function was to distribute cheap tracts controverting Jacobin propaganda. One of these tracts was a speech by Mainwairing himself attacking the Jacobins' visionary doctrines of social equality. The speech condemned the efforts of "evil-disposed persons" to "alienate the minds of the people from a due regard to the laws and our happy Constitution." It praised the equality before the law allowed under the constitution and derided the Jacobin chimera of equality of property:

> In this country the law is no respecter of persons. In our courts of Justice all are equal; high and low, rich and poor, all are alike under the care of our laws. This is the happy Equality which everyone is entitled to, and enjoys in this country—and it is the only equality consistent with any form of government, with any system of society. Equality in the sense in which it is now attempted to be inculcated into the minds of the people by crafty and designing men is, in the nature of things, impossible.[56]

Mainwairing was only one of a score of Tory politicians and propagandists who expounded upon the advantages of the British constitution. Hannah More, who was gifted with more semantic cunning and a more popular touch than Mainwairing, was deployed by the society to immunize the poor against the bacillus of Jacobinism. Her best-known tract, *Village Politics,* was a long dialogue between two rustics on the virtues of the English legal tradition:

> Tom: Why do our governors put many of us poor folks into prison against our will? What are jails for? Down with the jails, I say. All men should be free.

Jack: Harkee, Tom, a few rogues in prison keep the rest in order and then honest men go about their business afraid of nobody; that's the way to be free. And let me tell thee, Tom, thou and I art tried by our peers as much as a Lord is. Why the King can't send me to prison if I do no harm, and if I do, there's reason good why I should go there. I may go to law with Sir John at the great castle yonder, and he no more dares lift his little finger against me than if I were his equal. A lord is hanged for hanging matter as thou or I should be; and if it will be of any comfort to thee, I myself remember of a Peer of the Realm being hanged for killing his Man, just the same as the Man would have been for killing him.[57]

More was referring to the execution of Earl Ferrers in 1760 for the murder of his steward. This proof of English justice was served up to the poor repeatedly throughout the 1790s.

Given the depth of popular disaffection in the 1790s, it is not surprising that so much effort was expended to convince the poor that the law was fair. The government was particularly vulnerable to arguments that it had violated the rights of freeborn Englishmen. This "constitutionalist" attack had considerable appeal among the middle class, as evidenced in the Middlesex juries' stolid skepticism towards the government's case in the state trials. The repression, in other words, brought out a characteristic dilemma of class rule in times of social crisis. In suspending normal civil liberties so as to crush the Jacobins, the ministry ran the risk of eroding public respect for the law. Mainwairing's speeches and More's pamphlets were thus attempts to provide a patina of justification for a legal system that could easily be seen only as an instrument of class oppression.

The Middlesex election can be seen as a culmination of this ideological battle over the law. Mainwairing's chief propagandist, John Bowles, thundered that Burdett's campaign against the prison was a Jacobin attempt to discredit the whole legal system in the eyes of the poor:

For when the people are taught to view the magistrates with contempt or hatred and to consider every gaol a Bastille, annexing to that appellation some indefinite idea of severity and tyranny, it is greatly to be feared that their indignation will next be turned against the laws of the land; and the state of the country, the prosperity of which is so inseparably connected with a due respect for its laws and legal institutions will then be deplorable indeed.[58]

He warned the Middlesex electors that Burdett's real purpose was to incite the mob to "lay that prison in ruins and make its destruction a prelude to the overthrow of the British monarchy." Mainwairing's supporters seized on a small riot at the prison in the midst of the polling for the election as proof that Burdett was inciting both the mob and the prisoners. At lockup on July 17, a group of eight prisoners set up an outcry of "Murder! Bloody Murder! Starving Alive!" It was soon taken up by the other prisoners, and the noise attracted a large crowd outside the prison. A police magistrate arrived and appealed in vain to the prisoners to settle down. The women in the prison were particularly unruly, and several of them had to be gagged, chained, and dragged below to the dark cells.[59] The disturbance was less serious than the one two years earlier. When the prisoners were subdued, the crowd dispersed peaceably. Nevertheless, Mainwairing used the riot to hammer away at his theme that a victory for Burdett meant a victory for Jacobinism and revolution.

Sensing that respectable householders might be influenced by Mainwairing's allegations, Burdett replied with a nimble piece of hustings rhetoric designed to reassure the propertied without alienating the radical:

> An allusion had been made that day to a glorious circumstance which some years ago took place in a neighboring country—the destruction of the Bastille. He never contemplated that important event without participating in the joy which every independent mind felt on the occasion—and he felt still greater satisfaction whenever he reflected that there was no necessity for a similar act in this country; for he was confident that Englishmen by a firm, legal, and constitutional conduct might obtain without violence that which the unfortunate people of France could not have obtained by any other means.[60]

Though he paraded as a paladin of the common people, Burdett was careful to distance himself from the extremes of Jacobinism. He clothed his opposition to the Bastille in the rhetoric of strict constitutionalism. It was Mainwairing, not he, who was endangering the British monarchy by supporting measures of repression that brought the law into disrepute with the common people.

The voters were reassured by these arguments, as they were by the fact that Burdett was the son-in-law of the eminent London banker Thomas Coutts.[61] On election day they gave Burdett a narrow victory. When the result was announced, an immense crowd, estimated in some newspapers at half a million people, drew Burdett's carriage in a triumphal procession from the hustings at Brentford to his home in Piccadilly, stopping along the way to sing choruses of the French Revolutionary song "Ça Ira" in front of St. James's Palace. The *Morning Chronicle* described Burdett's victory as a "spontaneous and honest expression of indignation against the system of solitary confinement."[62] It also expressed the revulsion felt even among the franchise holders at the suppression of civil liberties during the Pitt years.

V I

In retrospect, it is obvious that Burdett used Coldbath Fields as a convenient but temporary issue, for after the election he let it drop completely. Aris, Glasse, and Mainwairing continued in their posts, and for the next five years the Whig opposition made no mention of the prison in Commons debates. The restoration of *habeas corpus* and the liberation of the last political prisoners took away all impetus to make the new prisons a political issue.

Yet the question of Coldbath Fields did not disappear. It was revived again in 1807 by Alexander Stephens, a member of the circle of radical Whigs, including Burdett, who met at John Horne Tooke's house for bibulous political luncheons.[63] Stephens became involved in Coldbath Fields while serving as foreman of the Middlesex grand jury. In July 1807, after it had finished its work on criminal indictments, the jury made its usual tour of the Middlesex jails. Stephens, naturally enough, subjected Coldbath Fields to particular scrutiny and found that the abuses denounced since 1798 still persisted. The prison loaves were underweight. A number of poor people were still being confined in solitary cells awaiting further examination on charges of felony, in violation of the recommendations of the commission of 1800. Debtors were confined indiscriminately with vagrants and felons. Stephens also heard allegations that Aris's son had been sleeping with some of the female prisoners.[64]

During his tour, Stephens heard cries and entreaties issuing from one of the cells. He ordered it opened and found inside a deranged and pathetic Frenchman, the Chevalier du Blin. A former aide-de-camp of General Dumourier, he had been arrested in May 1807 as a spy and had been detained in solitary confinement. After

three months of total solitude he began to lose his mind. He tore
his clothes and wrote confused messages upon them, which he
tried to have smuggled out of the prison. He screamed that he
could hear his wife and children being tortured in the cell below
him. The du Blin case raised the controversy about solitary
confinement once again.

Stephens drew up a petition with his findings and sent copies
to the Whig opposition, the Home Secretary, and Middlesex magistrates. He also enlisted the support of his friend Richard Phillips,
an influential publisher then serving as sheriff of London. Phillips
had personal acquaintance with prison having served eighteen
months in Leicester jail during the 1790s for having sold Paine's
Rights of Man. He supported Stephens's charges by sending a letter
to the Middlesex justices attesting to the deficiency of the prison
loaves that had been weighed before him at Guildhall. The Middlesex magistrates replied, predictably enough, that Phillips had been
"imposed upon."[65] The prisoners were never cheated on their
rations, they said, although individual loaves might be underweight upon occasion.

This time, however, official support for the prison and for the
magistrates was noticeably less enthusiastic than it had been in
1800. When Sheridan presented Stephens's petition in the Commons, the government admitted that "there had been neglect somewhere," and even Wilberforce confessed that "while many happy
effects had resulted" from the system of solitary confinement, "it
might be liable to abuse."[66] All sides of the House approved the
appointment of a second commission of inquiry.

Like its predecessor, the commission succeeded in avoiding a
censure of the justices or the governor by taking a literal-minded
approach to the charges made against them. It nevertheless confirmed the truth of Stephens's allegations. The commission acknowledged that du Blin had lost his reason during his
imprisonment, though it chose to interpret this as proof of the
susceptibility of the Gallic temperament to intemperate passions
rather than as an indictment of solitary confinement. It recommended his removal to the St. Luke's Hospital for the Insane. The
commission, like its predecessor, confirmed that debtors, vagrants,
and misdemeanants were not kept separate, while persons awaiting
trial continued to be held in solitude. Prisoners were confined in
their cells at night but were allowed to roam freely about the yards
and passages by day. The commission found them dirty, idle,

profligate, and foul-mouthed. It also confirmed that Aris's son had forced his attentions upon the women prisoners, but took the curious position that Aris senior could not be held responsible for his son's conduct in the institution.[67] Clearly, the old pre-1775 subculture of prisons, complete with its corrupt bargain between custodial staff and confined, had reemerged in an ostensibly "modern" institution.

There is no evidence to suggest that the 1808 report was heeded any more than the one in 1800 had been. Aris managed to survive this second indictment of his corruption and incompetence just as he had the first. The magistrates kept him on because there was no one else available to take his place.

If the management of the prison did not change, the attacks upon it over so many years had a permanent effect. Penitentiary and Bastille became indissolubly linked in the popular imagination. By 1811, the *Dictionary of the Vulgar Tongue*, a collection of slang popular in the streets of London, listed "Steel" as the poor people's word for houses of correction and for Coldbath Fields in particular. Steel or Stile was short for Bastille,[68] just as the Stone Jug became the slang term for Newgate.[69] These names stuck to their institutions. Journalists noticed in 1850 that poor boys just released from Coldbath Fields still referred to the place as the Stile.[70] The persistence of these terms indicates how deeply Burdett's campaign worked its way into the consciousness of the poor. Indeed, the term Bastille became a rallying cry for popular opposition to the framework of total institutions created in the nineteenth century. In the 1830s, it was applied by the poor to the bitterly hated Union workhouses. When Pentonville was opened in 1842, a small radical journal labeled it too a Bastille.[71]

The campaign against the Bastilles also had a disillusioning impact on advocates of prison reform. In 1808, Richard Phillips as sheriff of London wrote to the aging G. O. Paul, asking him to inspect the London prisons and to make recommendations for reform. Paul turned Phillips down with a letter that indicated how much his old enthusiasms had waned. He said he was convinced that the London aldermen would continue to ignore his recommendations as they had ignored Howard's. Referring to the Coldbath Fields agitation, he continued:

> And with regard to the popular voice of the Metropolis—if Howard had been living, as I was, at the end of the 18th century, he would have had the mortification to find his views and his designs,

like my own, made the subject of scurrilous libels, and, as I was, so he would have been obliged to defend himself from charges of an unfeeling cruelty regarding those very acts in the performance of which he had religiously felt himself executing the duties of a Christian and the policy of an enlightened philanthropist.[72]

Paul concluded tersely, "I am weary of ineffective labours."

The second generation of reformers, who emerged after the Napoleonic Wars to support Elizabeth Fry's ministry to the women of Newgate and to campaign for the construction of the national penitentiary at Millbank, were strongly influenced by the reaction against solitary confinement. They opposed total separation and took pains to reassure skeptical opinion that they were in favor of the association of prisoners and of group labor in workshops. To allay public anxiety about their proposals, they coined the euphemism "separate confinement" to describe their program.[73] This effort to reclothe Howardian ideas in more acceptable linguistic garb was not particularly successful. Resistance to solitary confinement remained widespread and was one major reason why penitentiary ideas spread so slowly in England after the years of innovation in the 1780s.

The Politics of Prison Reform

in the Peterloo Era

I

In December 1816, Elizabeth Fry led an apprehensive committee of wives of Quaker businessmen and bankers into the women's wards at Newgate. As one of them later recalled, they felt they were going into a "den of wild beasts." As the gate clanged shut behind them, they were surrounded by a "promiscuous assemblage" of "half naked" prisoners, begging for money, swearing, and fighting with each other to get closer. When the Quaker matrons succeeded in securing silence, Elizabeth Fry announced that the sheriff had given her permission to reform the wards and introduce new rules of discipline. "Not a rule would be made," Fry assured the prisoners, "without their full and unanimous concurrence. Each of the rules should be read and put to the vote." With their apparent agreement, the Quaker women set about imposing order upon the prisoners. First, the tried and the untried, the young and the old, the first offender and the "hardened, drunken prostitute" were divided and placed in separate wards.[1] The women's children were placed in a school within the prison, run by one of the prisoners. Having classified the prisoners and broken up their criminal "associations," Fry began to order their appearance. Earrings,

curled hair, and "all sorts of finery and superfluity of dress" were
forbidden. In order to promote "that humiliation of spirit which
... is [an] indispensable step to improvement and reformation,"
their hair was cut close and they were issued with white uniforms.
These were modeled on the plain and unadorned dresses worn by
the Quaker women.[2] Both sides of the philanthropic encounter
thus embraced a common asceticism.

Soon, Fry had set the women to work sewing. She adopted the
monitorial system of discipline used by her close friend and fellow
Quaker Joseph Lancaster in his school for poor children in South
London.[3] The prisoners were divided into groups of thirteen each
under the eye of a monitor chosen by them. Over the whole female
wing she appointed a working-class woman as full-time matron.

The results of Fry's work were dramatic. Passersby noticed
that the women had stopped begging from the cell windows. The
keepers discovered that when the first batch of "Mrs. Fry's" prisoners were sent down to the ships to be transported to Australia
they did not smash up their cells. Fry had convinced them to
abandon this "saturnalia."[4] In place of the idleness, fighting, and
swearing, she had substituted quiet industry and prayerfulness. As
her brother-in-law, Thomas Fowell Buxton, put it, she had turned
a "Hell on Earth," into a "well-regulated Manufactory."[5]

Within a year, Fry had become one of the celebrities of Re-
gency London. When Queen Charlotte stopped to talk to her
during a public gathering, "a murmur of applause" rippled
through the assembled crowd watching this encounter between
royalty and philanthropy.[6] Fry's Sunday services at Newgate chapel became one of the major philanthropic venues of the
city, attended by such personages as the Duke of Gloucester
and the Home Secretary, Lord Sidmouth. So popular did these
services become with the city's elite that there were frequently as
many visitors watching from the galleries as there were prisoners
in the pews. In 1820, Sir James Williams took his whole family to
the service and recorded his impressions.[7] After passing through
the "dark, stone-vaulted lobby," hung with fetters, and through the
"enormous, grated iron-guarded doors," they were admitted to the
chapel. Fry, seated in the center of the chapel, ordered a bell to be
rung to "give notice to the prisoners to get ready." On the second
ringing, they began to enter and filled up the pews in a tight,
serried mass of identical uniforms and bonnets. While about forty

visitors looked on, Fry read from the thirteenth chapter of the Epistle to the Romans:

> Let every soul be subject unto the higher powers. For there is no power but of God and the powers that be are ordained of God. Whosoever therefore resisteth the power, resisteth the ordinance of God; and they that resist shall receive to themselves damnation. For rulers are not a terror to good works but to the evil. Wilt thou then not be afraid of the power? Do thou that which is good and thou shalt have praise of the same.

In her sermon to the prisoners, Fry delivered a homily on the necessity of obedience and dwelt particularly on the verses of the epistle that read, "Bless them who persecute you; bless and curse not. Recompense to no man evil for evil." These injunctions were sorrowfully received. The visitors were gratified to observe that the silence that followed the sermon was punctuated by the sighs and sobs of the prisoners. At the end of the service, Sir James Williams came away musing on the universality of guilt. Fry had proved that the poor were as susceptible to the call of conscience as the rich. "Are we not all convicts under the divine law?" he asked himself.

Many visitors to Fry's services came away with the same reaction. She had shown that those whom she did not hesitate to call "the very lowest order of the people ... the scum of the city and country" could be transformed into dutiful, orderly, and pious penitents.[8] Her extraordinary celebrity in 1817 suggests that her work was taken up by people like Lord Sidmouth as a hopeful allegory for class relations in general.

The reception given Fry's work invites comparison with the experiences of Robert Owen, another philanthropist who took London by storm in the same year. Like Fry, he too became a celebrity because his model factory community, New Lanark, seemed to prove that the discontented poor could be transformed into obedient workers. When he came to London in 1816, Owen trumpeted such communities as a new instrument of social control, capable of suppressing criminal inclinations among the young and inuring the unruly to habits of industry.[9]

Yet while both Fry and Owen shared a faith in the reformative uses of discipline, they came from radically different traditions. For Fry the reformation of criminals represented the triumph of God's grace. The discipline she used to put prisoners in a frame of

mind ready to receive such grace was a secular version of her own
sectarian asceticism. Owen's faith in discipline, by contrast, harked
back to the intellectual ambience of the Manchester Literary and
Philosophical Society, whose meetings he had attended as a young
factory master in the 1790s. His ruling principle, that people's
characters are formed for them, not by them, in their encounter
with education and environment, was a product of the Hartleian
materialism of that milieu.

By the late 1790s, though, it was no longer fashionable to
legitimize factory discipline as improving. Conditions of trade
were becoming increasingly competitive, and the profit margins,
which had paid for "philanthropic" measures in the factory communities, were declining. Owen was one of the few masters who
remained true to the optimism of the 1780s. He believed that his
discipline at New Lanark had reconciled profit and moral reform.
He came down to London in 1817 seeking to publicize his discovery that his "animate mechanisms" were as susceptible to improvement as his machines.[10]

Despite their obvious differences of background and outlook,
Owen and Fry drew support from the same milieu, the Evangelicals and Quakers who were the mainstay of London charity in this
period. The central figure in this group was William Allen, a
wealthy Quaker businessman who managed a large chemical
works in the East End of the city.[11] As a young man in the 1780s,
he had been drawn into the Evangelical crusade against the slave
trade. This campaign, which finally secured passage of the Slave
Trade Abolition Bill in 1807, became the model for philanthropic
organization in the early nineteenth century.

In the late 1790s, Allen distributed soup to the starving weavers
of Spitalfields as part of another Evangelical charity, the Society
for Bettering the Condition of the Poor. By 1810, he had become
a philanthropic entrepreneur in his own right, as the editor of the
leading charitable journal, *The Philanthropist*. He was also the chief
organizer of voluntary relief for the poor of London's East End
and a regular prison visitor. It was he who introduced Elizabeth
Fry to Newgate and, in 1817, formed the Prison Discipline Society
to support her work. It became the major lobbyist for prison and
criminal law reform in the period. Its reports gently chided local
benches for abuses and urged the passage of a new jails act, establishing national standards for prison discipline. Besides Allen, the

key figures in the society were Thomas Fowell Buxton, a leading Evangelical politician, and Samuel Hoare, a Quaker banker.[12]

In its membership, the society represented the same fusion of religious zealotry and utilitarian rationalism as had emerged in support of Howard's program during the 1780s. The society brought Evangelical Quakers like Hoare and Allen together with Benthamites like Basil Montague and James Mill. As in the 1780s, the religious and rationalist wings of prison reform found common ground in a shared vision of discipline. Allen may have been affronted by Mill's militant agnosticism, but he was happy to accept Mill's articles on prison reform for *The Philanthropist*, and he felt free to praise Bentham's *Rationale of Punishment*, after assuring himself, "that it contains nothing at variance with my religious feelings."[13]

Allen, the Evangelical Quaker, and Bentham, the utilitarian agnostic, both served as trustees of New Lanark. Bentham's support is easy to explain. New Lanark had obvious affinities with the Panopticon. Both were disciplinarian utopias, inspired by the same confidence in the malleability of men. Allen's support was a more complicated matter. He soon became aware of Owen's increasingly militant atheism, but he agreed to serve as a trustee because he looked to New Lanark as an alternative to the rapacious industrialism of the urban north; as an attempt to reintroduce, albeit in a new and scientific form, the paternalism that had been sacrificed in the scramble for profits.

During a speech to the workers at New Lanark in 1818, Allen praised Owen for reconciling the employer's interest in profits with his obligation to the well-being of the labor force:

> Woeful experience in other places has shown that to endeavour to extract the greatest quantity of profit from such a concern, at the expense of the health and comfort of those employed in it is a policy, at once short-sighted and cruel; and calculated eventually to lead to results baneful to society.[14]

Believing that Robert Owen intended the same reform of the poor that Joseph Lancaster was attempting at the monitorial school in Walworth, and Elizabeth Fry was pursuing in Newgate, Allen swallowed his doubts about Owen's atheism and agreed to serve as a trustee.

The support of the Nonconformist bankers and industrialists for Owen's scheme was fragile. As his religious views became more pronounced, and as his experiment in scientific management was slowly transmuted into a vision of a socialist utopia organized on communitarian lines, his support among the benevolent elite of London and the provinces dwindled away. William Allen actually remained on the board of trustees until the early 1830s, but he had broken with Owen long before over the question of religious instruction at New Lanark.[15]

In 1817, however, it was still possible for the same milieu that supported Elizabeth Fry to endorse Owen's scheme. Enough has already been said about the hidden affinities between Quaker piety and Enlightenment materialism to explain how Fry and Owen could find common ground together. The question is one of timing. How are we to account for the renewal of prison reform activity in particular and attempts to reform the poor in general around the year 1817?

I I

The philanthropic revival among the Quakers after the Napoleonic Wars should be traced back to the impact of the Evangelical movement upon Dissent in the 1790s. The Evangelical revival began as a protest against the corruption of the Established Church, the tepid and accommodating deism of its doctrine, and the decline of moral earnestness among the Anglican upper and middle classes.[16] In doctrinal terms, the Evangelicals' most vehement criticism of the Church was that it excused sin as mere "error" and hence encouraged casuistry and moral equivocation among its members. Believers could only come to a full awareness of the moral dimension of their lives once they realized, as their leader, William Wilberforce, put it, that "man is an apostate creature, fallen from his high original, degraded in his nature and depraved in his faculties, indisposed to do good and disposed to do evil."[17]

Their powerful sense of guilt underlay their criticism of the materialist hedonism and religious indifference of their own class. In terms reminiscent of Hanway's anxious discussion of the effects of "luxury" in the 1770s, the Evangelicals argued that the social conscience and religious commitment of the rich had been weakened by "the success of their commercial speculations," by the wealth and prosperity of a growing empire. "The multiplication of great cities" and the "habit of frequenting a splendid and luxurious metropolis," Wilberforce warned, "would powerfully tend to accelerate the discontinuance of the religious habits of a purer age and to accomplish the substitution of a more relaxed morality."[18]

This anxiety about urban growth and economic prosperity gained new cogency with the coming of the French Revolution and the upsurge of Jacobin radicalism at home. Evangelicals viewed the revolution as God's visitation on an aristocracy that had allowed itself to be corrupted by sensual distractions and intellectual libertinism.[19] The receptivity of the poor to Jacobin propaganda appeared to confirm the Evangelicals' warning that the godlessness of the "higher orders" would end by "descending" among the lower.[20]

Though Evangelicalism may have begun as a purely private search for a faith that would overcome a sense of moral aimlessness, as a movement it could not escape involvement in the crisis of the 1790s. The Evangelicals interpreted the times as a warning writ large of the need for personal, inner reform. There was thus a close connection between their self-reproaches and their social criticism. Their activism had a special intensity because it served both personal and social needs, because self-reform and social reform were one and the same project.

The particular dynamism of their philanthropy owed a good deal to their emphasis on the efficacy of good works. They managed to introduce the Calvinist emphasis on original sin into the Established Church without at the same time accepting a fatalist, predestinarian view of salvation.[21] On the contrary, they believed that a person could earn redemption through philanthropy —that "labor in a calling" appropriate for the rich. Accordingly, Wilberforce and his followers, the London financiers and merchants known as the Clapham Sect, plunged into a host of benevolent projects: the campaign to abolish the slave trade; the Society for the Suppression of Vice, dedicated to the prosecution of brothel keepers and radical tract sellers; and the Society for Bettering the Condition of the Poor, whose most important work in the 1790s was the maintenance of soup kitchens in the East End.

The Evangelicals' call for social activism had a powerful effect on the Quakers, partly because it appealed to their long-standing philanthropic tradition, but also because its attack on materialism called them back from worldly success to the heroic rigors of their own past. In the seventeenth century, the Society of Friends had been the most uncompromising and radical of the Puritan sects, suffering constant harassment and imprisonment. As is often the case, persecution merely strengthened the determination of the faithful. Quakerism's most robust hours were in its time of trial. When the persecution was lifted by the Act of Toleration in 1685, the slow dissolution of the sect's militant separation from the world began.[22]

The decline of strict Quakerism was accelerated by the sect's phenomenal economic success in the eighteenth century. Weber has made us aware of the irony that it is precisely those who subject their passion for gain to some higher spiritual end who achieve the greatest wealth. The strict discipline of the Quakers gave them a decided aptitude for methodical acquisition. By expelling any Friend found guilty of dishonest business practice, they gained a reputation for probity that served them well as bankers. (It was one of Elizabeth Fry's enduring sorrows and embarrassments that her husband, Joseph, suffered expulsion in 1828 for a business failure that brought about the ruin of other Friends.)[23] Their sober assiduousness and impeccable credit-worthiness helped them to rise from struggling journeymen and artisans in the seventeenth century to leading positions in provincial banking and industry by the middle of the eighteenth.

The Quakers' ascent is epitomized by Elizabeth Fry's family, the Gurneys of Norwich. Her ancestors had been small clothiers who suffered imprisonment for their beliefs during the era of persecution. Barred from entry into politics and the ruling culture of Norfolk by the Test Acts, the Gurneys devoted themselves to their woolen business and built it into the largest in the county, employing thousands of outworkers. In 1770, using capital generated from the business, they entered provincial banking. In 1780 they capped their ascent by establishing their headquarters in Lombard Street, London, the center of the English banking world.[24]

Success, however, had a corrosive effect on their Quakerism. Elizabeth Fry grew up at the family's estate, Earlham Hall, amidst a degree of "luxury" that would have shocked her ancestors. The strict forms of speech and dress had been abandoned because they had become an embarrassment in the world of business and an obstacle to social acceptance among the local gentry. In place of Quakerism, the family adopted a free-thinking Unitarianism. Earlham Hall became a center of Nonconformist radicalism. Cartwright's pamphlets on parliamentary reform, Priestley's *Lectures on Government*, and Rousseau's *Emile* were all eagerly discussed. Looking back in the somber 1790s, one of Elizabeth's sisters said of this time, "we were truly in the wilderness of error."[25] The French Revolution, by demonstrating the fatal consequences of free thought, dampened the radicalism of Earlham Hall and prepared the family for the impact of Evangelicalism. First, one of Elizabeth's older sisters embraced Evangelicalism. Elizabeth's own religious crisis followed soon after. In late adolescence, acute attacks of anxiety about her estrangement from God prevented her from attending Meeting. In her diary, she castigated herself for her lack of faith and pined for the illumination of the "inner light" that Quakerism identified as the sign of grace.[26]

Her illumination came in 1798 in the form of a visit to the Norwich Meeting by the fiery and emotional Philadelphia Friend William Savery. Savery said he was ashamed of the "gayness" of the Norwich Meeting and added pointedly, "the marks of wealth and grandeur are too obvious in several families of Friends."[27] His visit, coming after the recent conversion of her sister, appears to have been the catalyst for Elizabeth's transformation into a strict Quaker. To the dismay of her sisters, she began to withdraw from the round of dances and singing parties at Earlham Hall in order to pray alone in her room. Her diary is filled with poignant signs of struggle over this decision. As she sat in her room, praying and meditating, she could hear the sound of music in the dining room below. If her brother came upstairs to ask her to join the dancing, she found herself sorely tried and having refused, poured out her regret in her diary. But she persevered in adopting the strict dress and speech of old Quakerism, and, after her marriage to the London businessman Joseph Fry, she became one of the leaders of a strict Meeting in the city. Her influence was largely responsible for the conversion of her brother, J. J. Gurney, to strict Quakerism.

These religious experiences heightened the family's self-consciousness about its wealth. In 1807 we find J. J. Gurney writing from the family countinghouse, "How important it is ... that we bankers and brokers should not suffer ourselves to be wholly immersed in Mammon."[28] While Gurney stayed with the family firm, he remained, in the words of his biographer, "an uneasy banker and an uneasy man of wealth to the end of his days."[29]

Gurney's brother-in-law, Thomas Fowell Buxton, was similarly affected by his contact with the Evangelicals. After 1810, his

diaries and letters record a growing conviction about the moral
emptiness of his work as a partner in the brewery firm of Truman,
Hanbury and Buxton:

> It is so unpleasant to wake and go to sleep with your head full of
> vats and tubs; and I disapprove it more than I hate it. No man, I
> think, can have more abstract conviction of the folly and futility
> of such engagement of heart upon objects so utterly trifling and
> unendurable. How sincerely I do often wish that I could direct
> this fervent energy about temporals into its proper channel—that
> I could be as warm about things of infinite importance as I am
> about dust and ashes![30]

In another letter, written shortly before he plunged into the work
of prison reform, Buxton confessed disconsolately:

> I am irritable about trifles, eager after pleasures and anxious about
> business: various objects of this kind engross my attention at all
> times: they pursue me even to Meeting and to church, and seem
> to grudge the few moments which are devoted to the higher
> considerations and strive to bring back to the temple of the Lord
> the sellers and buyers and the money changers. My reason tells me
> these things are utterly indifferent, but my practice says that they
> only are worthy of thought and attention. My practice says Thou
> art increased with goods and hast need of nothing; but my reason
> teaches me Thou art wretched and miserable and poor and blind
> and naked.[31]

These letters provide us with a glimpse of the inner turmoil
that the Evangelical revival unleashed among the Quaker business
people. In the passion of their self-castigation, the letters hint at the
immense spiritual energy that was seeking escape from the banal
convolutions of business. Buxton never did leave the brewery, but
philanthropy provided him with an outlet for his energies that
allowed him to be at peace with himself. He plunged into the relief
of distress in Spitalfields in 1811, and in 1817 successfully stood for
election as a Whig Member of Parliament. In the House, he became
the leading spokesman for prison and criminal law reform. Outside
the House, he was in constant attendance at Fry's Sunday services
at Newgate as well as a key member of the Prison Discipline
Society.

Philanthropic activism provided a vital emotional release for
men and women whose passions were so completely yoked to
religious ideals. Fry's control of her feelings extended even to her
motherly instincts. "The maternal feelings, when under subordination, are real and great sources of enjoyment," she once remarked,
"but they are apt to occupy the mind too much."[32] Likewise, she

confessed that singing gave her rather too much pleasure. "It carries me far beyond the centre; it increases all the wild passions and works on enthusiasm."[33] Benevolence was an essential avenue of release from her carapace of self-discipline, as we can gather from her intense description of the philanthropic emotions:

> There is a sort of luxury in giving way to the feelings! I love to feel for the sorrows of others, to pour wine and oil into the wounds of the afflicted; there is a luxury in feeling the heart glow whether it be with joy or sorrow.[34]

Fry's choice of prisoners as the object of her benevolent energies did not follow automatically from her conversion. It developed slowly, under William Allen's influence, and became fixed only in 1817 when she felt her children were old enough to enable her to turn her attentions elsewhere. In many ways, her attraction for prisoners was similar to Howard's. On one level, she sought to establish over the women the same surveillance that she had established over her own desires. On another level, she was drawn to them as fellow sinners. Her sympathy for criminals cannot be dismissed or ignored. She knew that "the bias of all men to evil is so powerful that if there be nothing to check and counter-check its influence it will soon obtain the mastery over them."[35] At the same time, her conversion experience in adolescence gave her a serene confidence that no one, not even the criminal, was excluded from God's mercy.

For Elizabeth Fry and others, therefore, prison reform as a spiritual vocation helped to resolve the religious tensions and inner turmoil unleashed by the Evangelical revival of the 1790s. Yet the rebirth of reform after 1815 cannot be explained only in these terms. Philanthropy is not simply a vocation, a moral choice; it is also an act of authority that creates a linkage of dependency and obligation between rich and poor. Of necessity, therefore, it is a political act, embarked upon not merely to fulfill personal needs, but also to address the needs of those who rule, and those who are ruled.

III

The politics of this renewed attempt to reform the poor through discipline make most sense when viewed against the backdrop of the social crisis of the period. For the prison reformers and the

middle class generally, the precipitous increase in the crime rates
and in the numbers of people receiving poor relief at the end of
the Napoleonic Wars were the most obvious indicators of this
crisis. During the period of mass unemployment that followed
demobilization and the post-1815 trade depression, relief costs doubled.[36] The increase in numbers committed for trial was equally
rapid.[37]

Table 2:   Numbers Committed for Trial
at Assizes, England and Wales

1805–1809	23,462
1810–1814	30,613
1815–1819	58,662
1820–1824	65,227

Between 1810 and 1819, the number of adult males committed for
trial soared from 66 per 100,000 population to over 210.[38] This
drastic increase brought chaos to the prisons. Between 1813 and
1820, the population of Newgate, which was built to hold five
hundred prisoners, never dropped below eight hundred. This burden fell on an institution that was still more or less as Howard had
found it in the 1770s. Felons were still confined in chains and were
still being plucked for fees. Despite the reformers' numerous warn-
ings about the dangers of "association," convicts, juveniles, and
persons awaiting trial were still confined together. Little attempt
was made to enforce discipline. At the height of the overcrowding,
there were no more than two custodial personnel for every one
hundred inmates at Newgate.[39] It is not surprising, therefore, that
the inmate subculture continued to flourish. It was still a regular
custom for convicts to smash up their cells the night before they
were taken down to the transport ships. Boxing matches, mock
trials, gambling, and even illicit sexual commerce with whores had
survived the reformers' condemnation.

A petition to the Lord Mayor by prisoners in the City of
London's Borough Compter in 1813 confirms that there was still
no regular diet, fires, or blankets for the inmates:

> ... your petitioners are in the greatest distress; we humbly pray
> that your Lordship will pardon the liberty they now take in
> stating their distressed situation, having no allowance whatever
> but one penny loaf per day which will scarcely support life; nor
> is there any allowance for coals or candles; we also beg leave to
> observe to your lordship that this is a very confined place, the yard

not being twenty foot square, and the house much incumbered for room; it therefore requires often washing and cleansing which we are not well able to do for want of necessities such as brooms, pails etc. and as to beds we may justly say there are none; there are a few old rugs with very few blankets, but not nearly sufficient for the prisoners now here, and there have been many more than we are at present.[40]

When T. F. Buxton visited the Compter in 1818 he was appalled by the conditions of the prisoners, especially one vagrant whom he found

lying on a straw bed, as I believed, at the point of death, without a shirt, inconceivably dirty, so weak as to be almost unable to articulate, and so offensive as to render remaining a minute with him quite intolerable; close by his side, four other untried prisoners had slept the preceding night inhaling the stench from this mass of putrefaction, his groans breathing the steam from his corrupted lungs and covered with myriads of lice from his rags of clothing.[41]

In blunt language Buxton laid the blame on the aldermen of London:[42]

This prison, within less than five minutes walk of London Bridge —a prison which outrages every feeling of humanity . . . has not . . . been visited by one single official person, capable of redressing the slightest of its atrocious evils for a period of more than six months.[42]

The overcrowding after 1815 might have been accompanied by epidemics of disease had Howard's hygienic program not been adopted. The widespread introduction of regular whitewashing, quarantine of the sick, and the provision of baths and uniforms for at least the dirtiest of incoming inmates prevented the outbreak of typhus during the overcrowding of 1815–1819. The last such episode in London had occurred in 1802–1803 when seventy-nine people died of an epidemic at Newgate.[43]

The crisis was perhaps most obvious in London, but its effects were felt across the country. The Prison Discipline Society estimated in 1818 that one hundred institutions, built to hold 8,545 prisoners, were actually being forced to accommodate 13,057.[44] The overcrowding forced the abandonment of solitary confinement in the penitentiary houses built in the 1790s. At the New Bayley in Manchester, 752 prisoners were crammed into 150 cells, while at Preston, there were two men per cell from 1817 until

1819.[45] In 1818, as we have seen, overcrowding brought the Gloucester experiment in solitary confinement to a close.

Conditions also deteriorated on the hulks, those floating prisons first established as a "temporary expedient" in the 1770s and since then continued as a cheap alternative to institutions constructed on land. As early as 1810 the hulks had become a scandal. The officers in charge reported that they never went into the prisoners' quarters below decks after lights out except in armed parties. They sealed up the hatches, posted a guard and allowed the fighting, drunkenness, and bestiality to boil below.[46]

From the perspective of the Quakers and Evangelicals in the prison reform movement, the crime statistics were symptoms not merely of an overstocked labor market or temporary distresses, but of a much more serious erosion of social disciplines. These reformers viewed the criminality in the manufacturing districts through lenses tinted by a nostalgic and backward-looking lament for the lost disciplines of the small workshop and the family productive unit. When Elizabeth Fry and her brother, J. J. Gurney, toured the Midlands and the North in 1819, they argued that the destruction of the small workshop and the rise of the new factories were a major cause of crime in the region.[47] Unlike the small master, they said, the factory owners did not bother to supervise their youthful workers after hours, and in the weaving sheds and spinning rooms they allowed boys and girls to inflame each other with criminal desires.

The philanthropists' anxiety about the dangers of the new industrialism—the estrangement of rich and poor and the breakdown of face-to-face controls—also extended to the metropolis of London. They seized on juvenile crime as the particular manifestation of this larger pathology. In 1816, after disclosures in the newspapers about the beggar boys who were sleeping in the porticoes of Covent Garden, Buxton, Hoare, and a young businessman named William Crawford formed a committee to investigate the problem. Their report attributed juvenile crime, not merely to unemployment or distress per se, but to the collapse of family discipline under the impact of economic stress:

> Of late the supply of labour in the Metropolis has been far greater than the demand; and the Committee are of opinion that the distress, to which the poor have been exposed, from this circumstance, has in great measure produced that laxity of morals, which has rendered a considerable number of parents regardless of the

welfare of their children. The want of employment, the prevalence of improvident marriages, the degrading tendencies of the Poor Laws and the increased facilities for the consumption of spirituous liquors have doubtless contributed much to deteriorate the moral character and consequently to weaken the natural affections of the lower classes of society.[48]

Earlier, in 1810, another committee of reformers had made a revealing attempt to understand the psyche of the young "predators" and the milieu that produced them. The Society for the Diffusion of Information about the Punishment of Death issued a tract for juveniles that took the form of a letter from Jack Wild, an imaginary convict on board the hulks, to one of his "mates" in St. Giles warning him against a life of crime. Into Jack's mouth the reformers put their own analysis of the criminal milieu:

> I was born in Dyot Street. I never remember my mother; but my father's companions sometimes spoke of her as one who had been transported for passing bad money.... Some people said she died broken-hearted in gaol but I never heard the truth of it. In our street he who thieved most cleverly was the most admired, and the only disgrace that could be incurred was the shame of detection. I sometimes saw people ride past in fine coaches and these I supposed had robbed still more succesfully.... I have heard of God and Hell and the Devil; and they once told me, when the bell tolled at St. Giles, that people went there to pray that they might go to Heaven; but I saw nobody who seemed to believe this, and I thought those words like so many others were only useful to swear by. The only thing I was taught to fear was a thief-catcher; and though I eluded his vigilance for some time, he caught me at last.... [49]

Here then was the reformers' quintessential criminal, alienated from the values of the rich, ignorant of religion, and raised from birth to a life of crime by vicious parents.

Much of this could be found earlier in the writings of Colquhoun or Hanway. Yet a distinctive new anxiety began to appear in the pamphlet literature that explained crime to the propertied classes after 1815. The writers dwelt on the connection between criminality and political disaffection among the working class. In 1819, W. L. Bowles, the poet and pamphleteer, attributed the increase of crimes to

> the alteration in the reasonings, feelings and habits of mind, particularly in the fermenting populous districts, in consequence of the French Revolution! The disciples of this terrific and once triumphant anarchy, under various names and aspects, have never slept!

All that made obedience to the laws "liberal" has been systemat-
ically and incessantly decried as delusions practised by the rich to
enslave the poor! All the kindlier virtues have drooped and withered under the extent of the influence of this poisonous opinion.
It has spread and infected the whole country.... It works on in
darkness and in light distempering religion or deriding it.[50]

A prominent spokesman for prison reform in Parliament,
George Holford, blamed the crime wave on the "tide of blasphemy and sedition which is poured incessantly from the public
press to subvert the principles and deaden the moral feelings of the
people."[51] Basil Montague, the criminal law reformer, was sufficiently worried about the "tide of sedition" to write a tract in 1819
warning the "lower orders" not to pay heed to "the vindictive and
discontented fancies" of radical agitators like the Whig MP Henry
Hunt and the journalist William Cobbett.[52]

This anxious drawing of connections between the crime wave
and the seditious doctrines of radicals should not be dismissed
simply as reactionary alarmism. The Peterloo era, after all, wit-
nessed the most dramatic flowering of radical popular agitation
since the 1790s. In a time of mass unemployment and depression,
the artisan's movement for parliamentary reform revived again,
taking form in strikes, marches, secret societies, and riots in London and the manufacturing centers. Government spies in the manufacturing districts filled the dispatch box of the Home Secretary,
Lord Sidmouth, with news of laborers drilling with guns and pikes
in moonlit fields and unemployed artisans plotting armed uprisings
in the back rooms of taverns and grog shops.

In June 1817, the stocking weavers, quarrymen, ironworkers,
and laborers of the villages around Pentridge in Derbyshire assembled under the leadership of Jeremiah Brandreth and began to
march on Nottingham, hoping to gather enough support to invade
London and overthrow the government. They were stopped by
the Hussars, dispersed, and the ringleaders sent to the gallows. In
London, the center of discontent was the Spitalfields's silk-weaving
district of the East End. In December 1816, a crowd of one hundred thousand weavers, laborers, and artisans gathered in Spa
Fields to roar their support for parliamentary reform and an end
to taxation and government extravagance. Following the meeting,
some sailors broke into a gun shop and made an attempt, easily
repulsed, to storm the Tower of London as a prelude to an armed
uprising in the city.

The agitation culminated in September 1819 at a huge rally held in support of parliamentary reform at St. Peter's Field in Manchester. A crowd of fifteen thousand was listening to the oratory of Henry Hunt when it was attacked by the Manchester Yeomanry, a cavalry militia composed largely of the sons of the city's manufacturers, merchants, and shopkeepers. In the wake of their sabre charge through the field, eleven people lay dead and one hundred sixty-one suffered sabre wounds. The Peterloo massacre gave its name to a whole era.[53]

With these events going on around them, it was natural for middle-class property owners to interpret crime and sedition as the common results of distress, and even to infer that seditious doctrines had inflamed the criminal mind. The propertied class was aware that the radical press was politicizing the question of crime and punishment. William Cobbett, for example, wrote in 1816:

> Poverty, misery, these are the parents of crime; and what adds to the pain of the reflection is that the crimes this produces are more likely to be committed by a brave than a cowardly part of the poor. When a man becomes a robber from want, it is because he cannot endure to be a beggar, or because he has resolved to set death at defiance rather than become a skeleton from starvation.[54]

The real criminals, he insisted, were the "placemen" and "sinecurists," those government hirelings who fattened themselves on taxes extorted from the poor. The theme that the real criminals were not in Newgate but in Whitehall and St. James's Palace became one of the most popular in radical invective. Consider, for example, this description of William Pitt in the *Black Dwarf* of May 1820:

> Again, had he escaped hanging or returned from Botany Bay and turned common swindler as an outcast of St. Giles might have done, what rewards would have been offered for his apprehension! He would have been hunted through society like a mad dog! Bow Street, Worship Street and the police office at Guildhall would have rung with his exploits.... But being enabled to swindle genteely and respectably on a grand scale, and by the help of miserable assistants, although he robbed that credulous old fellow John Bull, of hundreds of millions, and has brought him to actual beggary ... not one action has been ... mentioned against him.... Therefore let me entreat thee to be a *respectable rogue.*[55]

As in the 1790s, the government's renewed suspension of *habeas corpus,* its use of spies and informers to infiltrate the radical movement, its political arrests and state trials brought the law and its institutions into the center of political controversy. It is not surprising, therefore, that the legal system was a recurring target of radical polemic. Nor was it any wonder, the reformers asked, that the poor lost their respect for the law when they were able to read paragraphs like this one in the *Black Dwarf*:

> The laws are only intended to protect the rich. The poor have enough to do with them certainly; but they are only the subjects of the law—the safety of the rich is the constant object; which is no wonder as the rich make the laws and may very naturally be expected to make them for themselves. Some shadows of equity, they are compelled to effect; and therefore, they say—"The doors of all our courts are open; and the laws make no distinction of person." This is very true. The law makes no distinction—but the expense of the law makes a very material distinction. He who cannot obtain justice for less than £20 loses justice if he has not £20 to buy it with. . . . [56]

Just as the state trials made the courts vulnerable to radical polemic, so the use of prisons for the confinement of political prisoners once again brought them under radical scrutiny. The rioting that had broken out after a radical meeting at Spa Fields in London in December 1816, and the attack made upon the Prince Regent by a London crowd in early 1817, had provided the Home Secretary, Lord Sidmouth, with the pretext he needed to secure a suspension of *habeas corpus*. About fifty major radicals were subsequently imprisoned without trial.[57] They protested bitterly about their treatment in petitions that received wide publicity in the pages of the radical press and in parliamentary debates. They complained of confinement in "small, gloomy stinking felons' cells . . . surrounded by noisy brutal prisoners."[58] One of them recounted that he had been confined in the New Bayley in Manchester

> in a loathsome cell, without candle light, on a bag of rotten straw, without bedding of any sort, deprived of communication with wife or friend, half-poisoned by the non-removal for three days at a time of a pan, the receptacle of the voidings of nature, and treated in my native town, where my character had always been spotless, as if I had been a miscreant that had forfeited all claim to be considered a human being.[59]

Some radicals were forced to wear "felon's clothes," an indignity that they insisted was a violation of their rights as political prisoners.[60]

The most vociferous attack on the prisons came from Henry Hunt, sentenced to Ilchester jail for his part at Peterloo. During his confinement, Hunt managed to secure publication of two wild but effective attacks on "Ilchester Bastille".[61] Hunt alleged that the governor routinely placed women in the stocks and men in straitjackets for offenses against prison discipline. He also charged that the governor winked at the sexual exploitation of female prisoners by the turnkeys.

Interestingly enough, some of Hunt's most savage remarks were reserved for Thomas Fowell Buxton, who had praised the woolen manufactory in the jail in a widely read pamphlet on prison conditions. By conferring his imprimatur on the institution, Hunt charged, he had "lulled the magistracy" into believing that their prison was a "model of rectitude," and had "entrenched the officers in their negligence." Philanthropists who let themselves be gulled in this way, Hunt charged, were the prisoners' "bitterest enemy."[62]

A commission of inquiry appointed to look into Hunt's allegations did confirm some of his charges against the jailer. The commission condemned him not only for the excessive severity of his punishments but also for having allowed an election band to enter the prison yards and serenade him as an elector. In language reminiscent of Howard's indictment of keepers two generations before, the commission criticized his habit of ignoring the rules and resorting to "ancient usage" or "custom of the gaol" to justify his arbitrary practices.[63]

In addition to the attacks of the political prisoners, the government had some reason to fear the disaffection of ordinary convicts. In the reports of the Parliamentary Committees of Secrecy, investigating the radical threat in 1817, mention was made of a planned uprising in the London debtor prisons timed to coincide with a general rising of the East End poor around the Spa Fields meeting.[64] The agents of the Home Secretary had intercepted a crude broadsheet that had been slipped into Whitecross Street debtors prison. The broadsheet, signed by a mysterious body calling itself the Tricoloured Private Committee, told the prisoners to await the day when "a powerful body of your countrymen, armed for that purpose," would throw open the prison doors and reduce "your Lofty Bastille" to ashes. In anticipation of this day, prisoners were to wear a "tricoloured cockade" in their hats.[65] Later, in March 1817, the ministry got word of a plot in Manchester to "attack the barracks, the police office, the prison, the houses of magistrates and constables and the banks in separate parties."[66] The government used these rumored plots as justification for the suspension of *habeas corpus* in 1817.

Since the crisis in the prisons after 1815 coincided with massive popular disaffection and a sustained radical polemic against legal institutions, the prison reformers, like most of their class, could not help but interpret the increase in crime as an indication of the deeper political and social alienation of the poor. Likewise, they were forced to look upon the abuses of prisons not just as administrative problems but as political ones too. Thus, while the reformers liked to characterize prison reform as a neutral philanthropic crusade "above politics," they were, of necessity, drawn into the tactics and strategy of class rule in a time of conflict.

The reformers themselves did not support the deployment of troops at Peterloo, the use of police spies, the suspension of *habeas corpus*, and the passage of the Six Acts limiting freedom of speech and assembly. Henry Grey Bennet, Samuel Romilly, Thomas Fowell Buxton, and George Holford—the leading spokesmen for criminal law and prison reform in the Commons—steered a tortuous middle course between what they called "Tory reaction" on the one hand and "radical demagoguery" on the other. Buxton's response to the Peterloo massacre epitomized this middle course. In a letter to his uncle in 1819, he wrote:

> I quite agree with you in reprobating the radicals. I am persuaded that their object is the subversion of religion and the constitution and I shall vote for any measure by which the exertions of their leaders may be suppressed, but I fear we shall much differ as to the nature of those measures. I must strongly condemn the conduct of the magistrates at Manchester. . . . The wretched affair ought to be strictly scrutinized.[67]

For the Whig opposition, the Peterloo massacre was as dangerous as it was regrettable. They argued that the government had allowed itself to be panicked by the radicals into the use of means of repression that violated the constitution and alienated the poor from the institutions of justice. Buxton, Romilly, and Bennet believed that a strictly constitutional strategy of order should go hand in hand with a program of institutional reform to remove the sources of discontent. They urged the necessity of a moderate parliamentary reform as a stabilizing social gesture aimed at conciliating the unenfranchised lower middle classes. Bennet was quoted as telling the House of Commons in the wake of the Peterloo massacre:

> He felt himself bound to recommend to the House, if it wished to avoid civil dissention, if it wished to avoid that greatest of evils, the shedding of English blood by English hands, to examine fairly and freely into the state of representation and to show the people that, though it would oppose all such innovations as would tend to subvert the constitution, it was quite alive to the greatest of all questions.[68]

Even Wilberforce felt that some moderate reformers should come forward to "rescue the multitude out of the hands of the Hunts and Thistlewoods."[69]

This conception of social strategy also animated the philanthropy of the prison reformers. In an article in William Allen's *The Philanthropist*, the counterrevolutionary uses of benevolence were explicitly set out:

> To the objecting and cautious politician who believes all reform is dangerous and the precursor of revolution, it is in vain to urge that reform would in most cases, if judiciously introduced, be the preventive and antidote of revolution, and that all institutions are secure in proportion as they are accommodated to the circumstances, the manners and characters–in other words, the interest of the people for whom they are framed.[70]

Underlying this strategic conception of reform was a pervasive anxiety about the legitimacy of legal institutions. The reformers knew that the severity of the economic depression had forced many of the "respectable" poor into crime. While they themselves did not waver on the necessity of imprisoning such people, they did realize that the poor themselves questioned the justice of "punishing poverty." T. F. Buxton reflected pensively:

> Persons may steal for immediate sustenance. I do not contend that they are not criminal. True morality would tell them it is better to starve than to rob; but in truth such a sacrifice of life to principle is an effort of heroic virtue; and perhaps if those amongst yourselves who, free from every temptation, call aloud for rigid and inflexible justice, were placed in the same circumstances, they would have some difficulty in the choice of an alternative, and hunger might make appeals which honesty could hardly reject.[71]

William Allen's journal, *The Philanthropist*, went even further, arguing that the "vast proportion of the victims of our criminal laws" were driven to crime by the "neglect of their society." To punish the victims of such neglect was to inflict an act of gross injustice.

The Philanthropist kept its indictment of the neglect of the rich conveniently vague. It made highly charged but indistinct denunciations of the "sleek and glossy figure of English apathy, reposing within view of its ghastly brother, and calmly and complacently resigning him to his fate," but no names were named, no sustained analysis mounted.[72] Nevertheless, the reformers' qualms about the legitimacy of punishment cannot be dismissed simply as pious moralizing, for these qualms constituted the emotional force behind their involvement in gestures of conciliation.

One such gesture was the Spitalfields soup kitchen program administered by Samuel Hoare, William Allen, Peter Bedford, and T. F. Buxton. Because of its proximity to the centers of social power, Spitalfields was the most dramatic example of the distress of the poor during this period. Tens of thousands of silk weavers had been thrown out of work by the interruption of the supply of raw silk from Italy during the wars and by the depression that set in after 1815. Since Allen's chemical works, Buxton's brewery, and Bedford's silk business were in the East End, all three men had intimate acquaintance with the distress. They decided to establish a soup kitchen and a shop to sell dried fish and other food at a reduced rate, subsidized by charitable contributions. In line with their conception of "scientific philanthropy," the reformers set about determining the eligibility of the needy. They visited every family who applied, and issued tickets for soup or cheap food only to those who maintained discipline in the home, appeared to be looking for work, and eschewed the use of alcohol.[73]

It would be denigrating to the obvious moral concern of the reformers to interpret the Spitalfields project merely as a calculated political gesture. Yet, regardless of the reformers' motives, their charitable work was integrated, of necessity, into the government's strategy of social control. The ministers were keenly aware, from their spies, that Spitalfields was a center of radical discontent in the city, and that the unemployed weavers were among the most outspoken participants at the Spa Fields meeting of December 1816. Hence, after Buxton delivered a speech on the work of the relief committee, the government seized upon it as a useful piece of propaganda, vindicating the moral solicitude of rich for poor. It ordered thousands of copies of the speech distributed among the poor of the city as an antidote "to those wretched demagogues whose infamous doctrines would increase the evils they affect to deplore."[74]

The radicals, for their part, were keenly aware of the political uses of philanthropy. The Spitalfields relief scheme was a butt of jokes from the platform at the Spa Fields meeting. When one orator referred to the benevolent gentlemen who sought to placate the poor with "Oxcheek Soup and Oxbone Broth," the crowd roared, "Shame!" In William Cobbett's widely read *Letter to the Lord Mayor of London,* written in the wake of Spa Fields, he said bluntly that "the soup meetings . . . have a tendency to disguise [the real causes of the misery] and therefore a tendency to prolong the evil till a peaceable remedy shall become impossible." It was fear of the poor, not moral solicitude, he charged, that prompted the soup scheme. Subscriptions from the wealthy of the West End did not begin to roll in, he pointed out sarcastically, until Spa Fields made clear the dangers of ignoring the miseries of the East End.[75]

While Cobbett does not appear to have attacked Fry's reform of Newgate, it could also be seen in the same light as the Spitalfields soup kitchen project. Certainly, it was received with emotion by the propertied as a symbolic demonstration of their benevolence as a class. Fry's wards in Newgate became a showcase for what a regimen of obedience-training and ascetic discipline could accomplish among the poor. The prisoners' tearful and penitent responses in chapel seemed to offer hope that the poor could still be reached by the language of religion and duty.

At the same time, the Newgate project contained a measure of admonition to those in power. Fry and the Prison Discipline Society insisted on the futility of unmitigated repression as a strategy of deterrence:

> The prevention of crime will never be effected by the influence of fear alone. . . . In no Christian or civilized country has unmixed severity attained this object. The criminal thus treated . . . experiences a feeling of injury; resentment is excited in his bosom.[76]

As Howard had done two generations earlier, they warned that to tolerate abuses because of their deterrent value was to risk compromising the legitimacy of punishment itself. The significance of this line of argument is only apparent if we recall the times in which it was made. The seemingly inexorable increase of the crime rates convinced many magistrates that terror, not reform, was the proper prescription for the social dissolution around them. There was one London alderman who grumbled aloud in 1815 that the reformers would not stop until every prisoner had a "Turkey carpet" in his cell.

In 1818, when Buxton and Crawford wrote a letter to the *Times*, denouncing conditions at the Borough Compter, the London aldermen peremptorily barred them from making further visits and passed a minute in the Gaol Committee criticizing reforming zealots who, "under the pretense of improving discipline," seek out "distressing cases of which they make partial statements without making the proper inquiries, for no other purpose . . . than that of gratifying their own feelings."[77] Obviously, the reformers had struck a sore nerve.

In the face of increasingly astringent criticism of their weak-kneed humanitarianism, they continued to insist on the overriding importance of conserving the moral reputation of the institutions of justice by providing the prisoner with essential amenities.[78] In the eyes of many skeptical magistrates, this argument must have seemed dangerously wrong-headed. In their view, people like Elizabeth Fry seemed to be arguing that the state should assume obligations for the prisoner that it did not assume for free labor.

The reformers themselves were uncomfortably aware of this apparent contradiction. How were they to justify their conception of the state's commitment to the prisoner at a time when the state was withdrawing from its role in the supervision of the wage relationship; at a time when the wage regulation and apprenticeship clauses of the Statute of Artificers were falling into disuse; at a time when the leading authorities on the poor law were wondering aloud whether the state had any obligation to relieve poverty; at a time when ruling opinion denied that the state had the right to intervene in the market economy to safeguard the health and morals of the parish apprentices in cotton mills?[79] All in all, the ascendancy of *laissez faire* did not seem to make the moment propitious for the reformers' arguments.

In the face of criticism that their conception of deterrence violated the tenets of *laissez faire,* the Prison Discipline Society tried to reassure the middle-class public that it believed in maintaining the just terrors of the law as much as anyone:

> It is true that they [the society] consider it desirable that prisons should be clean, and the food given to the prisoners plain, wholesome and sufficient; but they are equally anxious that everything

which borders on sensual gratification or unnecessary comfort should be entirely prohibited.[80]

Nevertheless, they went on to insist that deterrence, to retain its effectiveness, had to be bound by the strictest considerations of morality:

> They are of opinion that the punishments contemplated by the law should alone be inflicted, and that no collateral evils, the horrors of disease and the corruption of principle, should be superadded.

Underlying this anxiety about legitimacy was a highly significant assumption: the treatment of prisoners was a symbolic test of the morality, not simply of the state, but of the "ruling powers" of society. William Allen's articles in *The Philanthropist* gave words to this, the crux of the reformers' position:

> In prisons, a part of the population ... [is] taken by the ruling powers and placed forcibly in a situation in which they cannot help themselves, in which they are necessarily defenceless and exposed to the last of evils, as well from neglect as from active cruelty. If a part of the population placed in this situation, so immediately under the eye of the ruling powers ... are not taken care of as they ought to be, is it not a matter of moral certainty that the other parts of the population are equally or still more neglected? ... The behaviour of government, therefore, in this department is a sample of its behaviour in all the rest.[81]

In other words, punishment, as the most extreme of the state's powers over citizens, was the test of its dealings with citizens in all lesser exercises of authority. The magistrates who supervised prisons were charged with nothing less than maintaining the state's reputation as a moral agent. On the legitimacy of the state as a moral agent rested, in turn, the legitimacy of the "ruling powers of society" and their continued hegemony in the social order. These were the social assumptions that connected the project of prison reform to the politics of class rule in the Peterloo period.

IV

The reformers' efforts to bolster the legitimacy of the law at a time of crisis were not confined to the symbolic display of Fry's work at Newgate. The Prison Discipline Society led the campaign for a new jails act, setting out standards for the treatment of prisoners and establishing uniform criteria for discipline. In their reports, they pointed out that the decentralization and localism of English administration had allowed an unjust and unequal variation in the rigors of discipline to emerge in institutions across the country. In some places, prisoners were confined in strict solitude and made to work eight hours a day, while in others, prisoners convicted of the same crimes were allowed to associate freely and were not forced to work. Such anomalies could only be corrected, they argued, by national legislation enforced by a salaried inspectorate. The society continued to defend the concept of localist voluntarism in prison administration, and at every annual meeting passed a resolution praising the diligence of the very magistracy whose neglect was palpably demonstrated in their reports. Yet their campaign for an inspectorate and a national bill of compulsory standards belied these pro forma resolutions. By the early 1820s, the society had concluded that the legitimacy of state institutions could only be safeguarded by centralization of control and administration by professionals.[82]

The society's activities culminated with the passage of the Gaols Act of 1823.[83] Because of the resistance of the magistracy to anything that smacked of direction from Whitehall, the measure fell far short of what the society would have liked. A large number of borough institutions were exempted from its provisions. No inspectorate was established, and the standards of diet, hours of labor, exercise, and visiting privileges laid down by the act were left for the magistrates to interpret and enforce as they wished. Nor did the act endorse solitary confinement. While acknowledging that it was desirable, the act allowed magistrates to abandon it whenever overcrowding made it necessary to do so. A generation later the idea of solitude was to be revived again, but in 1823 it was in retreat, tarnished by the excesses of its enthusiasts.

The 1823 act did contain one significant provision that went part way towards standardization of discipline. Magistrates were required to submit annual reports on their prisons to the Home Secretary and also to complete a questionnaire on the population, staff, and discipline of their institutions. These "Schedule B's," as they were called, were published annually in the parliamentary papers. They enabled the Home Secretary and Parliament to increase their scrutiny of the local magistracy. Robert Peel, an activist Home Secretary, further increased Whitehall's involvement in local prisons by circularizing magistrates on administrative and disciplinary questions and by corresponding with individual benches about particular abuses that came to his notice.

Besides campaigning for standardization of prison discipline, the reformers of the Peterloo period also fought to reduce the severities of the criminal code. Samuel Romilly, who initiated the campaign in 1808 by introducing legislation to commute the capital penalties for a number of minor larcenies, based his case on the same arguments used by the prison reformers: that arbitrariness and cruelty in the administration of punishment jeopardized public respect for the law:

> The frequent occurrence of the unexecuted threat of death in a criminal code tends to rob that punishment of all its terrors, and to enervate the general authority of the government and its laws. The multiplication of this threat in the laws of England has brought on them, and on the nation a character of harshness which evidence of a mild administration of them will not entirely remove.[84]

Underlying his case for reform was the conviction that public cooperation with the law was the basis of social order, especially in a society that objected on constitutional grounds to paid prosecutors and police. As Buxton put it in the debate on Romilly's bills:

> Our whole system of criminal jurisprudence proceeds on the presumption that the law will be aided by the public. Wanting a spy in every house, and a crowd of police officers in every street and a public prosecutor ever ready to undertake all the labour and all the expense, the presumption is that these deficiencies will be supplied by the active co-operation of the people.[85]

When they spoke of "public" respect for law, the reformers were concerned, first of all, with the middle-class public. Romilly claimed that "traders of the cities of London and Westminster" needed more efficient penalties against shoplifting, shopbreaking, and other petty crimes. They had complained to Romilly that they abandoned prosecutions for petty theft because of moral scruple at sending offenders to the gallows.[86]

The reformers were also concerned about the attitudes of the poor. Romilly pointed to the angry public reaction to the execution of the Spa Field rioters as evidence that the poor were alienated by gratuitous acts of severity. In 1817, Elizabeth Fry told him that the prisoners in Newgate opposed the execution of two women confined there on forgery charges. When they were executed the shouts of "Shame!" hurled at the sheriffs appeared to confirm Fry's and Romilly's impression that the poor in general opposed hanging as a punishment for minor forms of property crime.[87]

Romilly did not wish, of course, to weaken the just terrors of the law. As he summarized his position, "The law is nominally too severe, practically not severe enough."[88] Hanging discouraged prosecutors from prosecuting and juries from convicting. It also encouraged high pardon rates. He pointed out that of 1,872 people committed to Newgate for trial for larceny in a dwelling or a shop between 1803 and 1810, only one was eventually executed.[89] At the same time, he argued that when the penalty was inflicted, it aroused the resentment and resistance of the poor.

The solution to this dilemma of deterrence, he argued, was to replace the savage but rarely enforced penalties of the Bloody Code in property cases with the milder but inflexibly enforced penalty of sentences to a penitentiary. Alongside his proposals for commutation of the capital penalties in property cases, he advocated the revival of the idea of a national penitentiary, either along the lines of the original act of 1779 or else according to Bentham's Panopticon proposals.[90] The government, after toying with the idea of building a network of penitentiaries, finally settled for the construction of one penitentiary at Millbank, on the present site of the Tate Gallery. Construction was begun in 1812 and completed in 1816, under the supervision of a committee of MPs and prison reformers, chaired by George Holford.[91]

There are several reasons why the time was finally right for a national penitentiary. The judiciary was becoming increasingly dubious about the deterrent value of the hulks, which were a public scandal.[92] Even transportation seemed to lose its terrors as stories got back to England of the new start that could be made in Australia. A few judges actually encountered prisoners who had the effrontery to ask to be transported when brought into the dock for sentence.[93] The steadily declining rate of executions in capital cases itself increased doubts about the efficacy of public hangings. Whereas in the late 1780s about 50 percent of those convicted in capital cases in London and Middlesex were hanged, by 1808 the figure had dropped to a little over 10 percent.[94] The balance of those convicted were transported or imprisoned instead. Romilly capitalized on increasing uncertainty about the traditional deterrents by advocating that the national penitentiary would be an opportunity to experiment with an alternative—long-term imprisonments.

At the outset, however, the experiment proved to be an embarrassment. Construction cost the enormous sum of £450,000. The Millbank committee insisted that the expense was caused by unforeseen difficulties in sinking foundations into the soggy riverbank of the Thames, but allegations of scandal continued to hover over the prison long after the bills were paid.[95] When finally opened in 1817, it was a giant, turreted monstrosity, the biggest prison in Europe, capable of holding up to twelve hundred prisoners in its seven pentagons. These pentagons, which contained the cells, were clustered around the symbolic heart of the prison, the chapel building. Around the whole edifice was a perimeter wall and a moat. In theory, the prison was modeled on Bentham's inspection principle, but in practice the prison was a maze of endless corridors. There was an old warder in the prison who found the layout so baffling that he would leave chalk marks at the crucial turnings in his rounds so that he would be able to find his way back to the guardhouse.[96]

The early years of the penitentiary were a story of conflict and chaos. The difficulties with personnel that had dogged the reformers of the 1790s continued unabated. The first two governors had to be sacked for incompetence. Several turnkeys, wardens, and taskmasters were also dismissed for trafficking or for failing to enforce discipline. The Millbank rules proclaimed:

> [The turnkey] shall enforce his orders with firmness but shall be expected to act with the utmost humanity towards all prisoners under his care. On the other hand, he shall not be familiar with any of the prisoners or converse with them unnecessarily, but shall treat them as persons under his authority and control and not as his companions or associates.[97]

In practice, though, it proved impossible to find men capable of realizing this standard of glacial impartiality.

The prisoners, who had been used to the lackadaisical routines of the hulks or the county jails, revolted when subjected to the regimen of solitude, hard labor, and meager diet. Early in 1818 there was a mutiny over bread. At chapel, the prisoners tossed bread around and chanted, "Give us our daily bread! Better bread! Better bread!" The next day, when they were told that the bread ration would not be increased, they smashed up their cells, dislodged masonry from the edges of their windows and hurled it at the warders in the courtyards. Two men assaulted the governor. Bow Street runners had to be called in to restore order at gunpoint. The hapless governor was fired as a result of the disturbance.

In September 1826 and throughout the winter of 1827, a group of prisoners attempted to force their transfer to the hulks, where discipline was easier. Realizing that they could secure this object by making themselves incorrigible, they set about smashing up their cells, fighting with keepers, and rioting in the chapel. In March 1827, they hanged a hated warder's favorite cat and left it dangling from a beam in the infirmary with the following attached:

> You see yor Cat is hung And
> you have been the corse of it
> for yoor Bad Bavior to Those
> around you. Dam yor eis, yoo'l
> get pade in yor torn yet.[98]

In 1828, a deputation of prisoners appeared before the governor with a long letter itemizing instances of brutality by the guards:

> Who gave Mr. Bulmer authority to strike a lad named Quick almost sufficient to have broken his arm, indeed so bad that the lad could not lift his hand to his head? And who gave Mr. Pilling the same authority to strike a lad to the ground, named Caswell, with a ruler, the same as a butcher would a Bullock, without him making the least resistance?

With a flourish the prisoners signed themselves "Friends to the Oppressed." The spirit of the inmates in the 1820s is tersely and expressively epitomized in the little piece of doggerel found etched on one of their drinking cups:

> Yor order is   but mine is
> for me to go   that I'll go
> to chapel   to Hell first.[99]

The unity of the rebellious prisoners, perhaps only twenty-five in number, astonished the prison staff. When sealed away in the dark cells for punishment they continued to pierce the silence of the penitentiary with shouts of encouragement to each other. It was the solidarity of these rebels that led Whitworth Russell, the prison chaplain, to confess that he had never known an instance when prisoners were "untrue to their own body."[100]

The persistence of the prisoners eventually paid off. Some succeeded in getting themselves transferred to the hulks. When the Millbank committee realized that this had been their aim all along, they secured special legislation to authorize the use of the lash. In the more optimistic days when the prison was planned, the committee had believed that it would be possible to do away with corporal punishment altogether. By 1828, the humanity of the reformers had run dry. The cat-o'-nine-tails was laid upon the ringleaders of the disturbances, culminating in the hundred lashes inflicted on David Sheppard in April 1829 for "assaulting and repeatedly striking the machine keeper."[101] With that, the authorities regained control of the prison.

In the 1880s, Arthur Griffiths, who had been a penitentiary governor in the Victorian penal service, wrote a history of Millbank. Looking back on those early years, he pronounced the place a "bear-garden." Its management, he said gruffly, was "free and easy" and "over-tender."[102] These remarks reveal as much about his vantage point as they do about Millbank. Obviously, the full pitch of institutional repression of the high Victorian period had not been reached. There was a new generation of rigor yet to come.

CHAPTER SEVEN

Prisons, the State,

and the Labor Market, 1820-1842

I

The Peterloo era left the rulers of English society in a truculent mood. One sign of this spirit was the sustained attack on radicalism. While the Whig opposition and the philanthropic middle class pleaded for the arts of conciliation, Lord Sidmouth, the Home Secretary, pursued the politics of vengeance. By 1822, radicalism was in jail, in flight, or in hiding underground.[1] Another sign of the ruling mood was a marked hardening of opinion on issues of punishment.

It became fashionable in the 1820s, for example, to deride the "spurious benevolence" of Elizabeth Fry and the Prison Discipline Society. Fry was increasingly seen as a well-meaning but naive creature distracted by the "fallacious idea" of "reformation through the medium of moral persuasion." While both Fry and the society itself took pains to insist that they "were no friends to undue indulgence," the belief became current that their philanthropy had diminished the sting of imprisonment.

In county after county, magistrates came to the conclusion, as one Staffordshire JP put it, "that nothing but the terror of human suffering can avail to prevent crime."[2] An influential Tory MP, C. C. Western, spoke for many of the county gentry when he said in 1821, "The truth is that our gaols and houses of correction are generally considered by offenders of every class rather as a sure and comfortable asylum, whenever their better fortunes forsake them."[3] In 1828, a Commons committee investigating the causes of crime wondered aloud, in its report, whether the reformers' success in ridding the prison of the terrors of filth and disease had not compromised its deterrent value. The report also questioned the Prison Discipline Society's insistence on reformation as the central function of punishment: "As places of reform only, gaols have not succeeded; as places of reform only they ought not to be considered."[4] In 1831, a Wiltshire magistrate, addressing another Commons committee meeting on the question of punishment, said that "the state of a prisoner [is] infinitely preferable to that of, I am sorry to say, a large proportion of the peasantry at the present time in the southern and south-western districts of this country."[5]

Accordingly, magistrates set about devising ways to make confinement "as lonely and as inconvenient and irksome as the human mind could bear."[6] The tightening up at Millbank after 1818 exemplifies a general trend. George Holford, the chairman of the Millbank committee, was taunted in the House of Commons and in the press with charges that he was running a "fattening house."[7] The Millbank prisoners' bread riots of 1818 encouraged the myth that the administration was weak and indulgent. Dependent as he was on parliamentary approval of the prison estimates, Holford quickly bowed to the pressure. All reading material, even Hannah More's religious tracts, was withdrawn on the grounds that reading was an "amusement" that diverted the prisoners from sorrowful reflection.[8] In a similar spirit, visits were cut back to ten minutes in length. A warder with a sandglass was positioned between the prisoner and his visitor, with orders to time the conversation and listen for remarks critical of the prison. In 1820, when Holford discovered that prisoners were playing leapfrog during exercise hours, new rules were instituted requiring the inmates to walk in silent pairs around a circular pathway.[9]

The diet was steadily reduced. In 1817, prisoners received meat and vegetables at least once a week. In 1822, the Millbank committee announced that the "liberal" food allowances would be cut back, in view of the "material reductions which have taken place in the dietaries of several of the gaols and houses of correction."[10]

By 1823, prisoners were subsisting upon a monotonous round of bread, gruel, and a watery soup made from the "clods and stickings of beef." Such paring away had disastrous results. "The murdering rogues are starving us by inches," one prisoner was heard to whisper to his mother in the visiting hall, before being whisked back to his cell. In the winter of 1823, the inmates began to succumb to typhus, dysentery, and scurvy. Thirty-one died and four hundred others were incapacitated before the prison was closed temporarily and the remaining prisoners were pardoned or sent to the hulks.[11]

At first, the authorities attempted to disguise the causes of the tragedy. During a coroner's inquest on the deaths of the prisoners, a jury of Middlesex citizens reached a verdict of "death by dysentery caused by inadequate diet." The coroner, however, "strenuously impressed upon the minds of the jurymen the discontent such a verdict would occasion out of doors."[12] Obviously the prison had enemies: property owners who believed its presence was lowering the value of their holdings; opponents of the solitary confinement regime; and the poor who feared that it was a health hazard for the neighborhood.[13] In order to protect the administration against these constituencies, the jury bowed to the coroner's suasion and changed its verdict to accidental death.

Eventually, however, Holford and the Millbank committee were forced to explain themselves to a Commons committee of inquiry. Its report documented the connection between the reductions in diet and the deaths of the prisoners. It also observed that the "depression of spirits" induced by solitary confinement had acted as a "moral cause" of the epidemic, rendering the prisoners susceptible to disease.[14] When Millbank was opened again in 1824, the solitary regime was relaxed somewhat, sentence lengths were shortened, and a broth fortified by beef stock and vegetables was added to the fare of bread, water, and gruel.

The Millbank committee's experimentation with the outer limits of terror was extreme, but it was not anomalous. As they insisted in their defense, they had reduced their diets in response to a general reduction in jails around the countryside. In an effort to stem the surge of committals after 1816, county and borough magistrates introduced bread and water diets and banned the supply of outside food. By the early 1840s, the paring away of institutional diets had reached the point that the Home Secretary felt it

12. Kyd Wake, political prisoner at Gloucester Penitentiary, 1796–1801. Shown in his cell, clothed in the uniform of the penitentiary, wearing an iron ringlet on his ankle.

13. The treadwheel at Brixton Prison, 1821.

14. The cruelties of Ilchester Gaol, 1821, from a pamphlet by Henry Hunt.

15. Prisoners waiting to be weighed during medical inspection at Millbank Penitentiary, 1880s.

16. Henry Fielding.

17. Jeremy Bentham's Auto-Icon and mummified head. The Auto-Icon was a waxwork likeness of himself, dressed in his own clothes, which Bentham ordered made after his death. It is preserved in a cabinet at University College, London, and is exhibited upon ceremonial occasions.

18. Prisoners turning out for exercise, wearing masks. Surrey
House of Correction, Wandsworth, London.

19. Female convicts at work during the silent hour, Brixton Prison.

20. Millbank Penitentiary from the Thames, 1820s.

21. Vagrants working at the treadwell and exercising,
Coldbath Fields Prison.

Chief Warder,
Pentonville Peniten-
iary, and Principal
Matron, Brixton
Prison.

23. Prisoners picking oakum under the silent system, Coldbath Fields Prison.

24.

William Towens, 12 years of age; 4'5½", brown eyes, brown hair, born in Richmond, unmarried, no visible distinguishing marks. Place of Residence, 9 Botron's Place, New Richmond. Convicted at Richmond summary sessions, 20 December 1872, of simple larceny of two live tame rabbits. Sentence: 1 month hard labor, Wandsworth Prison. Wandsworth Prisoners' Register, 1872.

25.

Caroline Lightfoot, also known as Reyno[l] 51 years of age; 5'1", brown hair, blue eyes, p[a] complexion, born in Westminster, married. [No] trade or occupation. Deeply marked with sm[all] pox. Place of Residence, 35 Richmond Str[eet,] Lambeth. Convicted of stealing a drinking g[lass] worth sixpence. Previous conviction for ste[al]ing two frocks worth ninepence. Sentence[:] months hard labor, Wandsworth Pris[on.] Wandsworth Prisoners' Register, 1872.

26.

Sidney Lowman, 17 years of age; 5'4", dark brown hair, blue eyes, fresh complexion, born in Somerset, single. Butcher. No distinguishing marks. Place of Residence, 21 Wickersley Grove, Wandsworth Road. Convicted of simple larceny, stealing a can and a half pint of milk. Sentence: 6 weeks hard labor. Wandsworth Prisoners' Register, 1872.

necessary to warn JPs against using diets as "an instrument of punishment."[15]

Besides reducing diets, magistrates introduced the treadwheel. Credit for its invention must go to Samuel Cubitt, a founder of the giant English firm of building contractors that today bears his name. Magistrates in his native Ipswich were at a loss to find a deterring form of hard labor for their prisoners. Cubitt devised a huge revolving cylinder with steps on it like the slats of a paddle wheel.[16] Prisoners mounted the steps of the wheel, making it turn with their feet while gripping a bar to keep themselves upright. Usually the wheel was set to turn at between forty-eight and fifty steps a minute. While some were geared to grind corn or raise water, most did nothing more than "grind the air." To the influential pamphleteer Sydney Smith, the sheer uselessness of treadwheel labor was a salutary terror:

> We would banish all the looms of Preston jail and substitute nothing but the treadwheel or the capstan, or some species of labour where the labourer could not see the results of his toil, where it was as monotonous, irksome and dull as possible....[17]

The JPs' enthusiasm for the treadwheel was boundless. It was, as one gratified justice observed, "the most tiresome, distressing, exemplary punishment that has ever been contrived by human ingenuity."[18] First publicized in a Prison Discipline Society report in 1818, it spread to twenty-six of the counties by 1824.[19] In many institutions, the treadwheel ran ten hours a day, with prisoners going on for twenty-minute stretches followed by twenty-minute rest breaks. At first, magistrates spared no one in their enthusiasm. Onto the wheel they forced pregnant women, broken-down tramps with bad legs, and laborers with hernias. The miscarriages of several of the women and the collapse of several of the older men forced a more careful medical scrutiny and selection of those put on the wheel.

At Leicester and Swaffham, the machine itself claimed three prisoners, crushed and mangled in its gearing.[20] But such accidents did not prevent the county benches from giving it a ringing endorsement. Most credited it with having checked the criminality of "vagrants, refractory husbandry servants and other small offenders."[21] Right through the 1870s, the wheel became one of the shared humiliations of the English poor. There were tramps in the 1850s who could count the time they had spent on the "shin-scraper" in years of their lives.

Besides the treadwheel and the bread and water diet, the period saw the extension of the rule of silence. The reformers of the 1780s had been ambiguous about silence. It was regarded as an essential precondition for sorrowful introspection in the cell, but it was not prescribed for periods of exercise or associated labor. At Millbank, at least the prisoners were allowed to whisper to each other in the cell areas and the yards. The Gaol Act of 1824 did not include silence in its disciplinary provisions.[22] However, in the associated workshops in the American penitentiaries at Auburn and Sing Sing strict silence became a key element of discipline. After 1830, their example became influential in England.

One of the first English prisons to convert to strict rules of silence was Coldbath Fields House of Correction in London. In 1834, all speech and gesture among inmates were banned. By 1835, nineteen counties had followed suit by introducing similar rules.[23] At Coldbath Fields, the governor, G. L. Chesterton, proudly reported:

> Prisoners are kept under constant and secret inspection day and night, lights being burned in the sleeping rooms all night and night watches on the alert; every movement of the prisoners is made so as to prevent their faces being turned to each other; they are never allowed to congregate or cluster together; they move in solitary lines in single file.[24]

Additional guards were hired to police the new regulations— on a ratio of one guard for every twenty inmates, as opposed to one for every forty before the change.[25] With the introduction of the silent system, the prison governor and his staff began a savage battle against what was left of the prison subculture. The number of punishments for prison offenses rose precipitously, from one punishment for every 191 inmates in 1825, to one punishment for every 3.4 inmates in 1835.[26] Irons, bread and water, the dark cells, and floggings followed every attempt to speak or protest. The inmates, however, proved to be both stubborn and imaginative. A prison semaphor of winks, hand signs, and tapping through the pipes emerged, and its secret alphabet became one of the cultural inheritances of the London underworld.[27] After one determined attempt to wipe out "association" altogether, Chesterton and his staff resigned themselves to policing a silence that actually hummed with secret language.

The silent system, the bread and water diet, and the treadwheel each mark a stage in the tightening up of prison discipline after

1820. At the end of this process stands Pentonville. While the Prison Discipline Society as a whole quickly got in step with this renewed cycle of severity, there were those among the old generation of reformers who looked askance at the new mood. In 1835, for example, Elizabeth Fry warned the Lords committee on prisons against excessive use of the treadwheel, bread and water diets, and undiluted solitary confinement. "In some respects, I think there is more cruelty in our Gaols than I have ever before seen," she confessed.[28]

II

This escalation of terror followed the upward course of the rate of crime. The number of males committed for trial at assize and sessions for serious offenses rose from 170 per 100,000 population in 1824, to 240 by 1828, and to 250 in 1830. After a pause from 1830 to 1835, the rate began to climb again, reaching its peak in 1842, the year Pentonville opened, at 326 per 100,000 population.[29]

The numbers sent to prison for minor summary offenses increased even faster than the numbers committed to stand trial for major indictable crimes. For example, in London and Middlesex, the number of people committed for summary offenses more than doubled between 1814–21 and 1822–29, while the number of persons committed for trial rose by only 28 percent.[30] Nationally, the numbers committed for vagrancy rose by 34 percent between 1826 and 1829, and by 65 percent between 1829 and 1832—more than double the rate of increase for indictable committals.[31]

Hence, by the 1840s summary offenders (vagrants, poachers, petty thieves, disorderlies, and public drunkards) accounted for more than half of the prison population, while those awaiting trial or serving sentences for indictable crime represented only 25 percent of the inmates, with deserters and debtors making up the balance.[32] The tightening up of prison discipline, therefore, was directed especially at minor delinquency and work-related offenses: vagrancy, absconding from service, destruction of tools, theft of wood, theft of produce in the fields, desertion of family, public drunkenness, disorderly conduct, poaching, and common assault. In trying to explain this delinquency, magistrates and politicians of the 1820s put the demoralization of the agricultural laborer at the center of their analysis.

Farmers testifying before the Committee on Criminal Committals in 1826 admitted that the increasingly casual character of
hiring in the rural labor market acted as a cause of crime. While
"improvement" increased the demand for unskilled labor—in
ditching, draining, and hedging—the labor was increasingly sea-
sonal and temporary in character. Since laborers were no longer
boarded and maintained through the off-season by their employers,
rural prisons filled up during the winter months. Young, unmarried laborers in particular followed the harvest gangs until the
autumn and then stole poultry in order to get committed to houses
of correction when they could not find work.[33]

While the abolition of "living in" obviously served the interests
of the agricultural employers, many of them professed to be anxious about maintaining effective social control over laborers who
no longer lived under their supervision:

> Servant lads are not taken into the farm-house, and kept in subjec-
> tion as they used to be, but live more at home with their own
> parents, and are their own masters; in consequence they go where
> they please, instead of being kept in orderly habits. . . . There is not
> the same accommodation in the present farm-houses which there
> used to be in the old ones. . . . The farmers' wives dislike having
> 2 or 3 servants in the house to attend to, one cause of which is that
> labourers are so ill brought up, and their moral conduct so bad. . . .
> There is not that attachment between employer and the employed
> which there used to be; they seem to make it more a separate
> interest.[34]

Some of the farmers who were enclosing common lands, con-
solidating tenancies, and evicting cottagers admitted the social
costs of these measures. A Huntingdonshire farmer admitted that
enclosure of the commons of a nearby village had been an "injury"
to the "little people who kept a cow or two cows" on the common.
Other farmers admitted that the elimination of the small holdings
and the gradual squeezing out of the small tenants had destroyed
the dreams of independence that had spurred the industry of the
cottage laborer.[35]

Repeatedly in the 1820s, crime was defined mainly as a rural
problem, a sign of the breaking of the "bond of union which
formerly existed between the labourer and his employer."[36] An-
thony Collett, an east Suffolk parson, told a Commons committee
in 1824 that within his memory the two classes had considered
"their interests as one and the same." The "husbandman then
worked for years, perhaps for life on the same farm; he was consid-

ered as part of the establishment, rejoiced in his master's prosperity and sympathized with him in his misfortune." Now, however,

> the labourer is . . . in general the mere servant of the day or of the season; and is cast off, when the task is done, to seek a precarious subsistence from other work, if he can find it, if not from the parish rates. It has most rapidly effected the demoralization of the lower orders and while the pittance allowed to sustain life has driven those to despair who still cherish the feelings of honesty, it has made those who are more void of principle poachers, thieves and robbers.[37]

Ten years later, in the wake of the agricultural laborers' riots of 1830 that engulfed the southern counties, Edwin Chadwick quoted Collett's testimony in the 1834 Poor Law Report, adding the significant coda:

> And yet this was said in the year 1824, a time to which those who witnessed the events of 1830 in the disturbed districts . . . must look back as a period of comparative comfort.[38]

For Chadwick as for Collett the causes of both rural crime and the rioting of 1830 were to be sought "among those gangs who had scarcely any other employment or amusement than to collect in groups [on the parish road gangs or in the beershops] and talk over their grievances."[39]

Low wages, of course, were the most persistent of these grievances. While most rural magistrates and clergymen accepted the farmers' pleas that overpopulation and depressed conditions in the grain market left them no option but to lower wages or rely on relief-subsidized labor, they pointed out the social costs in terms of crime, demoralization, and unrest. As Reverend Philip Hunt, a Bedford magistrate, put it in 1824:

> [The] laborer cannot lay by any money against the time he may wish to marry; he can scarcely indulge any temporary gratification without having recourse to other means than labour; and in counties where game preserves are very numerous, the resource of poaching immediately presents itself to him. If detected he cannot pay the penalty, and is consequently sent to prison. . . .[40]

Besides the price slump and overpopulation, the poor laws themselves were usually blamed for low wages. Sure that the parish would subsidize wages up to subsistence levels, employers pared away at wages and employed parish-subsidized paupers in place of laborers hired on long-term contracts. The poor relief system thus helped to weaken the bonds between farmers and laborers:

> The farmer, finding himself charged for a greater quantity of labour than he requires, naturally endeavours to economise, by discharging those labourers of whom he has the least need and relying upon the supply furnished by the parish for work, hitherto performed at his own cost. . . . The steady, hard-working labourer employed by agreement with his master is converted into the degraded and inefficient pensioner of the parish.[41]

At the same time, these magistrates and clergymen argued, the certainty of relief eroded whatever incentives to industry remained in a low wage economy. As a result, the able-bodied were "slovenly at their work and dissolute in their hours of relaxation." On the parish road-gangs, they leaned on their tools or ventured into the woods nearby to steal firing or into the fields to steal turnips, only bestirring themselves when a farmer or overseer rode by.[42] Always discontented, always embroiled in quarrels with the overseers and farmers over their right to relief, the laborers gradually lost their respect for their social superiors and their property. Thus, all restraints from crime had disappeared.

While most of the committees inquiring into the causes of pauperism and crime in the 1820s concentrated on the agricultural districts, they also identified a similar breakdown of master-servant relations in the manufacturing districts. By the late 1820s, some anxious magistrates were beginning to rediscover the disciplinary virtues of the apprenticeship statutes that had been allowed to lapse in the interests of a free labor market. John Eardley Wilmot, chairman of the Warwickshire quarter sessions, blamed juvenile crime in Birmingham on the erosion of the paternal supervision of the master class over their young workers:

> Formerly the apprentice was taken into the house of the master; he was considered one of the family, and he was boarded, lodged, and educated by the master, who was answerable for his conduct; now the master has ten or a dozen apprentices and perhaps never sees them. They work . . . and then are allowed to go where they please and we know at that time of night with boys it is exactly the worst time that they could be their own masters and the consequence is that they are all thieves.[43]

This sort of elegy to the disciplines of paternalism in the small workshop also found expression in attacks upon the masters of the steam-powered mills in the manufacturing towns, who did not scruple to throw their work force onto the streets whenever there was a slump in demand. They were contrasted nostalgically with the employers in the rural, water-powered factories of the 1780s, who had provided housing, schools, and a guarantee of steady employment for their labor force. The employer of the 1820s, however, washed his hands of his workers when they left the mill at the end of the day. Like the improving farmer, he left the burden of relieving the distress of the unemployed and controlling the young to the parish or the prison.[44]

In cities like London, without a strong industrial base, the committees of inquiry defined the problem of crime in different terms. There the problem was the inability of a traditional, highly fragmented, and inefficient employment structure of small shops, artisanal trades, and garret sweatshops to provide steady employment for the constantly increasing numbers of unskilled juveniles.[45] The result was a drastic overcrowding of the few trades, particularly the street trades, in which entrance was easy.

Without a detailed study of the London labor market, it is impossible to document the relation between crime and employment conditions in the three decades after the Napoleonic Wars.[46] It is clear, however, that by 1816 middle-class authorities were keenly aware of the existence of an underemployed, semi-vagrant juvenile population who worked an hour or two a day sweeping crossings, holding horses for gentlemen, hauling carts, or selling newspapers. The investigators of the juvenile delinquency committee in 1816 had found large numbers of them sleeping huddled up under barrows in the porticoes of Covent Garden. As we have seen, the Evangelicals and the Quakers on the committee took their existence as a sign of the erosion of family disciplines and the failure of the traditional structure of workshop employment to provide steady work.

It was within this general framework, therefore, that the magistrates and politicians who formulated penal and poor relief policy in the 1820s analyzed the meaning of the rise in criminal committals. Crime was interpreted as a sign of an ongoing crisis in labor market disciplines and class relations, especially in the agricultural districts of the south, but also in the manufacturing districts and in the juvenile labor market of the metropolis. Even those farmers and industrialists who stood to gain by the whittling away of the vestiges of paternalism, the introduction of labor-saving machinery, and the beating down of wages were worried about the social costs of these measures in terms of crime and pauperism. Like the philanthropists of the 1770s who worried about the corroding impact of "luxury," their successors in the 1820s were keenly aware of the contradiction between their interest in social stability and their desire to transform the economic and technological basis of their relationship with the classes below them. The very violence of this transformation threatened the foundations of their hegemony.

Their dilemma was to pursue the capitalist transformation of the social order without somehow destroying its stability. Eric Hobsbawm and George Rudé have put this point well in *Captain Swing:*

> A fundamental contradiction lay at the heart of English agrarian society in the period of the Industrial Revolution. Its rulers wanted it to be both capitalist and stable, traditionalist and hierarchical. In other words, they wanted it to be governed by the universal free market of the liberal economist (which was inevitably a market for land and men as well as for goods), but only to the extent that suited nobles, squires and farmers; they advocated an economy which implied mutually antagonistic classes, but did not want it to disrupt a society of ordered ranks.[47]

It is in this context that the introduction of the treadwheel, the silent system, and the bread and water diet should be located. The strictness of these new measures reflected the desires of magistrates and politicians in the 1820s to restore an older, nostalgically remembered social stability in a market economy.

These policymakers also realized that, in a free labor market, the state would have to assume disciplinary functions formerly discharged by "paternalist" employers. As a result, measures were taken in the 1820s to make it easier for employers to turn the business of discipline over to local justices of the peace. Four new acts, passed between 1824 and 1831, gave the local JPs the authority to adjudicate cases of assault, poaching, malicious trespass, and damage to property, as well as certain categories of petty theft.[48] This saved prosecutors in such cases the expense and delay of jury trial. Observers in the 1820s agreed that the new acts helped to increase the frequency with which petty offenses were brought before the justices. The committee on rural crime in 1828 was told, for example, that farmers who used to beat their servants for misbehavior now took them before a justice to receive a dose of the treadwheel. Children who used to be "corrected on the spot" for stealing apples were now brought before the JP for admonition or punishment.[49]

This new severity towards petty crime was accompanied by measures to improve policing, especially in London. The most frequently mentioned failing of the ramshackle system of Bow Street runners, amateur constables, and parish beadles who policed London before 1828 was that they ignored petty offenders because no rewards were offered for their arrest. As one indignant magistrate put it in 1816, the Bow Street runners tended to regard the crowd of petty thieves in the "flash houses" and brothels of St. Giles like game in a preserve, watching and tending them until they became big enough to be worth the sport of catching.[50]

The new police were introduced in 1828 to hunt down the small game. Eighty-five percent of their arrests in the 1830s were for vagrancy, prostitution, drunkenness, disorderly behavior, and common assault, while only 15 percent were for indictable offenses, most of these being petty larceny and pickpocketing.[51]

Though the new police were not much more successful than the old in detecting or deterring burglaries, robberies, and other major crimes, they revolutionized the enforcement of laws against vagrancy and public drunkenness.[52] In fact, to prevent their courts from being clogged with drunkenness cases, the magistrates had to insist that the police could only arrest those whom they intended to charge and prosecute. In the case of vagrancy, between 1829, the year the police were introduced, and 1832, when they reached full strength, vagrancy committals in Middlesex increased by 145 percent.[53]

The real increase in crime rates after 1828, combined with the new volume of petty arrests by the police, acted to produce severe overcrowding in the London prisons. Two of them doubled their capacity to cope with the pressure. Four hundred new cells were added to the Westminster bridewell, while the capacity of the vast plant at Coldbath Fields grew from 600 inmates in 1825 to 1150 in 1832.[54] The "Steel" became the largest prison in England, a huge machine of cells, workrooms, treadwheels, dormitories, and mess halls crammed within the walls built in 1794. More than ten thousand vagrants, beggars, disorderlies, drunks and petty thieves passed through its gates every year. Many of them were there simply because they were poor. The journalist Henry Mayhew found in 1851 that 48.1 percent of the Coldbath Fields population were in prison because they were unable to pay fines in police court.[55] The London poor came to know well its hammock beds, its raucous visiting pens, its wheel, and its gruel.

The introduction of the silent regime at Coldbath Fields in 1834 can be seen, then, as part of a general crackdown on petty disorder among the metropolitan poor. Commenting on this pattern in 1851, Mayhew wrote, with pardonable exaggeration:

> Now-a-days, it is almost impossible for a poor man to escape jail. A slip of the foot as he walks the street may cause him to break a pane of glass, and so, if he cannot pay for the damage, gain for him admission within the prison walls. Let a cab man murmur at his fare—a street trader in his desire to obtain an honest living obstruct the thorough fare—a sweep shout out his calling in the streets—a dust man ring his bell—or other commit a host of such like petty offences—and to prison they must go, to wear a prison dress and do the work of felons.[56]

To the degree that the poor themselves were victims of crime, they too benefited from patterns of stricter enforcement. After all, the new police not only arrested the man seen climbing into the mansion in Grosvenor Square, but also the one seen stealing washing off a line in Brick Lane. Had the police served only the employers and the rich, it would have been impossible to introduce them into the streets of London. The first commissioners, Rowan and Mayne, were keenly aware that the effectiveness of the police depended on securing some measure of grudging cooperation from the "respectable" working class. Hence, the enforcement of the Police Act (which wags called the Breathing Act because grounds could be found in its multifarious provisions for arresting a man for breathing) was never so total as might be imagined.[57] Magistrates and police superintendents realized, for example, that a stringent pursuit of popular disorder could become counterproductive if too many of the poor became habituated to the inside of a prison. As one of them put it in 1836, "The mere fact of having been sent to prison is likely to deprive a man of the greatest moral restraint, the dread of being marked out as a criminal in the face of his country."[58]

Magistrates were particularly concerned about the "criminalizing" effects of small imprisonments on juveniles. A London magistrate in the 1830s cited, as an example, the arrest record of one Thomas McNelly, aged 14:[59]

1836	15 April	Wilfully breaking several squares of glass, St. Saviour's Church.	7 Days
	30 April	Sleeping in the open air at St. Olave's	Discharged
	29 May	Stealing 14 lbs. of coal from a barge	1 month
	6 July	Stealing a bag containing brushes	3 months
	17 Nov.	Stealing 2 bundles of wood	Discharged
	23 Dec.	Stealing carrots from a barge	14 Days
1837	31 Jan.	Stealing a piece of cheese from a shop, St. Saviours	3 Months
	29 April	Stealing a pair of drawers at Bermondsey	1 month

This sensitivity to the dangers of making a criminal out of a boy like Thomas McNelly only highlights the dilemmas of the new strategy of bearing down on minor forms of disorder. Though the strategy was designed to widen the gulf between the "criminal" and the "respectable" working class, it bore down on everyone in the casual labor market who was vulnerable to unemployment. The petty imprisonments handed out by the police courts thrust together in the same oakum picking rooms and dormitories of Coldbath Fields professional criminals and young boys caught breaking church windows; the London "mobsman" and the London street-seller working off a fine for public drunkenness. Magistrates could only hope that the enforcement of strict silence at Coldbath Fields would curtail this dangerous kind of fraternization.

III

Hand in hand with the tightening up of penal deterrence and policing went the centralization of prison administration. By 1831, the Prison Discipline Society and its allies in Parliament were agreed that the measure of centralization initiated by the Gaols Act of 1823 had not gone far enough. Many boroughs had secured exemption from its provisions altogether, and of the 130 required to submit annual reports to the Home Secretary, only 80 had bothered to do so. The Home Secretary, in turn, lacked even the power to order the closure of the small town lockups where abuses were worst.

There was still no uniformity in prison discipline from county to county. Some kept their vagrants on the wheel for four hours a day, some for ten; some fed them meat once a week, others provided only bread and water. The Prison Discipline Society, noting the increasingly national character of the labor market and the huge distances that men were wont to tramp in search of work, worried aloud in its reports that vagrant laborers would take to congregating in counties where they were guaranteed an "easy lag" in prison.

Samuel Hoare and William Crawford of the Prison Discipline Society argued for a national prison inspectorate. Such an inspectorate was the only way, they maintained, of countering the inevitable tendency of institutional discipline to decline into a slack and unthinking routine. Crawford and Hoare cited the Irish prison inspectorate established in the 1820s, the factory inspectorate established in 1833, and the poor law commissions of 1834 as precedents for government intervention in local administration.[60] However, when an inspectorate was actually established in 1835, its powers were limited. In order not to tread on the prerogatives of the magistracy, the inspectors were only given authority to publicize abuses, not to close prisons or order changes. As a result, their early reports were a litany of frustration. Many of the practices that Howard had denounced fifty years before still persisted in small borough jails and in the London prisons. Howard, for example, would have recognized this scene, as described in the inspectors' report on Giltspur Street Compter in London in 1841:

> Looking through the inspection hole, we saw a party of prisoners playing at pitch and toss; others of the prisoners were lying on their beds amusing themselves with looking on. We called the attention of the governor who himself saw the prisoners gaming. They appeared so unaccustomed to be overlooked that they were quite unconscious . . . we were observing them; and until the ward door was unlatched and we entered the room, they continued their amusement.[61]

While there was less disease than in Howard's day, and a more concerted attempt to enforce sentences of hard labor, prisoners did not sleep in separate cells at night, free association of prisoners in the day yards was tolerated, and in one or two places garnish was still exacted by the prisoners.[62]

While the inspectors were careful to avoid direct denunciations of the JPs, their documentation of abuses helped to undermine support in Parliament for the traditions of local administration. As a result, the inspectors were able to accumulate power. By the early 1840s they were approving architectural plans, dietaries, and solitary-cell designs submitted to them by the local magistracies.[63] The establishment of the inspectorate institutionalized the reform movement. With the appointment of Whitworth Russell, the former chaplain of Millbank, and William Crawford, a London businessman and member of the Prison Discipline Society, as inspectors, the Prison Discipline Society fell into desuetude. Henceforth, until the founding of the Howard Society in the 1880s, the most influential voices of reform were to come from within the prison system itself—from the inspectors, prison chaplains, and governors.

The professionalization of reform was accompanied by the professionalization of prison and police staff. Tighter prison discipline, like tighter supervision of the streets, depended on the recruitment of men with an aptitude for the exercise of strict authority. But where were such men to be found? The earlier reformers had looked in vain for effective subordinate staff in prison. At the end of the Napoleonic Wars, however, a large number of half-pay officers and NCOs began to move into careers in institutional discipline. In the 1820s and 1830s, they took positions in the Metropolitan Police, the prisons, the prison inspectorate, the poor law administration, and later the rural constabulary, bringing with them the habits of command that they had learned in the forces. This infusion of trained disciplinarians provided the personnel necessary for the centralization and rationalization of the machinery of public order in the 1830s.

Typical of the new disciplinarians was George Laval Chesterton, the governor of Coldbath Fields who supervised the imposition of the silent system in 1834. He was a half-pay officer and a veteran of the Peninsular Campaign.[64] So was Colonel Rowan, the police commissioner who turned a motley band of veterans, tradesmen, and laborers into the Metropolitan Police. He took his disciplinary program for the new police force from the regimental drill manual used by Sir John Moore in the Spanish Campaign.[65] At Millbank, another army veteran, Colonel Chapman, was brought in during 1824 to bring order to the prison. At Preston, the jailers of the 1820s—a former army sergeant, a butler to a county magnate, and a publican—were followed in 1827 by the appointment of a former captain in the navy.[66]

The movement of gentlemen officers into positions formerly the preserve of petty tradesmen attests to the increasing importance of prisons as institutions in the minds of the middle-class public. Those who specialized in prison administration came to be seen as vital and, therefore, respectable public servants. How else can we explain the fact that men like Chesterton and Reverend Clay of the Preston House of Correction became important public figures in their own right? To a bourgeoisie that could no longer take public order for granted, those with front-line experience with the criminal poor became eagerly sought-after and esteemed public servants. No less a personage than Lord Brougham is reputed to have told Clay that his reports on the Preston prisoners had kept him up reading half the night.[67] Chesterton, for his part, corresponded with Dickens when the novelist was seeking firsthand information about the "dangerous classes."

The change in the social composition of prison officers and in their functions was reflected in language. As early as 1807, Robert Southey noted that the old eighteenth century term "keeper," with its rude connotations of animal taming, had been replaced by the more impersonal and commanding term "governor," while "turnkey" was being discarded for "warder."[68] At the same time, eighteenth century institutional usages with familial connotations were also being discarded. Howard had used the word "family" to refer to the inmate population, as when he said, "I know not why an house of correction may not be conducted with as much regularity as any other house where the family is equally numerous."[69] This usage, which died out in the 1820s, was also common in most eighteenth century pamphlets on workhouse management. It was usual to refer to the master of the workhouse as the house father, to his wife as house mother, and to the paupers as the family. Likewise, when John Jebb discussed the discipline or routine of a prison, he used the term "economy," which referred to the distribution of tasks and the allocation of expenditure in the family household.[70]

Around the end of the Napoleonic Wars, a language of discipline free from familial or animal-taming connotations began to make its appearance. The word "cell" replaced the word "apartment," with its association to the household dwelling. Discipline displaced economy. Prison populations, not families, were referred to in official parlance. The metaphors of command also became increasingly military in derivation. The new army-trained disciplinarians used the language of the parade ground and the regiment. In his report for 1837, one of the prison inspectors, William J. Williams, himself a former army officer, argued that the government of prisons

> should be made as analagous as possible to that of a battalion; with the same graduated responsibility among the officers, the same inflexible regularity extended even to trivialities, the same promptitude in punishments, the same nice divisions of time. Under such a rule, leagued with a rigid and uniform system of corrective discipline, unswervingly applied, prisons may at least be relieved from the reproach of tending more to the extension than the repression of crime.[71]

The militarization of prison discipline was not achieved without a struggle both against the old guards and the inmates. When Chesterton took over Coldbath Fields in 1828, he found a vivid subculture flourishing in the overcrowded cells and day yards:

> As the yard was approached, the ear was assailed with a discordant buzz of voices, occasional singing and whistling and ever and anon an interjectional shriek. This hubbub proceeded from a heterogeneous mob of persons of all ages, from 16 years and upwards, who were moving about in a confused mass, without supervision, order or wholesome system of any kind. No sooner was my presence discerned than all this din became suddenly stifled and the yardsman, generally the most subtle villain of the whole lot, would assume an air of solemn severity, pull off his cap and bow reverentially and look the very image of primitive simplicity.[72]

Before he could silence this din, Chesterton had to regain control of the guards. They were turning a good penny on rackets in the prison, the most imaginative involving a hidden trapdoor through which, for a consideration, they allowed male prisoners entry into the female prisoners' quarters.[73] Using prisoner informants, Chesterton was able to gather evidence to secure the dismissal of the corrupt guards, but it took six years before he felt sure enough of his staff to embark on the imposition of the rule of silence in the prison.

As part of the silent discipline, Chesterton attempted to ban all fraternization between guards, prisoners, and their families:

> Turnkeys... are strictly forbidden to hold familiar conversations with the prisoners or to communicate with them on any subject whatsoever unconnected with their duties. Neither are they to entertain applications without the prison gates of the friends or

relatives under the pleas of extending favor to those within the walls. Moreover, it is expected that they will carefully abstain from forming intimacy or acquaintanceship with discharged prisoners of any class or description but maintain their respectability by avoiding the company of all such people.[74]

Chesterton's struggle with his staff recalls Rowan and Mayne's difficulties in forging a reliable police force out of the motley "rascals," as Rowan called them, who volunteered for the job.[75] A whole range of disciplinary expedients was employed to separate the police from the class they were intended to discipline. They were drilled in military style, clothed in uniforms, and imbued with loyalty to their corps. They were placed on regular salary to render them independent of the control of their community. They were housed in barracks or dormitories in the station house. They were forbidden to frequent haunts of their class like the pub or the penny theater. They were even forbidden to swear or make use of street slang. The rules enjoined a sober and impartial demeanor in all dealings with the public and strictly forbade fraternization or familiarity.[76]

As might well be imagined, the police commissioners had trouble finding men capable of such self-restraint. Of the 2,800 who were taken on in 1830, only 562 remained in 1834, the rest having been fired or having resigned.[77] These high turnover rates reflected not only the simple incapacity of some of the recruits but also the rigidity of the discipline to which they were subjected. They were being asked nothing less than to renounce the language, customs, and loyalties of their class. This would be difficult at any time, but especially so in face of the massive popular hostility manifested in the demonstrations of November 1830. Called out to guard the route of the King's procession to Parliament, the police were attacked by a crowd of laborers and small shopkeepers who abused the police physically and chanted "Down with the Peelers!" and "Down with the Lobster Backs!" (a reference to their red coats). Popular hatred of the new police was renewed in 1833 when a detachment of policemen charged into a radical demonstration near Coldbath Fields, dispersing the crowd with blows of their staves. These confrontations were a forceful reminder to a young recruit that he was, in some measure, regarded as an enemy by his community.[78]

Thus, while the tightening up of public order required the creation of a reliable cadre of working-class disciplinarians, demarcated from their class by the regimens of their corps, it proved difficult in practice to find sufficient men capable of adopting the controlled institutional persona envisaged by prison and police reformers.

I V

The opening of Pentonville in 1842 represents a point of culmination in the tightening up of social controls underway since 1820. At the same time it was an effort to vindicate penitentiary discipline after the failures of Millbank. Whitworth Russell, formerly a chaplain of the prison and now, in the 1840s, a prison inspector, believed that discipline at Millbank had not been strict enough. Prisoners at Millbank had worked alone in their cells, but the doors were left open during the daytime, and wardsmen and taskmasters circulated freely throughout the corridors, collecting finished work, handing out new material, or instructing novices. These wardsmen and taskmasters were usually prisoners, and they provided the leadership for a network of resistance to the guards. As Russell said in a confidential memo to the Home Secretary:

> The employment of prisoners in these situations enables them also to act as spies upon the officers' movements, so as effectually to prevent him from restraining or detecting misconduct or irregularity.[79]

There was always a low buzz of conversation in the corridors, carried on *sotto voce* from cell to cell:

> If as frequently happens the officer hearing the noise returns into the ward, a signal given by the wardsman or tailor's instructor at once stops the uproar, and baffles the endeavour of the officer to detect the transgressor.

In this way, Russell gloomily concluded, "the prisoner is the superintendent of the officer rather than the officer of him." In Russell's view it was not enough to outlaw the wardsman system and enforce a strict rule of silence. The whole design of the prison was at fault. There were so many blind spots on the circular corridors that it was impossible to keep the prisoners under effective surveillance.

To vindicate solitary confinement, it was necessary, Russell believed, to develop a prison architecture that would expose the prisoner in his cell before the eye of authority. In his opinion, Millbank represented a botched attempt to put Bentham's Panopticon inspection principle into practice. Now Russell and his colleague, William Crawford, set about finding another design that would harmonize the imperative of strict seclusion and omnipresent inspection. They found the model they were looking for in America.

By 1830, the reports of the Boston Prison Discipline Society and the travelogues of English visitors like Captain Basil Hall had made English authorities familiar with the Haviland design for the Philadelphia penitentiary. Instead of ranging the cells around the periphery of a circular tower, as at Millbank, Haviland devised the cell block, three tiers of cells ranged around three sides of a huge open corridor. These blocks radiated from a central inspection point, offering clear lines of sight throughout the building. The design for Pentonville drew heavily on the Philadelphia model.[80]

America also offered two competing models of discipline for the English to chose from: the solitary confinement regime at Philadelphia and the silent associated system used at Auburn and Sing Sing. In the Auburn plan, prisoners were confined separately in cells by night, but worked by day in associated workshops under the rule of silence. In 1829, Basil Hall described the "moral machinery" of the Auburn system for his English readers:

> A narrow dark passage runs along the back part of all the workshops from whence the convicts sitting at their tasks as well as their turnkeys can be distinctly seen through the narrow slits in the wall, half an inch wide and covered with glass, while the superintendent himself can neither be seen nor heard by the prisoners or by their keepers. The consciousness that a vigilant eye may at any given moment be fixed upon them, is described as being singularly efficacious in keeping the attention of all parties awake to an extent which no visible and permanent scrutiny, I am told, has the power of commanding.[81]

The Philadelphia system struck Hall much less favorably. Prisoners were made to endure as much as five years in total seclusion broken only by visits from prison staff. The prisoners worked and slept in their cells and took exercise in tiny walled pens attached to each cell. This was the system pursued at Reading in the 1780s that Howard had condemned as an excessively zealous application of his ideas. Basil Hall, likewise, thought Philadelphia went too far. "There really is no torture more severe even to a virtuous mind than absolute solitude," he said, coming out firmly in favor of the associated Auburn system.

In 1834, the Home Secretary sent William Crawford to investigate both systems and report back on their merits. Crawford criticized the Auburn system for concentrating on the exploitation of the prisoner's labor at the expense of moral reformation. Prisons, he insisted with an emphasis true to Howard and Paul, should never be converted into "mere manufactories." He was also appalled by the uncontrolled use of the lash at Auburn. The Philadelphia system, by contrast, placed primary emphasis on sorrowful and solitary repentance, and it relied for the maintenance of order, not on the lash, but on the subduing force of solitude itself:

> In judging of the comparative merits of the two systems it will be seen that the discipline of Auburn is of a physical, that of Philadelphia of a moral character. The whip inflicts immediate pain, but solitude inspires permanent terror. The former degrades while it humiliates; the latter subdues but it does not debase. At Auburn the convict is uniformly treated with harshness, at Philadelphia with civility; the one contributes to harden, the other to soften the affections. Auburn stimulates vindictive feelings; Philadelphia induces habitual submission.[82]

Crawford was also impressed by Philadelphia's success in stamping out the illicit associations of the prison subculture. He liked to tell the story of the Philadelphia prisoner who asked a warder whether his accomplice had been arrested, little knowing that they had been confined side by side in adjacent cells for ten months.[83]

Besides making the case for separate confinement on the Philadelphia model, Crawford also went to some length to prove the English pedigree of penitentiary discipline, citing the 1779 act and the institutions at Gloucester and Horsham as precedents in order to rebut potential criticism of the penitentiary as a foreign innovation. He insisted that it was in fact "British in its origin, British in its actual application, British in its legislative sanction."[84]

On his return, Crawford teamed up with Whitworth Russell to lobby for the construction of a model prison. They both agreed, however, that the American example was defective in one crucial respect. Sentences at Philadelphia commonly ran for five and sometimes ten years. Russell's experience at Millbank convinced him that prisoners could not be subjected to such terms of solitude without danger to their health. Hence, in their proposal to the Home Secretary for the construction of Pentonville, they recommended that eighteen months should be the maximum allowable period in solitude.[85]

They emended the American model in another particular as well. At Philadelphia (and at Millbank too), prisoners were returned to the community after their release. In 1831, Basil Hall referred to American anxieties about the steady accumulation of numbers of released convicts and expressed relief that Britain could still dispose of offenders by banishing them to Australia.[86] While both Crawford and Russell had doubts about the deterrent value of transportation, they agreed that it was unthinkable to replace it with sentences that returned ex-offenders to the community. Hence, they recommended that Pentonville be used to inflict a probationary period of solitude on offenders under sentence of transportation prior to their embarkation. They also recommended that only first-time offenders with a stout constitution and an apparent willingness to reform be exposed to the rigors of the Pentonville regime.[87]

These concessions did little to satisfy critics of solitary confinement or win over advocates of the Auburn system in England. The chief exponents of the rival system were G. L. Chesterton, who had introduced it into Coldbath Fields, and Peter Laurie, a superintending magistrate of the prison.

In two influential pamphlets, Laurie inveighed both against the increasingly intrusive role of the prison inspectors in local prisons and against their dogmatic attachment to separate confinement. He poked fun at their disciplinary fanaticism:

> Thieves may be drilled to march with all the gravity and regularity of the parade, from the washing tub to the treadwheel, from the treadwheel to their meals and back again to labour and at night to bed; they may be taught to sit in decent clothes and clean apartments in rows a certain distance apart; half an inch too close being synonymous with contamination, and half an inch too far being grievous insubordination; they may profess to admire picking oakum and eschew picking pockets; be civil to their officers and respectful to visitors—the women may be taught to knit stockings and plait caps; to ask for tracts instead of tea and prefer spinning to spirits; cry at good advice and curtsey becomingly; yet this may be just as feasible a mode of diminishing crime and reforming criminals as Mrs. Partington's attempt to mop out the Atlantic.[88]

Carried away by his piquant sallies against Crawford and Russell, Laurie was apt to forget that advocates of the silent associated system proved to be no less insistent on lockstep routine and no less easily taken in by the prisoners' guileful masquerades of reformation. Nonetheless, the associated system attracted some extremely influential support. Charles Dickens came out against the Philadelphia system in his *American Notes:*

> I hold this slow and daily tampering with the mysteries of the brain to be immeasurably worse than any torture of the body; and because its ghastly signs and tokens are not so palpable to the eye and sense of touch as scars upon the flesh; because its wounds are not upon the surface, and it extorts few cries that human ears can hear.[89]

Opposition to the separate system reached into the bureaucracy itself. Crawford and Russell's fellow inspectors, William J. Williams and Bisset Hawkins, used their reports to register "an earnest dissent" against the system, citing the cost of converting existing prisons to the cellular plan, and expressing doubts as to the morality of strict solitude.[90] Williams also demurred from the extravagant claims that Crawford and Russell advanced for solitude as a reformative agent. Crime, he said, depended too much on the economy, technological change, the state of the working-class family, and other "uncertain and uncontrollable circumstances" to be "permanently and extensively influenced by any system of prison discipline."[91] Faced with divided counsel from their own inspectors and influential opposition among the public, it is no wonder that the successive Home Secretaries, Russell, Normanby, and Graham, embarked hesitantly upon the construction of Pentonville.

Nonetheless, as a trial of an unproven discipline, Pentonville turned out to be an enormous success, exciting emulation throughout the county institutions in England and in the prison systems of Europe. By 1850, ten new prisons had been built on the Pentonville model, and ten more had been converted to the separate system.[92] Although the sniping from advocates of the silent associated system continued, Pentonville assured the triumph of separate-system discipline. It had many obvious attractions. Chaplains found that the cellular system gave them extraordinary power over the psyche of offenders. As Reverend Clay put it, solitude was a "terrible solvent":

> . . . a few months in the solitary cell renders a prisoner strangely impressible. The chaplain can then make the brawny navvy cry like a child; he can work on his feelings in almost any way he

pleases; he can, so to speak, photograph his thoughts, wishes and opinions on his patient's mind, and fill his mouth with his own phrases and language.[93]

Of the thoughts that the chaplain sought to "photograph" on the mind of his "patient," the most important was the justice of his sentence. The chaplains exhorted the criminal to "lay aside the angry feelings against his prosecutor, to acknowledge the justice of his sentence, to take his own punishment patiently, and to endeavour to allay discontent and repress turbulence in others."[94] As the penitentiary's technician of guilt, the chaplain provided the constant legitimization of institutional practice required for its functioning. It was he who presented the penitentiary as a moral universe of benevolent intention. It was he who prevented offenders from escaping their guilt by taking refuge in contempt for their captors.

If the chaplain failed, as he often did, to adjust the prisoner to the institutional order, there were plenty of expedients available to the prison authorities to bring the prisoner to heel by force. Stoppage of diet and curtailment of letters and visiting privileges proved to be as effective instruments of control as chains and the lash. When Henry Mayhew asked the Pentonville guards in 1856, "Do you find that you have inmates of the jail under the same control now as in the days of 'thumb screws', and 'gags' and 'brandings'?" he received the significant reply:

> I think we have greater power over them, sir. For at present you see, we cut off the right of receiving and sending letters, as well as stop the visits of their friends and a man feels these things more than any torture that he could be put to.[95]

While chaining and whipping continued to be used to punish major acts of insubordination, the new "micro-punishments" were necessary additions to the arsenal of control mechanisms because the older corporal punishments were no longer considered appropriate for the tiny new offenses—winking, nodding, scratching initials on a drinking cup, and so on, that were created by the new rules.

The intensity of institutional scrutiny in turn required a higher ratio of custodial staff to prisoners. In the new prisons on the Pentonville model, it was common to employ one custodian for every ten to fifteen inmates.[96] This involved higher costs for the counties, but in the mood of severity that accompanied the seemingly inexorable increase in the crime rates in the mid 1840s, the JPs were prepared to foot the bill.

Penitentiary routine appealed, therefore, as much for its severity as for its reformative potential. Indeed, advocates of the Pentonville system liked to argue that it was reformative because it was severe. As the Earl of Chichester, one of the commissioners appointed to superintend Pentonville, put it in 1856:

> Human nature is so constituted that when a man has been long addicted to a life of crime or sensual indulgence it requires a severe affliction to force him to reflect—he must be providentially deprived of those sources of animal pleasure and excitement which have hitherto enabled him to silence his conscience and to shut out from his mind all thoughts of the future—there must be something external to afflict, to break down his spirit, some bodily suffering or distress of mind, before the still small voice will be heard and the man brought to himself.[97]

The disturbing question about Pentonville was whether its discipline went too far in producing "distress of mind." Almost immediately, the Pentonville commissioners began to receive reports from the prison doctor about the psychological effects of solitude. Prisoners came to him complaining of delusions. One of them said "there was something the matter with his head, and something was eating away his nose." Another had "various fancies that insects have got inside his head, that he has seen his mother, and raves about his father's spirit which he said was in his inside."[98] Convict 1364 told the prison doctor that his body was being galvanized with tin, while another became obsessed that a small bird that appeared every morning in the exercise yards was a sign portending the death of his wife and children. Convict 222 was removed, first to the infirmary and then to an asylum, after being found in his cell muttering "in a very incoherent way about the Queen."[99] Each new case provided embarrassment for the Pentonville commissioners and ammunition for their opponents.[100]

The commissioners would only admit publicly to fifteen cases of madness in the first eight years of the prison's operation, but this figure did not include those temporarily removed to the infirmary suffering from delusions or depression. While their reports put a bold face on the experiment, the commissioners began to have doubts about the solitary regime, and when the most militant of their number, William Crawford, died in 1847, they reduced the solitary period from eighteen to twelve and finally to nine months.[101] In the 1850s they abandoned other features of the solitary regime such as the separate stalls in the chapel, the solitary exercise pens, and the masks that prisoners wore in the corridors to prevent them from recognizing each other.[102]

Faith in the reformative promise of Pentonville barely survived the 1840s. In the next decade, it became fashionable once again to insist that the "dangerous classes" were incapable of reformation. While solitude remained an essential element of prison discipline throughout the rest of the century, it was retained more as an instrument of terror than as an aid to reform. As early as 1854, influential voices, like that of Joseph Kingsmill, chaplain of Pentonville, were to be heard admitting:

> Separate confinement is no panacea for criminal depravity. It has been supposed capable of reforming a man from habits of theft to a life of honesty, of vice to virtue. It has no such power. No human punishment has ever done this.[103]

One sign of the public disenchantment with Pentonville was that the crocodile tears of the penitentiary inmate became a matter of public ridicule. Charles Dickens, ever attuned to his audience, knew he was sure of drawing a laugh from his readers by concluding Uriah Heep's career as a model penitent in Pentonville:

> "Well, Twenty-Seven," said Mr. Creakle, mournfully admiring him, "how do you find yourself today?"
> "I am very umble, sir!" replied Uriah Heep.
> "You are always so, Twenty-Seven," said Mr. Creakle.
> Here, another gentleman asked, with extreme anxiety, "Are you quite comfortable?"
> "Yes, I thank you, sir!" said Uriah Heep, looking in that direction. "Far more comfortable here than ever I was outside. I see my follies now, sir. That's what makes me comfortable."[104]

V

Doubts about the penitentiary increased after the suspension of transportation in 1853. As a result of protests from the Australian colonies and questions at home as to the deterrent value of sending a convict to an increasingly settled and prosperous colony, the government began in 1848 to replace transportation with a national system of convict prisons. Between 1848 and 1863, imprisonment, which had once been used for summary offenses and petty felonies, was transformed into a punishment for all the major

crimes, except murder, formerly punished by either public hanging or transportation. As a result, the authorities were for the first
time faced with the task of administering long-term sentences.
Until the late 1840s, the longest sentences in English prisons were
three years.[105] Most offenders served six months or less. Lord John
Russell was only repeating a commonplace when he said in 1837
that a ten-year imprisonment would be "a punishment worse than
death."[106] By the mid-1850s sentences of such a length had become
common as replacements for the abandoned sentences of transportation.

Instead of transportation, convicts were sent to work at a number of public-works prisons, administered by the central government, and set to work quarrying stone for public monuments,
building breakwaters or laboring in Her Majesty's naval dockyards. This period of hard labor followed a six-month dose of
solitude at Pentonville or Millbank. At the end of their sentences,
convicts were released on a ticket of leave, a parole that required
them to report to the police at regular intervals, maintain a steady
job, and avoid associating with other ex-offenders.[107]

The first ticket-of-leave men were released at home in 1853
amid general public panic. Almost immediately they found themselves blamed for every crime, large or small. While the director
of convict prisons, Joshua Jebb, insisted that the recidivism rate for
ticket-of-leave men was lower than for those released from county
and borough prisons, the ticket-of-leave men bore the brunt of the
public's anxiety at the fact that they could no longer count on
transportation to rid England of its most serious criminals.[108] The
ticket-of-leave men found themselves barred from most employment, harassed by the police, and vilified in the press.

While most of them had no evident political convictions, they
were quickly identified as a potential source of danger to the state.
Some alarmists, notably the editorial writers of the *Times* and Earl
Grey himself, ominously referred to the role that ex-convicts had
played in the revolution of 1848 in Paris. Gangs of liberated "for-
çats," the *Times* intoned, had "been the main instruments in the
hands of the demagogues for perpetrating the turmoils of the
French republic." Closer to home, they pointed out the numbers
of pickpockets and petty criminals circulating among the huge
Chartist demonstration at Kennington Common in June 1848.
While these statements are not to be taken seriously as sociologies
of either the Paris or London crowds in 1848, they do express the
cluster of political and social fears triggered by the suspension of

transportation and the conversion to a system of deterrence based entirely on penitentiary imprisonment.[109]

The ticket-of-leave men, for their part, did not hesitate to protest against their stigmatization by the public. At two meetings . convened by Henry Mayhew, one in March 1856 and the other in January 1857, the men recounted their stories of police harassment and rejection by employers. Most of the men, the *Times* reported, "bore the appearance of belonging either to the costermongering fraternity or to the class of bone-gatherers and pickers up of other unconsidered articles."[110] One of them told how he had been walking through Tothill Street, Westminster, carrying a bag of rabbit skins, when he was taken up by the police, brought before the magistrate, and threatened with imprisonment. When he protested his innocence of any charge, the magistrate burst out, "Oh, you are an insolent fellow and a disgrace to society—if the Secretary of State knew about your doings he would banish you."

In the January 1857 meeting, their deeply felt sense of victimization at the hands of the middle-class press vented itself even against Henry Mayhew, the most sympathetic exponent of their cause in the London press. The meeting was proceeding with Mayhew on the platform and the Earl of Carnarvon in the chair when one of the men shouted from the audience:

> Friends, be careful. You are doing wrong to come here so publicly and betray yourselves to a man who only wants to gain his own purposes (loud disapprobation). Henry Mayhew is the worst enemy you have got. He only wants to get it out of you and put it in his book (laughter and hisses). You may hiss me, but I am telling the truth.[111]

Like the ticket-of-leave men outside, the prisoners within the walls did not endure the change from transportation to long-term imprisonment with Heep-like masks of contrition. For them, the change abruptly ended the chance of a new start in Australia. At the same time, it introduced a host of inequities in sentences. Convicts under terms of seven years' transportation, for example, had their sentences commuted to 3½ years followed by 3½ on ticket-of-leave supervision, while prisoners under the new penal servitude sentences were required to serve a straight four-year term with no ticket of leave.[112] Both groups felt cheated when they compared notes. From 1853 to 1858, the convict prisons were swept by strikes, sit-downs, group assaults on warders, and escape attempts, all designed to bring pressure on the convict prison directors to eliminate sentence anomalies and restore transportation in place of imprisonment.[113].

Some of the most violent resistance came from the women convicts in Brixton and Millbank.[114] Between 1853 and 1859 a small group of them waged a dogged protest against the conversion of their sentences from transportation to imprisonment. They tore up their bedding, set fire to their uniforms, banged on their cell doors, stripped naked before their astonished matrons, and broke the silence with swearing and chants. The prison directors were both fascinated and dumbfounded by these women who so exuberantly violated the code of female docility. They seemed to resist dark cells, straitjackets, and bread and water punishments. In 1859, the director of convict prisons confessed that the Brixton women were "entirely beyond control, beyond the bonds of all propriety and decency, beyond hope save in the exercise of some miraculous agency."[115] He realized, however, that the women's protests were founded on a real grievance. He admitted that women released from prison suffered more stigma than men and consequently found it much more difficult to secure employment.[116] The women were conscious of this and were determined to pressure the prison directors to let them go to Australia.

While the directors refused to give in to the women's demands, the disturbances taught them that their power inside the penitentiaries was by no means as total as they had imagined. The women's riots made them realize that they could only secure order as long as they conformed to the prisoners' standards of fairness. Accordingly, in 1856 new legislation was passed standardizing penal servitude and transportation sentences.[117] Yet the convicts remained unsubdued.

Whenever the authorities attempted to alter institutional practice, they found themselves confronted with a similarly militant opposition. In 1861, when the prison directors ordered a major reduction in diet as part of an attempt to tighten up deterrence in the convict system, prisoners at Portland and Chatham staged a two-day riot that caused substantial damage. The prisoners doused the principal warder with gruel from their soup tins, overpowered the guards, unlocked the cells, and took over complete control of Chatham for several hours, until a contingent of armed Royal Marines succeeded in retaking the institution.[118]

It was only in 1864 that the riots within the prison and public anxiety outside began to subside. The public gradually accustomed itself to the transition from transportation to imprisonment and to the release of ex-offenders at home. The process of adjustment was made easier by a gradual falling off in the rate of criminal commitals after 1855.

The prison directors did their best to regain public confidence in their institutions. Sensing that public opinion supported stringent severity, they reduced institutional diets and imposed increasingly sharp restrictions on the ticket-of-leave men.[119] After 1862, they began to revoke tickets for failing to report and for association with undesirables. In 1870, a branch of the Metropolitan Police was established to supervise the ticket-of-leave men in London and to maintain records of their features and characteristics for use in court.[120] Photographing of ex-inmates was introduced in the late 1860s, and fingerprinting followed in the 1890s as part of a general attempt to improve the identification and surveillance of "habitual criminals."[121] By the 1890s, a national system of criminal record keeping had been established in Whitehall to keep track of the "criminal class" and to ensure that recidivists were identified for retributive sentencing.

This attempt to extend the surveillance exercised within the institution to offenders upon release attests to the general disillusionment with the reformative promise of penitentiaries. It also signals a change in tactics in social control strategy. Having discovered that there were offenders who resisted all attempts to reform them, the state moved towards a policy of identifying this subpopulation as accurately as possible, supervising their movements on the street and then incapacitating them as quickly as possible by renewed confinement. In this strategy the institution was used, not for purposes of reformation, but for penal quarantine.

Thus the penitentiary, which had been introduced in the 1840s as an instrument for remaking human character, survived into the late nineteenth century by virtue of its penal features. Solitary confinement, initiated as an instrument of reform, was retained as an instrument of punishment. In 1863, the Lord Chief Justice gave utterance to the orthodoxy that was to rule in the convict prison system for the next quarter century:

> The reformation of the offender is in the highest degree speculative and uncertain, and its permanency in the face of renewed temptation exceedingly precarious. On the other hand, the impression produced by suffering inflicted as the punishment of crime, and the fear of its repetition are far more likely to be lasting. . . .[122]

VI

By 1877, the major elements of the modern penal system were in place. The last remaining vestiges of voluntary and local administration had been wiped out with the transfer of all borough and county jails to a central prison commission administered from Whitehall. The public ritual of execution had been replaced by the private hanging within the prison walls. In place of the public spectacle of death, there was now only the small, ominous gesture of flying a black flag over the prison to announce the dispatch of the offender. The last convicts had been sent out to Australia and the hulks had been broken up. Imprisonment had become established as the punishment for every major crime except murder. The foundations of the modern system of parole had been established in the ticket-of-leave system, and a national system of criminal records, photographs, and dossiers had been set up. The principle of separate institutions for juveniles had been confirmed, with the creation of the first industrial schools and reformatories. Most of all, the huge glowering presence of the Victorian prison had been placed in the heart of the city, as the new symbolic representation of the state's ultimate power. That presence endures. While the night refuges, union workhouses, industrial schools, settlement houses, and model dwellings have fallen to the wrecker's ball and to the vagaries of philanthropic style and state policy, the Victorian prisons survive as the most unchanging element in our institutional inheritance. As late as 1969, over 40 percent of the prisons in use in England dated back to the Victorian era.[123]

Up the Caledonian Road in north London, for example, the old cattle market is gone, and the working-class housing in the area has been renewed at least three times since 1842, but Pentonville remains, inwardly changed of course, but still the same dominating presence it was 125 years ago. It is no longer the "model" it was in its Victorian heyday. The Home Office would prefer to show you the modern psychiatric facility at Grendon Underwood in Buckinghamshire. There, group therapy and psychiatric counseling have replaced solitude and religious exhortation as the latest vogue in the technology of reformation. Pentonville is used for the detention of petty offenders, immigration cases, alcoholics, and addicts. In the cells once built for one man's solitude there are now crammed three and sometimes four prisoners, and in the corridors that used to be as silent as catacombs, televisions blare, young men argue over a ping-pong game, and old men shuffle by, smoking absently and talking in monotones. In place of masks and dun-colored uniforms with number badges, they wear jeans and T-shirts.

Of the whole elaborate nineteenth century disciplinary ritual of lockstep processionals and inspections accomplished according to the cadence of bells and barked commands, only a few essential vestiges have survived—the body count at dusk and dawn and the cell check during the hours of darkness. The discipline that the building was built to enforce has broken down. But the huge machine that Jebb, Crawford, and Russell built still survives through all of the changes of fashion in prison reform, as a melancholy monument to the deeper continuities in the state's use of its ultimate power.

Conclusion

I

It is tempting to look upon the history of prison reform as a cycle of recurring ironies. One wonders, for example, what Howard would have made of Pentonville had he lived to see it. We can recall his condemnation of the zealots who used his name to justify the confinement of prisoners in solitude for weeks on end. What would he have thought then of solitude enforced for eighteen months; of the walled pens where prisoners exercised alone; of the masks, the drills, the silence? Hearing the screams issuing from the dark cells, would he have begun to think again about replacing "punishment directed at the body" with "punishment directed at the mind"?

One wonders too what he would have said about the circumstances surrounding the suicide of fifteen-year-old Edward Andrews in Birmingham borough prison in 1854. In that prison, constructed on the Pentonville model and opened in 1849, the governor routinely ordered petty offenders to be confined in solitude and to be kept turning a hand crank weighted at thirty pounds pressure, ten thousand times every ten hours. Those who failed to keep the crank turning or who sought to resist were immobilized in straitjackets, doused with buckets of water, thrown into dark cells, and fed on bread and water. One who resisted was Edward Andrews. After two months of refusing to work, being dragged below, doused, "jacketed," and fed on bread and water, he hanged himself from his cell window. The prison schoolmaster saw him on his last night alive,

> going up the steps to his cell; had the straitjacket last Sunday morning two hours. It made shrivelled marks on his arm and body. A bucket of water stood by him in case of exhaustion. He stood with cold, red, bare feet soaked in water. He looked very deathly and reeled with weakness. Had been sent regularly to the crank except when confined in the jacket.... Food, usually bread and water.... Too weak and jaded to be taught....

A commission of inquiry, hurriedly convened after Andrews's death, recalled in its report that crank labor had the explicit sanction of Parliament. While censuring the governor for excess of zeal, it did not recommend his dismissal or a relaxation of the Birmingham "system." It concluded that Edward Andrews's death was unfortunate but not a matter for criminal prosecution.[1]

This sort of episode recurs so frequently in prison history that we could easily miss what was historically specific about the case to the reform era. While one can never be sure, it is a good guess that a petty offender like Andrews would not have been sent to prison at all in the eighteenth century. Had he been apprehended or prosecuted—unlikely in itself, given the state of the police—he would have been whipped or reprimanded and delivered back to his master. In the nineteenth century, he was sent to endure a new, historically specific type of pain—the straitjacket, the hand crank, the hallucinations engendered by solitude—and he was sent to endure them alone. In the "reformed" prison, the inmate collectivity that might have intervened to prevent his total victimization had been broken up and silenced. The crowds of outsiders whose presence in the yards of eighteenth century institutions acted as a rough check on custodial power were all but barred by the victory of reform. The inspectors who Howard hoped would keep an eye on guards and governors were either ignored as in the Birmingham case, or chose to offer supine justifications of the conduct of prison officers. In the institution that the reform tradition built for Edward Andrews, there was no one to support him, no one to hear his defiance. His death in a "reformed" institution was not, therefore, an irony of reform but its inevitable consequence. Had Howard lived to see his offspring, he might well have denied paternity; but the Birminghams and the Pentonvilles were his children nonetheless.

To interpret the history of reform as a cycle of good intentions confounded by unintended consequences is to see it as a history of failure. But reform was a success. By 1860, most prisoners in Europe and North America marched to Howard's cadence and endured the solitude of his visions.

Yet if it is success that needs explaining, it is a success full of paradox. The movement that began with Howard established among a skeptical, middle-class public the ideal that prisons ought to reform, without ever having to convince them that penitentiaries actually did so. Indeed, the movement felt it did not even have to try. Typically, few reformers ever bothered to torture the recidivism rates into a validation of the penitentiary. In fact, faith in the reformative potential of incarceration among the middle class proved able to survive repeated demonstrations of its failure.

Similarly, episodes like the suicide of Edward Andrews continued to dog the new prisons' reputation for "humanity"; yet the public appears to have accepted the claim of the reformers that such abuses could eventually be checked by vigilant inspection and formalized systems of institutional accountability. While the further bureaucratization of prison command structures has done little to lessen the vulnerability of inmates to victimization, the reform tradition and the general public continue to this day to put their trust in creating new watchdogs to watch the old ones. Likewise, faith in penitentiaries as deterrents has persisted in the face of evidence that levels of crime do not vary significantly with levels of penal severity. The general decline of crime rates after 1855 in England, for example, owed little or nothing to the consolidation of the penitentiary system, and much more to the general rise in real wages among the working class.

The failure of the penitentiary to live up to its promise was obvious to Victorian critics like Charles Dickens and Henry Mayhew. Yet even they found it impossible to extricate themselves from the logic of Howardian premises. Their attacks upon the penitentiary lacked the internal consistency of a radical dissent. Both criticized the penitentiary for being too severe on the one hand and not severe enough on the other. Their inability to suggest a genuine alternative strategy of social control suggests that public debate about penitentiaries masked a consensus at a deeper level.

Yet it was a curious consensus, since it did not rest on the demonstrated effectiveness of the institution as an agency of deterrence or reform. The critics had made its shortcomings all too obvious. Still, we cannot conclude that this consensus was sustained simply by an absence of alternatives. Institutions cannot survive the volume of criticism that penitentiaries received simply because no one can think of anything better. The penitentiaries had to offer something to justify their enormous expense, even if it wasn't functional efficiency.

The persistent support for the penitentiary is inexplicable so long as we assume that its appeal rested on its functional capacity to control crime. Instead, its support rested on a larger social need. It had appeal because the reformers succeeded in presenting it as a response, not merely to crime, but to the whole social crisis of a period, and as part of a larger strategy of political, social, and legal reform designed to reestablish order on a new foundation. As a result, while criticized for its functional shortcomings, the penitentiary continued to command support because it was seen as an element of a larger vision of order that by the 1840s commanded the reflexive assent of the propertied and powerful.

In elaborating this new strategy of order, the prison reformers convinced their class of the gravity of crime by illustrating its connection to the deeper social and economic transformations of the age. This new environmentalism used the perspective of associationist psychology to illuminate the idea that a criminal career could be initiated by bad social associations and economic misfortune. Using this perspective, reformers drew a connection between the rising tide of property crime and the erosion of the estate, household, and artisanal economies that sustained "paternal" social relationships. They pointed particularly to the aggregation of masterless urban populations and the resulting estrangement of rich and poor. In this analysis, crime figured as a form of social envy, resentment, or desperation. In place of a traditional view of crime as merely an immemorial form of human wickedness and sin, the reformers succeeded in popularizing a new vocabulary of alarmism that interpreted crime as an indictment of a society in crisis.

The reformers' ideological success has been such that there is nowadays an unreflecting bias in favor of environmentalist criminology. Hence it can only seem paradoxical that this environmentalism acted historically to legitimize heightened intolerance not only for crime, but for other forms of popular disorder like the riot, which now seemed linked to crime as another manifestation of the collective estrangement of a class.

Since this environmental analysis implied that the rich bore some responsibility for the social genesis of crime, its premises helped to activate a wave of guilt-ridden philanthropic activism, especially among liberal, scientific, commercial Dissenters. Many historians have been convinced that this tradition was powered by a new sense of affinity with the poor and a revulsion at the accepted cruelties of existing class relations. But if one returns to the pages of Howard, Hanway, or Colquhoun, one encounters the language of "police," not "humanity."

While the social doctrine of the new philanthropy was often backward-looking and paternalist in tone, its actual prescriptions represented an attack on the traditional social order for resting on a weak state, tolerance of popular disorder, and a tacit acceptance of popular privileges and customs. The reformers insisted on the fragility of this order, especially its dependence on ritual displays of terror. Such terror, they insisted, could only secure grudging compliance from the poor. In a period of tumultuous economic and social change, coerced compliance was no longer enough. Social order, they argued, had to be guaranteed by something stronger than a frayed and increasingly hollow paternalism, backed up by hangings. Social stability had to be founded on popular consent, maintained by guilt at the thought of wrongdoing, rather than by deference and fear.

This conception of social order took shape in the writings of the Nonconformist radicals Burgh, Price, and Priestley. Their critique of a political system oiled by patronage at home and sustained by arbitrariness abroad echoed and reinforced Howard's exposure of prison abuses. Both underlined the corrupt, threadbare reality of paternalism and suggested the fragility of an order based ideologically upon it. The possibility of social breakdown loomed large once the turbulence of the Wilkes and Liberty agitation of the 1760s, the uproarious disorders of the Tyburn processional, the Gordon Riots of 1780, and the crime epidemic of 1783–85 were viewed through the bifocals of alarmism. The suspension of transportation in 1775 offered the reformers a pretext not only to devise an alternative to banishment, but to create a new concept of punishment embodying a more stringent and rational strategy of order.

This approach, articulated best by Bentham, envisaged fortifying the bonds of popular consent by means of enfranchisement, extension of civil and religious rights, and administrative reform, while at the same time tightening the grip of the law over the disobedient. In contrast to a paternalist conception of order that allowed only a constricted political right, but tolerated a wider range of customary, popular liberties, liberalism extended formal political rights while sharply reducing public tolerance for popular disorder. Hence Bentham's two personae—the advocate of parliamentary reform, and the publicist for the Panopticon—were not contradictory, but complementary. The extension of rights within civil society had to be compensated for by the abolition of the tacit liberties enjoyed by prisoners and criminals under the *ancien régime*. In an unequal and increasingly divided society, this was the only way to extend liberty and fortify consent without compromising security.

Alexis de Tocqueville was struck by the Janus-faced character of democratic liberalism during his tour of America in 1835. While brooding on his work about American democracy, he was also inspecting America's prisons. At one point, he and his companion, Gustave de Beaumont, remarked, "While society in the United States gives the example of the most extended liberty, the prisons of the same country offer the spectacle of the most complete despotism."[2] Outside was a scrambling and competitive egalitarianism; inside, an unprecedented carceral totalitarianism. Indeed, the creation of the "total institution" in America during the 1820s coincided exactly with the flowering of Jacksonian democracy. This seems paradoxical only if we assume that liberal egalitarianism advances hand in hand with tolerance. In fact, as Tocqueville so clearly sensed, the advent of democracy was characterized by an increasing intolerance towards "deviant" minorities. The tyranny of the majority took as its symbol and instrument the silence, the lockstep, and the bullwhip of Auburn penitentiary. It also expressed itself in a new attempt to mold and "reform" the criminal conscience.

Howard's success in presenting the reformative ideal as a vision of humane moral reclamation has obscured its function as a legitimation for an intensification of carceral power. In much the same way, the historians of liberalism have neglected the way in which the extension of popular sovereignty was accompanied by the elaboration of institutions and the deployment of philanthropic strategies designed to implant the inner disciplinarians of guilt and compunction in working-class consciences. As Howard and Bentham saw it, the penitentiary was conceived as a machine for the social production of guilt.

The same psychological assumptions that inspired Condorcet's and Helvetius's faith in human perfectibility, served, when applied to questions of punishment, to validate the notion that criminals were defective mechanisms whose consciences could be remolded in the sensory quarantine of a total environment. The social anxieties of the middle class in the 1790s ensured that this hard faith in human malleability soon received operational formulation at the hands of the medical profession, in asylums for the insane, Houses of Industry for paupers, hospitals for the sick, and penitentiaries for the criminal. In each environment, the poor were to be "cured" of immorality, disease, insanity, or crime, as well as related defects of body and mind, by isolation, exhortations, and regimens of obedience training.

In the penitentiary, the agency of cure was contrition. Yet the anguish of guilt could only be aroused, the reformers realized, in an environment whose self-evident humaneness confirmed the moral authority of the state and forced prisoners to recognize their culpability. Solitary confinement appeared to offer this perfect reconciliation of humanity and terror. It epitomized the liberal utopia of a punishment so rational that offenders would punish themselves in the soundless, silent anguish of their own minds.

The reformative ideal had deep appeal for an anxious middle class because it implied that the punisher and the punished could be brought back together in a shared moral universe. As a hopeful allegory for class relations in general, it proved capable of surviving the repeated frustrations of reality because it spoke to a heartfelt middle-class desire for a social order based on deferential reconciliation. Just how heartfelt and how wishful this desire was can be seen in the repeated credulity of Victorian chaplains in particular and the middle class in general towards patently contrived criminal repentances. It has also been reflected in the willingness of so many later historians to accept the reformers' project as a simple humanitarian crusade to bring prisoners into the fold of civil society.

To be sure, the reformers' rejection of the idea of incorrigibility opened up the possibility of recognizing criminals as human beings entitled to protection from extortion, brutality, and disease.

Yet this very claim of the inmates to social protection, as the reformers articulated it, was made conditional on their willingness to reform. The reformers did extend the state's obligations to prisoners, but not on the basis of a full recognition of their rights as human beings. Their right to decent treatment remained conditional on their willingness to reenter the moral consensus.

In the Victorian philanthropic tradition, prisoners were not the only ones whose right to be treated as human beings was made conditional on their submission to moral improvement. No attempt to raise the housing, educational, or sanitary standard of the poor was made without an accompanying attempt to colonize their minds. In this tradition, humanitarianism was inextricably linked to the practice of domination. The extension of the state's obligation to its citizens was invariably justified in terms of recasting their characters into that caricature of ascetic rectitude that the rich adopted as their self-image.

At first, the severity of this reformative vision repelled traditional paternalists accustomed to ignoring or tolerating the moral waywardness of the poor. Even some reformers like Howard drew back from the implications of their own disciplinary vision. Other liberal reformers, Romilly for one, felt that Bentham's adjudication of the claims of liberty and the claims of order in civil society had erred too far on the side of order. Outside the reform camp successive waves of political prisoners hammered away not only at solitary confinement and the penitentiary routine, but also at the willingness of ruling classes, when faced with radical opposition, to suspend or ignore the constitutional rights of subjects in the name of order and stability. While this tradition of radical opposition did not succeed in deflecting or delaying the consolidation of a network of total institutions, it did prevent the rich and powerful from successfully legitimizing such institutions to the poor as neutral arbiters above class conflict.

In the face of this opposition, the penitentiary slowly inserted itself into the realm of the taken-for-granted. Its silent rows of cells, the shaved heads of its prisoners, and the metronome of its routine gradually lost their strangeness. The institution took its place within a structure of other institutions so interrelated in function, so similar in design, discipline, and language of command that together the sheer massiveness of their presence in the Victorian landscape inhibited further challenge to their logic.

It was no accident that penitentiaries, asylums, workhouses, monitorial schools, night refuges, and reformatories looked alike, or that their charges marched to the same disciplinary cadence. Since they made up a complementary and interdependent structure of control, it was essential that their diets and deprivations be calibrated on an ascending scale, school–workhouse–asylum–prison, with the pain of the last serving to undergird the pain of the first.

Nor was it accidental that these state institutions so closely resembled the factory. As we have seen, Wedgwood, Strutt, and Boulton, the creators of the new factory discipline, drew inspiration from the same discourse on authority as the makers of the prison: Nonconformist asceticism, faith in human improvability through discipline, and the liberal theory of the state. The intensification of labor discipline went hand in hand with the elaboration of the freedom of a market in labor, just as the extension of popular suffrage proceeded together with the extension of a structure of carceral power.

Given the economic, ideological, and social connections between prison reformers and the new industrial employers, it is not surprising that the reformers assumed that a prison should be run like a "well-ordered manufactory," as Buxton put it. In this way, penal and industrial discipline developed along the same trajectory of severity.

It was just this resonance with the well-ordered manufactory, the workhouse, the asylum that made the penitentiary plausible, despite its evident failure to reform or deter. Its order was the order of industry; its "humanity," the conscience of philanthropic activism. By 1850 to challenge its logic was to challenge not just one discrete institution, but the interlocked structure of a whole encircling industrial order.

I I

It is easier to explain the coming of the penitentiary than it is to decide how that history continues to constrain the present and define the future. In one sense, Pentonville is gone. Its silence has been broken and its routine has been shattered. In another sense, it is still there, a Victorian carapace of spaces and walls that continues to constrain any attempt at a new start.

In much the same way, it is difficult to establish the historical significance of the present impasse in punishment, the decade of riot, the rising public disillusionment with incarceration, and the outpouring of proposals for reform. Criticism of the penitentiary, as we have seen, has been endemic to its history. Riots have happened before. Yet this time many people seem to believe something fundamental is beginning to happen. One historian has even suggested that the last decade has seen the beginning of the end of the "total institution."[3] This would imply that the 1970s are witnessing a fundamental departure from the traditions and vision described in this book.

It is true that there has been a trend underway since the mid-1950s to divert offenders from the "total institution" by means of probation, early parole, and the expansion of community treatment options. This attempt to expand the alternatives to confinement has resulted in an estimated decline in the American prison population from 120.8 per 10,000 population in 1961 to 96.7 a decade later. "Decarceration" has also been gathering momentum in the mental health field, with the closure of state mental hospitals and their replacement by drug maintenance and outpatient treatment schemes. The resident population of state and county mental hospitals in the United States has declined from 504,600 in 1963 to 215,600 in 1974.[4]

There is a growing consensus that the penitentiary ought to be used only for the confinement of the "dangerous" 10 to 15 percent of the prison population serving sentences for violent personal or property offenses. In addition, the new institutions envisaged for such offenders would carry further the relaxation of internal discipline already observable in prisons in the last twenty-five years. Inmates would recover opportunities for choice in dress, personal timetable, and room decoration. They would also have increased access to family, friends, and the press. More important, they would be free to choose whether to participate in rehabilitation programs. The length of their sentences would no longer be contingent on willingness to accept therapy.[5]

Decarceration and a liberalization of institutional regimes would indeed be significant if they represented a fundamental move to reduce the social distance between deviance and the community and to extend the bounds of social tolerance. However, a recent study has concluded that decarceration represents an attempt to meet the growing "fiscal crisis of the state" by cutting back on costly institutional treatment and replacing it with cheaper noninstitutional forms of control. The numbers arrested for criminal offenses continue to rise, and an increasing range of interpersonal unhappiness is being brought within the jurisdiction of state psychiatric and psychological "services." In fact, the proportion of the population sent to the "carceral archipelago" has not been reduced, since the archipelago has added some new islands, the halfway house, drug treatment centers, restitution centers, and outpatient clinics. In many instances, these supposedly noncarceral alternatives continue to rely on the threat of reimprisonment to maintain discipline and compliance among their "clients." In the case of mental patients released following closure of state mental hospitals, the hopeful rhetoric of "community treatment" often conceals a cruel irony. Many patients released from hospitals for outpatient treatment find themselves living a twilight existence of welfare checks and drug maintenance in inner-city ghettos, harassed and victimized by local criminals.[6]

Within the new institutions built to replace the Victorian penitentiary, the liberalization of discipline appears to represent a belated attempt, often under pressure of riot, to raise the level of institutional amenities to the standard made possible on the outside by the economic expansion in the sixties and the spread of easy-credit consumerism among the working class. Some of the new prisons look like college campuses, the cell blocks like dormitories, and the prisoners like students. Technological developments in security, such as the TV camera and heat and metal detectors, have made it possible to do away with the intensive personal surveillance of the Victorian institution and its panopticon architecture. The prison's power may be less perceptible in these settings, but it is hard to see how it has become less total.

This is not to suggest that nothing has changed within the last decade. Decarceration, more probation, faster parole, and shorter sentences have benefited many prisoners and will continue to benefit them as long as there are liberal-minded administrators brave enough to stand up to the vociferous opposition that these measures have aroused. Simply for the men and women who have been saved from the death-in-life of long-term imprisonment, these measures have been worthwhile.

What is much less clear is whether the scope of public tolerance for "deviance" has enlarged at all during the recent decade of reform. The rhetoric of the "permissive" society might encourage one to think so, as might the recent hard-won victories of homosexuals and women against sexual and economic discrimination. Yet the welcome liberalization of sexual codes and hiring practices may be deceptive, first because of the oft-discussed ability of the shapers of mass opinion in this society to incorporate forms of "deviation" without fundamentally broadening the bounds of the permissible; and second, because the apparent increase of toleration in one field often seems to bring its contraction in other fields. Judging from the current discussion of rape, for example, one can easily imagine that the public's awakening to the extent of sexual crimes against women may result in an increasingly punitive and intolerant attitude towards rapists. This is a familiar paradox of toleration in a liberal society. The increasingly permissive public attitude towards choices of sexual and personal life style may then be no indication that definition and treatment of the lawbreaker are likely to become more tolerant.

Such toleration does not appear to increase with the consolidation of social order. Despite the fact that the modern state has appropriated to itself a degree of power that would have thoroughly terrified our eighteenth century ancestors, public discussion about social control in Western society conveys the impression of a state barely able to hold the line against criminality and terrorism. This alarmism, which seems so exaggerated if looked at from the vantage point of a Londoner of the riotous 1770s, acts to legitimize ever more intrusive police deployment. Whatever the sources of this deep-seated anxiety about disorder in modern societies, it is significant that the historical consolidation by the 1860s of a structure of total institutions and policing did not succeed in quieting fears of disorder but only exacerbated them. Apparently, order breeds not peace of mind but greater anxiety and recurring demands for more order. It is a need that knows no satisfaction, at least not in this type of society.

In this society, the imperative to control, to dominate, and to subdue is written deep into the structures of those ways of thinking we call the "human sciences." At the genesis of these sciences in the eighteenth century, their premise that men could be scientifically described and understood was immediately translated into institutional strategies of control and "reform." The very act of describing human activity as scientifically knowable implied that it could be subdued, modified, and improved. This was so because these human sciences took their purpose from a context of demands within the ruling class for new techniques of social control. In much the same way, the philanthropic impulse in such a context found itself channeled into projects of coercive "improvement."

Today, the elaboration of the human sciences is canalized by its "field" work in the rationalization of human activity for corporations and the state. In the factory personnel office, in the courtroom, in the schools, at the welfare office, psychologists and social workers use the diagnostic tests—the IQ, Rorschach, TAT—as well as the whole conceptual apparatus of the psychological and behavioral disciplines to select, compare, position, hire, improve, and control individuals. Hence, as theoretical discourses, these "sciences" are of necessity enmeshed in the development of further diagnostic and interpretive instruments of a similar nature. As professions, behavioral science, medicine, and psychology derive so much of their authority from the service of corporations and the state that it is difficult to see how they can visualize a person scientifically except as an object to be predicted, controlled, and improved.

This is not to deny that the medical, psychological, and behavioral sciences have succeeded in devising chemical and therapeutic agents of demonstrated effectiveness in controlling symptoms of genuine personal unhappiness and disorientation. Nor do I wish to deny the value of the psychological therapies that attempt to make personal dilemmas bearable or comprehensible. It is simply that the advent of a therapeutic society has hidden costs.[7] The very prestige of these sciences of the mind seems to make possible a range of new types of abuse, abuses typically endured not by property-owning, law-abiding male adults, but by children, women, minorities, the propertyless, and the politically voiceless. In a society whose law-abiding adults are medicating themselves in such numbers, it is scarcely surprising to find school boards tranquilizing "hyperactive" children, or prisons and mental hospitals maintaining their charges in chemically induced states of nausea, fatigue, and dependency. Such abuses are not ironies, but necessary consequences of a tradition of trust in scientific devices for the control of human activity. The taste for therapy of verbal or chemical varieties is more than a fad. It has two hundred years of tradition behind it. The abuses of behavior modification and token economy schemes in prison are the fruits, not simply of the behaviorist zealotry of individuals, but of a tradition of psychological thinking that dates back to the blithely reductive assertions of Cabanis and Offray de la Mettrie that men were malleable things.

The point being made here is not a Luddite condemnation of the "human sciences" in toto, but simply the observation that the

prospects for increasing social tolerance appear dim as long as we
continue to apprehend and comprehend "deviance" through traditions of thought so deeply implicated in the business of finding
new ways of controlling and subduing it. Yet it would be fatalistic
to conclude that such sciences exclusively define the modes of
public perception or that they have driven from our cognitive field
any possibility of alternative vision. This would appear to be the
conclusion of Michel Foucault's *Discipline and Punish*, his account
of the coming of the penitentiary in France; and yet of course his
own work is a triumphant demonstration of the falsity of his own
fatalism.

As Foucault and others have proved, history, as one of the
human sciences, has a discrete but important role to play in com-
bating carceral power and the coercive structures of thought that
underpin it. It can explicate the genesis of structures of scientific
argument about human nature and deviance and can establish the
connections between this structure and the imperatives of class
rule. Above all, it can help to pierce through the rhetoric that
ceaselessly presents the further consolidation of carceral power as
a "reform." As much as anything else, it is this suffocating vision
of the past that legitimizes the abuses of the present and seeks to
adjust us to the cruelties of the future.

List of Abbreviations Used

Beds. R.O.	Bedfordshire Record Office
Berks. R.O.	Berkshire Record Office
C.L.R.O.	City of London Record Office
D.N.B.	Dictionary of National Biography
Econ. Hist. Rev.	Economic History Review
Gloucs. R.O.	Gloucestershire Record Office
H.O.	Home Office Papers, Public Record Office
J.H.C.	Journals of the House of Commons
Lancs. R. O.	Lancashire Record Office
Mepol	Metropolitan Police Commission Records, Public Record Office
Msex. R.O.	Middlesex Record Office
O.E.D.	Oxford English Dictionary
Oxon R.O.	Oxfordshire Record Office
P/COM	Prison Commission Files, Public Record Office
P.P.	Parliamentary Papers
P.R.O.	Public Record Office
Proceedings	Old Bailey Sessions Papers, Guildhall Library, City of London; Law School, Harvard University
S.P.	State Papers Domestic, Public Record Office
Staffs. R.O.	Staffordshire Record Office
W. Sussex R.O.	West Sussex Record Office

Notes

PREFACE

[1]Tom Wicker, *A Time to Die*, 1975, p. 46. See also New York State Special Commission on Attica, *Attica: The Official Report*, 1972.

CHAPTER ONE. Pentonville

[1]Thomas Carlyle, "Model Prisons," in *Latter-Day Pamphlets*, 1850; Uriah Heep ends his career as a "model prisoner" at Pentonville; see Charles Dickens, *David Copperfield*, also Philip Collins, *Dickens and Crime*, 1962; for more items in the controversy about Pentonville see "The Model Prison or Poor Man's Palace," in *The Penny Satirist*, December 19, 1840; Peter Laurie, *Killing No Murder; or the Effects of Separate Confinement on the Bodily and Mental Condition of Prisoners in the Government Prisons*, 1846; U. R. Q. Henriques, "The Rise and Decline of the Separate System of Prison Discipline," *Past and Present* 54, 1972.

[2]P/COM/2/86, October 1846. Prince Napoleon Bonaparte visited Pentonville; the Duke of Wellington was another visitor.

[3]The version of a day at Pentonville is taken largely from Henry Mayhew's incomparable account in his *Criminal Prisons of London*, 1861, pp. 113–99. I have taken further details of the daily routine from P/COM/2/84–86; and from P.P. 1843, XXIX; P.P. 1844, XXVIII; P.P. 1846, XX; P.P. 1847, XXX; P.P. 1847–48, XXXIV; P.P. 1849, XXVI.

[4]From 1842 to 1848 the period in solitude was 18 months; from 1848 to 1852, 12 months; and thereafter, 9 months. On completion of their sentence, Pentonville prisoners were sent to the public works prisons at Portland, Dartmoor, and Chatham, or transported. The penitentiary stage of their sentence was only a preliminary penance.

[5]Mayhew, *Prisons*, p. 141.

[6]Psalm 100.

[7]John Clay, *Twenty-Five Sermons Preached to Inmates of a Gaol*, 1827, p. 136; also W. L. Clay, *The Prison Chaplain: Memoirs of the Reverend John Clay*, 1867.

[8]George Withers's "characteristics" are taken from a series of prisoner dossiers to be found in P/COM/3/30–31.

[9]Mayhew, *Prisons*, p. 146; also Anon., *Five Years Penal Servitude by One Who Has Endured It*, 1878, p. 156, for a convict's description of the medical ritual of initiation.

[10]Mayhew, *Prisons*, p. 146.

[11]P.P. 1847, XXX, p. 372.

[12]Psalm 102.

[13]These cases are taken from P.P. 1852–53, LI, p. 12, p. 34; also P/COM/2/84–86.

[14]P.P. 1854, XXXIII, p. 22.

[15]Mayhew, *Prisons*, p. 104.

[16]P.P. 1864, XXVI, p. 43.

[17]P/COM/3/21; P.P. 1856, XXXV, p. 91; P.P. 1859, XIII, p. 81; P.P. 1846, XX, p. 12; 148 of the 616 prisoners at Pentonville were punished during the year 1845.

[18]Mayhew, *Prisons*, p. 132.

[19]P.P. 1847, XXX, p. 42; H.O. 21/4.

[20]P/COM/2/88. Officers on board the ships transporting Pentonville convicts to Australia reported that many of the convicts had "hysterical convulsions" and crying fits on the days following their release. For a description of the experience of release from solitary confinement, see Alexander Berkman, *Prison Memoirs of an Anarchist*, 1912.

[21]R. B. Pugh, *Imprisonment in Medieval England*, 1968; R. H. Tawney and Eileen Power, eds., *Tudor Economic Documents*, 1924, II, p. 332; Sidney Webb and Beatrice Webb, *English Prisons Under Local Government*, 1927, pp. 4–12.

[22]C. P. Hill, *Society and Puritanism in Pre-Revolutionary England*, 1964, p. 483; A. L. Beier, "Vagrants and the Social Order in Elizabethan England," *Past and Present* 64, August 1974; Frank Aydelotte, *Elizabethan Rogues and Vagabonds*, 1913; C. J. Ribton-Turner, *A History of Vagrants and Beggars and Begging*, 1887, pp. 120–21.

[23]J. T. Sellin, *Pioneering in Penology: The Amsterdam House of Correction in the Sixteenth and Seventeenth Centuries*, 1944.

[24]*Ibid.*, frontispiece; Webb and Webb, *Prisons*, p. 4.

[25]Georg Rusche and Otto Kirchheimer, *Punishment and Social Structure*, 1939, p. 24; T. S. Ashton, *The Eighteenth Century*, 1955, p. 39; William A. Bonger, *Criminality and Economic Conditions*, 1916, pp. 246–90.

[26]Dudley W. R. Bahlman, *The Moral Revolution of 1688*, 1957; Leon Radzinowicz, *A History of English Criminal Law*, 1947–1956, II, p. 15; Robert Nelson, *An Address to Persons of Quality and Estate*, 1715; Sidney Webb and Beatrice Webb, *English Poor Law History*, 1927, I, pp. 91–110; Bristol Corporation, *An Account of the Proceedings of the Corporation of Bristol . . . for the Better Employing and Maintaining of the Poor*, 1700; Thomas Firmin, *Some Proposals for the Employing of the Poor . . .* , 1678; John Bellers, *Proposals for Raising a Colledge of Industry . . .* , 1696;

John Locke, "Report to the Board of Trade" (1696), in H. R. Fox-Bourne, *The Life of John Locke*, 1876, II, pp. 377–91.

[27]Anon., *An Account of Workhouses*, 1724, p. 1; Webb and Webb, *Poor Law History*, I, p. 216.

[28]Dorothy Marshall, *The English Poor in the Eighteenth Century*, 1926, p. 128; Matthew Marryott, *An Account of Workhouses*, 1730; John Marriot, *A Representation of Some Mismanagements by Parish Officers*, 1726.

[29]Richard Burn, *History of the Poor Laws*, 1764, p. 192; F. M. Eden, *The State of the Poor*, 1795, II, pp. 619–23; Marshall, *English Poor*, p. 153; Arthur Young, *A General View of the Agriculture of Suffolk*, 1794, appendix by Thomas Ruggles; Isaac Wood, *Some Account of the Shrewsbury House of Industry*, 1792.

[30]R. Potter, *Observations on the Poor Laws . . .*, 1775; Webb and Webb, *Poor Law History*, I, pp. 139–43; Reports of the Committees of the House of Commons, 1715–1801, IX, Poor Law Committee Returns, 1775–1786.

[31]Jonas Hanway, *The Defects of Police . . .*, 1775, p. 134; Bentham Mss., 107/15/48; John Howard, *An Account of the Principal Lazarettos of Europe*, 1789, p. 210; Howard disapproved of the practice of the "workhouse test" as an abridgment of the rights of the poor to relief. See Chapter 5, p. 111 above.

CHAPTER TWO. **Eighteenth Century Punishment**

[1]*Proceedings*, Old Bailey, 1770–1774 (Harvard Law School Collection); see also J. M. Beattie, "Punishment in England, 1660–1800," an unpublished paper, 1972, on sentencing patterns in Surrey assize and sessions.

[2]*Proceedings*, 1763, session 3; 1764, session 4; 1767, session 6; 1771, session 1; see also George Rudé, *Wilkes and Liberty*, 1962, pp. 65–103.

[3]Calendar of Home Office Papers, Geo. III, October 25, 1773.

[4]Douglas Hay, "Property, Authority and the Criminal Law," in Hay et al., *Albion's Fatal Tree*, 1975, pp. 17–64.

[5]Leon Radzinowicz, *A History of English Criminal Law*, 1947–1956, I, p. 4.

[6]E. P. Thompson, *Whigs and Hunters*, 1975, passim.

[7]William Blackstone, *Commentaries on the Laws of England*, 1769, IV, pp. 233–37.

[8]Thompson, *Whigs and Hunters*, p. 22.

[9]Blackstone, *Commentaries*, IV, p. 246; also Peter Linebaugh in Society for the Study of Labour History, *Bulletin*, no. 25, 1972.

[10]Radzinowicz, *History of Criminal Law*, I, p. 156.

[11]PRO/SP/44/92, Criminal Letter Book, April 8, 1775.

[12]John Howard, *An Account of the Principal Lazarettos of Europe*, 1789, table 1, Appendix; on the operation and ideological function of pardons see Hay, "Property, Authority and Criminal Law."

[13]Beattie, "Punishment," p. 4; J. S. Cockburn, *A History of English Assizes, 1558–1714*, 1972, p. 128.

[14]Blackstone, *Commentaries*, IV, p. 363, on benefit of clergy; on housebreaking, p. 240.

[15]Beattie, "Punishment," p. 38.

[16]Blackstone, *Commentaries*, IV, pp. 132, 241.

[17]Radzinowicz, *History of Criminal Law*, I, p. 150.

[18]Blackstone, *Commentaries,* IV, p. 390; Samuel Romilly, *Observations on a Late Publication . . . ,* 1786, p. 42.

[19]Blackstone, *Commentaries,* IV, pp. 277–78; Richard Burn, *The Justice of the Peace and Parish Officer,* 1st ed., 1755, II, "Summary Justice."

[20]*Hansard,* XIX, March 29, 1811, col. 638.

[21]Radzinowicz, *History of Criminal Law,* II, p. 74.

[22]Such tenderness by prosecutors does not begin in the 1750s. See R. H. Tawney and Eileen Power, eds., *Tudor Economic Documents,* 1924, II, p. 341, for pleas by prosecutors in 1596.

[23]*Proceedings,* 1770–1774.

[24]*Ibid.,* 1770.

[25]Georg Rusche and Otto Kirchheimer, *Punishment and Social Structure,* 1939, p. 32.

[26]*Proceedings,* 1770–1774.

[27]Surrey R.O., QS/2/1/24, 1775.

[28]E. P. Thompson, "The Moral Economy of the Eighteenth Century Crowd," *Past and Present* 50, 1971, pp. 76–136.

[29]Place Mss., B. M. Add. Mss. 27826/178.

[30]Peter Linebaugh, "The Tyburn Riot Against the Surgeons," in Hay et al., *Albion's Fatal Tree,* pp. 65–118.

[31]C.L.R.O., Crooke, *Sermons,* 1695, p. 2.

[32]*Proceedings,* 1770.

[33]Ordinary of Newgate *Account,* June 16, 1693 (Guildhall Library Collection).

[34]Newgate *Calendar* or Malefactors' Bloody Register, London, 1773, IV, p. 79 (Guildhall Library Collection). The editor of the *Calendar* approved of Sheriff's Janssen's decision to request disbanding the military power, called out to guard against a rescue of Bosavern Penlez, on October 18, 1749.

[35]Bernard Mandeville, *An Enquiry into the Causes of the Frequent Executions at Tyburn,* 1725, p. 33.

[36]William Paley, *Principles of Moral and Political Philosophy,* 1811 ed., p. 434; Radzinowicz, *History of Criminal Law,* I, p. 28.

[37]Olwen Hufton, *The Poor of Eighteenth Century France,* 1974, p. 221.

[38]John Fielding, *A Plan for Preventing Robberies Within Twenty Miles of London,* 1755; William Smith, *Mild Punishment Sound Policy,* 1778.

[39]David D. Cooper, *The Lesson of the Scaffold,* 1975.

[40]Blackstone, *Commentaries,* IV, pp. 277–78.

[41]Richard Burn, *Justice of the Peace and Parish Officer,* 1st ed., 1755, II, "Summary Justice."

[42]17 Geo. II, cap. 5; also Radzinowicz, *History of Criminal Law,* III, pp. 68–71.

[43]W. E. Minchinton, ed., *Wage Regulation in Pre-Industrial England,* 1972, p. 11; C. P. Hill, *Reformation to Industrial Revolution,* 1967, pp. 40–41.

[44]"Report of the Committee . . . Appointed to Consider the Several Returns . . .", April 1, 1779, House of Commons Papers, Geo. III, XXXI (Scholarly Resources Reprint Series, 1975), p. 8.

[45]J. M. Beattie, "The Pattern of Crime in England: 1660–1800," *Past and Present* 62, 1974, p. 57.

[46]Blackstone, *Commentaries,* IV, pp. 174–75.

[47]Burn, *Justice of the Peace*, p. 445.

[48]Sidney Pollard, *The Genesis of Modern Management*, 1965, p. 31; D. S. Landes, *The Unbound Prometheus*, 1969, pp. 44, 54, 56, 71, 82, 118–19.

[49]T. S. Ashton, *The Eighteenth Century*, 1955, p. 102; Peter Linebaugh in Labour History Society, *Bulletin*, 1972; P.P. 1802–03, V, p. 16.

[50]P.P. 1806, III, p. 101; Burn, *Justice of the Peace*, "Embezzlement."

[51]Ashton, *Eighteenth Century*, p. 210.

[52]P.P. 1802–03, V, p. 16; Landes, *Unbound Prometheus*, p. 59; Ephraim Lipson, *A History of the Woollen and Worsted Industries*, 1921, p. 253.

[53]K. G. Ponting, *A History of the West of England Cloth Industry*, 1957, p. 115; J. de L. Mann, *The Cloth Industry in the West of England from 1640 to 1880*, 1971, p. 114.

[54]Henry Fielding, *An Enquiry into the Causes of the Late Increase of Robbers ...*, 1751, p. 15.

[55]Radzinowicz, *History of Criminal Law*, III, p. 67.

[56]"Report from the Committee Appointed to Make Inquiries Relating to the Employment, Relief and Maintenance of the Poor ...," May 21, 1776, schedule 4, House of Commons Papers, Geo. III, XXXI (Scholarly Resources Reprint Series, 1975).

[57]For example, see G. O. Paul's *Address to the Justices of the Peace ...*, 1789, p. 49.

[58]John Howard, *The State of the Prisons in England and Wales ...*, 1777, appendix.

[59]Minchinton, *Wage Regulation*, p. 22; Hill, *Reformation to Industrial Revolution*, p. 39.

[60]Howard, *State of the Prisons*, pp. 235–41.

[61]P.P. 1814–15, IV, pp. 18–19.

[62]*Ibid.*, p. 21; Howard, *Lazarettos*, p. 219.

[63]*Ibid.*, appendix.

[64]Howard, *State of the Prisons*, p. 35.

[65]Latimer, *Annals of Bristol: The Eighteenth Century*, p. 454.

[66]Howard, *State of the Prisons*, p. 4.

[67]House of Commons Reports, 1776, XXXI, schedule 4.

[68]Pollard, *Modern Management*, p. 46.

[69]Howard, *State of the Prisons*, p. 4.

[70]Jacob Ilive, *Reasons Offered for the Reformation of the House of Correction, Clerkenwell*, 1757; also his *Scheme for the Employment of All Persons Sent as Disorderly to the House of Correction in Clerkenwell*, 1759.

[71]House of Commons Papers, Geo. III, XXXI, 1779, p. 8.

[72]J.H.C. XXXII, 1770, pp. 878–83.

[73]C.L.R.O., Gaol Committee, 1760, 1813, Accounts for Bread.

[74]House of Commons Papers, 1779, pp. 7–8.

[75]Howard, *Lazarettos*, p. 145.

[76]Geoffrey Mynshul, *Essays and Characters of a Prison and Prisoners*, 1618.

[77]P.P. 1813–14, IV, p. 59; P.P. 1817, VII, p. 347.

[78]Howard, *State of the Prisons*, p. 14.

[79]Surrey R.O. QS 5/1, Committee Minute Books, 1769–1779, 1771.

[80]C.L.R.O., Small Mss. Box tr. 8. (1755).

[81]George Holford, *Thoughts on the Criminal Prisons of this Country*, 1821; Webb and Webb, *Prisons*, p. 11.

[82]Howard, *Lazarettos*, p. 233.

[83]Howard, *State of the Prisons*, p. 243; Ilive, *Reasons Offered*, p. 11.

[84]C.L.R.O., Gaol Committee Papers, Newgate, 1813, fee table; Surrey R.O. QS/2/24, Order Books; 1775–79; Anon., *An Accurate Description of Newgate*, 1724.

[85]Howard, *Lazarettos*, pp. 131–43; John Norris, *Shelburne and Reform*, 1963, pp. 202–29; H.O. 42/10, on organization of Home Office fee system and bureaucracy.

[86]Beds. R.O. QGR/3/1849.

[87]Berks. R.O. Q/SO/24/ f. 38, 1772.

[88]22 Geo. III, cap. 64, x.

[89]Gresham Sykes, *The Society of Captives*, 1958; Donald Cressey, ed., *The Prison: Studies in Institutional Organization and Change*, 1961.

[90]"Report from the Committee ... Appointed to Consider the Several Returns....," April 1, 1779, House of Commons Papers, Geo. III, XXXI, (Scholarly Resources Reprint Series, 1975), pp. 363–91.

[91]C.L.R.O., Gaol Committee, Rough Minute Books, 1760–65; also Misc. Mss. 249.12.

[92]See Schedule B Returns persuant to the Gaol Act, 4 Geo. IV cap. 64, P.P. 1830–31, XII; P.P. 1835, XLIV.

[93]Howard, *State of the Prisons*, appendix.

[94]Robin Evans, "A Rational Plan for Softening the Mind: Prison Architecture in the 18th and 19th Centuries," unpublished Ph.D. thesis, Essex University, 1975, p. 74.

[95]P.P. 1836, XXXV, pp. 86–87.

[96]C.L.R.O., Misc. Mss. 249.12.

[97]Mandeville, *Enquiry*, p. 16.

[98]On counsel for prisoners see Thomas Wontner, *Old Bailey Experience*, 1833; Sydney Smith, "Counsel for Prisoners" in *Works*, II, 1854.

[99]Natalie Davis, "The Reasons of Misrule," in *Society and Culture in Early Modern France*, 1975, p. 97; E. P. Thompson, "Rough Music: Le Charivari anglais," *Annales E.S.C.* 27, 1972.

[100]T. F. Buxton, *An Inquiry Whether Crime and Misery Are Produced or Prevented by Our Present System of Prison Discipline*, 1818, pp. 48–49.

[101]*Hansard*, XXVIII, June 14, 1814, col. 74.

[102]Buxton, *Inquiry*, p. 132.

[103]P.P. 1813–14, IV, pp. 21–24.

[104]As quoted in Anon., *Life of Howard*, 1790, p. 60.

[105]Place Mss., B.M. Add. Mss. 27826.

[106]Buxton, *Inquiry*, pp. 45–50; P.P. 1813–14, IV, pp. 14–24; Howard, *State of the Prisons*, pp. 15–20; P.P. 1836, XXXV (Home District).

[107]John Wesley, *Journal*, 1913 ed., IV, p. 52; p. 416; VII, p. 41; Mandeville, *Enquiry*, pp. 15–20; J.H.C. XXI, 1728, cols. 274–83; Thomas Bray's report is in W. Hepworth Dixon, *John Howard and the Prison World of Europe*, 1849, introduction.

[108]Alexander Wedderburn (Earl of Rosslyn), *Observations on the State of the English Prisons*, 1793, p. 6.

CHAPTER THREE. **Cords of Love, Fetters of Iron: The Ideological Origins of the Penitentiary**

[1] John Howard, *An Account of the Principal Lazarettos of Europe,* 1789, appendix.

[2] C.L.R.O., Misc. Mss. 185.6; Gaol Committee, 1750–55; S. T. Janssen, *A Letter to the Gentlemen of the Committee Appointed . . . for the Rebuilding of Newgate,* 1767.

[3] C.L.R.O., Misc. Mss. 185.6; T. A. Marcus, "The Pattern of the Law," *Architectural Review* 116, October 1954.

[4] C.L.R.O., Misc. Mss. 185.6.

[5] John Pringle, *Observations on the Nature and Cure of Hospital and Jayl Fevers,* 1750; also his *Observations on the Diseases of the Army,* 1775.

[6] J. H. Hutchins, *Jonas Hanway, 1712–1786,* 1940, p. 16.

[7] James Lind, *An Essay on the Most Effectual Means of Preserving the Health of Seamen in the Royal Navy,* 1762; Howard, *Lazarettos,* pp. 181–83.

[8] Hugh Amory, "Henry Fielding and the Criminal Legislation of 1751–2," *Philological Quarterly* 50, no. 2, April 1971, pp. 178–79.

[9] Henry Fielding, *A Proposal for Making Effectual Provision for the Poor,* 1753, p. 71.

[10] *Ibid.,* pp. 153–54.

[11] J.H.C. XXXII, 1770, cols. 878–93.

[12] Numbers committed for trial at the Old Bailey were 70 percent higher in the 1770–1774 period than in the 1760–1764 period. Old Bailey *Proceedings,* 1760–1775.

[13] 14 Geo. III, cap. 59.

[14] C.L.R.O., Misc. Mss., 85.2; Surrey R.O. QS/5/1, Gaol Committee Minute Books, 1769–1779; *Hansard,* XVI, April 10, 1770, cols. 929–43.

[15] Calendar of Home Office Papers, Geo. III, October 25, 1773.

[16] William Eden, *Principles of Penal Law,* 1771, p. 32.

[17] John Aikin, *A View of the Character and Public Services of the late John Howard,* 1792, p. 9.

[18] *Ibid.,* p. 43.

[19] Waldegrave Mss., Howard to Whitbread, Vienna, October 12, December 16, 1786.

[20] John Field, *The Correspondence of John Howard,* 1855, p. 26; Aikin, *View,* p. 46.

[21] Benjamin Rush, *Medical Inquiries and Observations on the Diseases of the Mind,* 1812, p. 355.

[22] Bodleian Misc. Eng. Mss. e. 401, 1789.

[23] *Ibid.*

[24] J. B. Brown, *Memoirs of the Public and Private Life of John Howard, Philanthropist,* 1818, p. 84.

[25] Bodleian Misc. Eng. Mss., e. 399.

[26] Henry Fielding, *An Enquiry into the Causes of the Late Increase of Robbers . . . ,* 1751, p. 71.

[27] W. A. Guy, "John Howard as Statist," *Journal of the Royal Statistical Society* 36, 1873, pp. 3–16.

[28] Howard, *State of the Prisons,* p. 40.

[29] J. P. Vilain, *Mémoire sur les moyens de coriger les malfaiteurs et les faineants,* Brussels (1774), 1841 ed. A copy of Vilain found its way into the library of G. O. Paul, Gloucester prison reformer.

[30]Gloucs. R.O., Paul Mss. Library Inventory D 589.

[31]Emmanuel Chill, "Religion and Mendicity in Seventeenth Century France," *International Review of Social History* 7, 1962, pp. 400–25; H. O. Evennett, *The Spirit of the Counter-Reformation,* 1968.

[32]Aikin, *View,* p. 97.

[33]Anon., *Hanging Not Punishment Enough* (1711), 1812 ed., p. 23.

[34]See W. Hepworth Dixon, *John Howard and the Prison World of Europe,* 1849, introduction.

[35]Bernard Mandeville, *An Enquiry into the Causes of the Frequent Executions at Tyburn,* 1725, p. 16.

[36]Jacob Ilive, *Reasons Offered for the Reformation of the House of Correction, Clerkenwell,* 1757, p. 41; H. Fielding, *A Proposal,* pp. 153–54; Joseph Butler, *Fifteen Sermons,* 1792 ed., pp. 40–65.

[37]Hutchins, *Hanway,* pp. 16–30.

[38]Jonas Hanway, *Solitude in Imprisonment,* 1776, p. 118.

[39]Waldegrave Mss., Howard to Whitbread, May 25, 1788; Aikin, *View,* p. 188.

[40]John Wesley, "The Great Assize," preached before the assizes held at Bedford, March 10, 1758, in *Wesley's Standard Sermons,* ed. by E. H. Sugden (1921), 1945 ed.

[41]Bodleian Misc. Eng. Mss. e. 401, 1789.

[42]Howard, *State of the Prisons,* p. 12.

[43]*Ibid.*

[44]Bodleian Misc. Eng. Mss. e. 401, 1789.

[45]Howard, *Lazarettos,* p. 221.

[46]W. L. Bowles, *Sonnets and Other Poems,* 1794, p. 49.

[47]Elizabeth Isichei, *Victorian Quakers,* 1970, pp. xx–xxi; E. D. Bebb, *Nonconformity and Social and Economic Life, 1660–1800,* 1935, pp. 60–70.

[48]John Bellers, *Proposals for Raising a Colledge of Industry* ... , 1696; Samuel Tuke, *Description of the Retreat, An Institution Near York for Insane Persons of the Society of Friends,* 1813; Philadelphia, *Report* of the Society for Alleviating the Misery of Public Prisons, 1786.

[49]Arthur Raistrick, *Quakers in Science and Industry* (1950), 1968 ed., pp. 290–301.

[50]Howard, *Lazarettos,* p. 133.

[51]See also J. C. Lettsom, *Of the Improvement of Medicine in London on the Basis of Public Good,* 2nd ed., 1775   o his *Hints Respecting the Prison of Newgate,* 1794.

[52]J. M. Good, *A Dissertation on the Diseases of Prisons and Poorhouses,* 1795, p. 27.

[53]Daniel Layard, *Directions to Prevent Jail Distemper,* 1772, pp. 5–6.

[54]Benjamin Rush, *The Autobiography of Benjamin Rush,* ed. by G. W. Corner, 1948, p. 94; David Hartley, *Observations on Man* (1749), 1792 ed.

[55]Thomas Percival, *Medical Ethics,* 1803, pp. 128–29.

[56]Jonas Hanway, *The Neglect of the Effectual Separation of Prisoners and the Want of Good Order and Religious Economy in our Prisons* ... , 1784, p. 4.

[57]William Turner, "An Essay on Crimes and Punishments" (1784), in *Memoirs of the Literary and Philosophical Society of Manchester,* II, 1785; A. E. Musson and Eric Robinson, *Science and Technology in the Industrial Revolution,* 1969, p. 196; Brian Simon, *Studies in the History of Education,* 1960, pp. 18–32.

[58]Neil McKendrick, "Wedgwood and His Friends," *Horizon* 1, no. 5, May 1959, pp. 88–96, 128–130; Arthur Raistrick, *Dynasty of Iron Founders: The Darbys and Coalbrookdale*, 1953, p. 98; Eric Roll, *An Early Experiment in Industrial Organization*, 1930; S. D. Chapman, *The Early Factory Masters*, 1967, p. 196.

[59]R. S. Fitton and A. P. Wadsworth, *The Strutts and the Arkwrights*, 1958, pp. 97–98; Chapman, *Factory Masters*, p. 157; Neil McKendrick, "Josiah Wedgwood and Factory Discipline," *The Historical Journal* 4, no. 1, 1961, pp. 30–55.

[60]P.P. 1815, III, p. 217.

[61]McKendrick, "Wedgwood and Factory Discipline," p. 34.

[62]McKendrick, "Wedgwood and His Friends," pp. 90–94.

[63]Aikin, *View* p. 229; John Fothergill, *Chain of Friendship: Selected Letters of Dr. John Fothergill of London, 1735–1780*, ed. by Betsy C. Corner and Christopher C. Booth, 1971, p. 492; Christopher Wyvill, *Political Papers*, IV, 1794, pp. 236–37; Caroline Robbins, *The Eighteenth Century Commonwealthman*, 1961, p. 354.

[64]John Jebb, *Thoughts on the Construction and Polity of Prisons*, 1785.

[65]Ian Christie, *Wilkes, Wyvill and Reform*, 1962, p. 85; Josiah Dornford, *Nine Letters . . . to the Lord Mayor and Aldermen of London*, 1786; William Smith, *State of the Gaols in London, Westminster . . .* , 1776; on Smith see Surrey R.O. QS 2/1/25; William Blizard, *Desultory Reflections on Police*, 1785; see also D.N.B.

[66]A. G. Olson, *The Radical Duke*, 1961, pp. 52–54; West Sussex R.O. QAP/4, 1778.

[67]Anthony Lincoln, *Some Political and Social Ideas of English Dissent*, 1763–1800, 1938, pp. 24–25.

[68]Aikin, *View*, pp. 58–64.

[69]Robbins, *Commonwealthman*, p. 336.

[70]Bernard Bailyn, *The Ideological Origins of the American Revolution*, 1967, pp. 40–41.

[71]Quoted in Lincoln, *Dissent*, p. 133.

[72]Fothergill, *Chain of Friendship*, p. 492; also his "Considerations Relative to the North American Colonies" (1765) and "An English Freeholder's Address to his Countrymen" (1779) in *Works*, ed. by J. C. Lettsom, 1803, pp. 444–83; Richard Price, *Observations on the Nature of Civil Liberty*, 1776, pp. 14, 73; Joseph Priestley, *An Address to the Dissenters on the Subject of the Difference with America*, 1775.

[73]John Norris, *Shelburne and Reform*, 1963, p. 83; Joseph Priestley, *Memoirs: Written by Himself to the Year 1795*, 1902 ed., pp. 47–54.

[74]Samuel Romilly, *Letters Containing An Account of the Late Revolution in France*, 1792; *Thoughts on the Probable Influence of The French Revolution on Great Britain*, 1790.

[75]Romilly, *Memoirs of the Life of Sir Samuel Romilly Written by Himself . . .* , 1840, I, p. 227.

[76]Priestley, *Memoirs*, p. 47.

[77]Bodleian Misc. Eng. Mss. e. 399.

[78]Aikin, *View*, p. 225.

[79]Robbins, *Commonwealthman*, p. 7; Lincoln, *Dissent*, p. 2.

[80]Hartley, *Observations on Man*, pp. 15–17.

[81]Jeremy Bentham, *Letter to Lord Pelham*, 1802, p. 5; *Panopticon*, 1791, p. 40; Samuel Denne, *Letter to Sir Robert Ladbroke . . .* , 1771, pp. 58–59.

[82]James Burgh, *Political Disquisitions*, III, 1775, pp. 176–78.

[83]Bentham, *Letter to Lord Pelham*, p. 6; Robert Owen, *A New View of Society...*, 1813, p. 95; McKendrick, "Wedgwood and Factory Discipline," p. 34.

[84]Julia Wedgwood, *The Personal Life of Josiah Wedgwood*, 1915, p. 295.

[85]Bentham, *Letter to Lord Pelham*, p. 6.

[86]P. J. G. Cabanis, *Sketch of the Revolutions of Medical Science and Views Relating to its Reform*, 1806, pp. 304–11; Claude Adrien Helvetius, *A Treatise on Man*, 1777 ed., II, pp. 440–47; Cabanis, *Rapports du physique et du moral de l'homme*, 1830 ed., I, p. 455.

[87]Offray de la Mettrie, *Man a Machine*, 1750 ed., pp. 43–44; Harvey Mitchell, "Nature, Knowledge and Power: Hospital Reform, Poverty and Medicine in France, 1774–1800," unpublished paper, 1977, University of British Columbia; Michel Foucault et al., *Les Machines à Guérir: Aux origines de l'hôpital moderne*, 1976; L. S. Greenbaum, "Health Care and Hospital Building in France: Reform Proposals of Dupont de Nemours and Condorcet," *Studies in Voltaire and the Eighteenth Century* 152, no. 2, 1976, pp. 895–930; Jean-Pierre Peter, "Disease and the Sick at the End of the Eighteenth Century," in Robert Forster and Orest Ranum, eds., *Biology of Man in History*, 1975, pp. 85–124.

[88]Philippe Pinel, *A Treatise on Insanity*, 1806 ed.; M. Foucault, *Madness and Civilization*, 1965.

[89]Tuke, *Description of the Retreat*; Kathleen Jones, *Lunacy, Law and Conscience*, 1955; William Parry-Jones, *The Trade in Lunacy*, 1972.

[90]Nathan G. Goodman, *Benjamin Rush: Physician and Citizen*, 1934; Sarah Reidman and C. C. Green, *Benjamin Rush*, 1964.

[91]Benjamin Rush, *An Enquiry into the Influence of Physical Causes Upon the Moral Faculty* (1786), 1839 ed., p. 21.

[92]Rush, *Autobiography*, p. 80; David Rothman, *The Discovery of the Asylum*, 1971, pp. 92–93.

[93]Duke de La Rochefoucauld-Liancourt, *A Comparative View of Mild and Sanguinary Laws*, 1796, p. 20.

[94]Goodman, *Rush*, p. 267.

[95]Hanway, *Defects of Police*, p. xii.

[96]Bentham, *Rationale of Punishment*, p. 28.

[97]G. O. Paul, *Considerations on the Defects of Prisons*, 1784, p. 50.

[98]Turner, "Essay on Crimes and Punishments."

[99]John Locke, *An Essay Concerning Human Understanding*, ed. Peter H. Nidditch, I, iii, 5–12.

[100]Robbins, *Commonwealthman*, p. 14.

[101]Butler, *Fifteen Sermons*, p. 47.

[102]J. L. Axtell, ed., *The Educational Writings of John Locke*, 1968, p. 177.

[103]Quoted in H. Fielding, *A Proposal*, p. 77.

[104]Locke, *The Second Treatise of Government (1698)*, Laslett ed., 1968, II, 8; VI, 85.

[105]Howard, *Lazarettos*, p. 222.

[106]John Brewster, *On the Prevention of Crimes*, 1792, pp. 4–5.

[107]Eden, *Principles*, p. 13; Romilly, *Life*, II, p. 486.

[108]Price, *Observations*, p. 14.

[109]Benjamin Rush, *An Enquiry into the Effects of Public Punishments and Upon Society,* 1787, p. 13; also his *Considerations on the Injustice and Impolicy of Punishing Murder by Death,* 1792.

[110]Price, *Observations,* p. 6; Joseph Priestley, *Lectures on History and General Policy,* 1826 ed., pp. 342–44.

[111]Burgh, *Disquisitions,* p. 216.

[112]John Howard, *The State of the Prisons in England and Wales . . . ,* 1777, p. 39.

[113]*Ibid.,* pp. 39–40.

[114]Brewster, *On the Prevention of Crimes,* pp. 4–5.

[115]Jeremy Bentham, *Rationale of Punishment,* 1830, p. 21; A. C. Ewing, *The Morality of Punishment,* 1929, p. 5; H. L. A. Hart, *Punishment and Responsibility,* 1968, p. 10.

[116]Brewster, *Sermons for Prisons,* 1790, p. 15.

[117]Bentham, *Rationale of Punishment,* p. 82.

[118]Joseph Priestley, *An Essay on the First Principles of Government,* 1768, p. 129; *Lectures on History,* p. 398; William Godwin, *Enquiry Concerning Political Justice,* ed. by K. C. Carter, 1971, p. 68.

[119]The centrality of punishment as the chief instrument of the state is clearly outlined in Locke, *Second Treatise,* I, 6.

[120]Jebb, *Prisons,* p. x; Hutchins, *Hanway,* p. 35.

[121]Society for Bettering the Condition of the Poor, *Reports,* 1798, p. xii; Eileen Yeo, "Social Science and Social Change: A Social History of Social Science and Social Investigation in Britain, 1830–1890," unpublished Ph.D. thesis, University of Sussex, 1972, for discussion of Bernard; David E. Owen, *English Philanthropy, 1660–1960,* 1964, p. 97.

[122]G. O. Paul, *An Address to His Majesty's Justices of the Peace . . . ,* 1809, p. 48.

[123]Howard, *Lazarettos,* p. 174; Beds. R.O. PE 254/1801; Berks. R.O. QAG/3/1; Lancs. R.O. QGV/2/2/1793; for examples of early penitentiary rules.

[124]Bentham, *Panopticon,* p. 39.

[125]Brewster, *On the Prevention of Crimes,* p. 27.

[126]Hanway, *Solitude in Imprisonment,* p. 141.

[127]Mettrie, *Man a Machine,* p. 43.

CHAPTER FOUR. **Preaching Walls: The Penitentiary in Practice**

[1]J.H.C., 1778, XXXVI, cols. 926–32; J.H.C., 1799, XXXVII, cols. 306–14.

[2]J.H.C., XXXVI, 1778, cols. 926–32.

[3]*Proceedings,* Old Bailey, 1760–1794.

[4]J.H.C., 1779, XXXVII, cols. 306–14.

[5]John Howard, *An Account of the Principal Lazarettos of Europe,* 1789, p. 232.

[6]*Proceedings,* Old Bailey, 1775–1785.

[7]J. M. Beattie, "The Pattern of Crime in England: 1660–1800," *Past and Present* 62, 1974, p. 93.

[8]Phyllis Deane and W. A. Cole, *British Economic Growth, 1688–1959,* 1969.

[9]Leon Radzinowicz, *A History of English Criminal Law,* 1947–1956, III, pp. 1–11.

[10]Jonas Hanway, *The Defects of Police . . . ,* 1775, pp. xxii–xxiii.

[11]Hanway, *Solitude in Imprisonment,* 1776, p. 141.

[12]*Ibid.,* p. 63.

[13]Hanway, *Defects of Police*, p. 11.

[14]Patrick Colquhoun, *A Treatise on the Police of the Metropolis*, 1797, p. 32.

[15]William Blizard, *Desultory Reflections on Police*, 1785, p. 30.

[16]For the provenance of the debate on the social effects of luxury see Dudley W. R. Bahlman, *The Moral Revolution of 1688*, 1957; Radzinowicz, *History of Criminal Law*, II, p. 15; Robert Nelson, *An Address to Persons of Quality and Estate*, 1715; Joseph Butler, *Fifteen Sermons*, 1792 ed.; Ellen Ross, "The Debate on Luxury in Eighteenth Century France," unpublished Ph.D. dissertation, University of Chicago, 1975.

[17]Reports of the Committees of the House of Commons, 1715–1801, IX, 1776–1786, Poor Law Returns.

[18]Howard, *Lazarettos*, p. 247.

[19]H.O. 42/4, January 19, 1784.

[20]H.O. 42/3, August 6, 1783.

[21]H.O. 42/3, November 10, 1783.

[22]H.O. 42/4, January 26, 1784.

[23]H.O. 42/5, July 25, 1784; G. O. Paul, *Considerations on the Defects of Prisons*, 1784, pp. 3–12; Gloucs. R.O., R.O.L., C/5, "Proceedings of a Committee ...", 1783.

[24]Blizard, *Desultory Reflections*, p. 5.

[25]S.P. 37/15, September 20, 1781.

[26]H.O. 42/5, December 14, 1784.

[27]H.O. 42/4.

[28]H.O. 42/8, May 23, 1786.

[29]H.O. 42/7, July 20, 1785.

[30]H.O. 42/1, September 23, 1782.

[31]*Proceedings*, Old Bailey, 1780–1785.

[32]P.P. 1818, XVI, p. 183.

[33]*Proceedings*, Old Bailey, 1783, VII.

[34]Martin Madan, *Thoughts on Executive Justice ...*, 1785, p. 137; Samuel Romilly, *Observations on a Late Publication ...*, 1786.

[35]S.P. 37/15, f. 474, September 20, 1781; for recollections of the mass executions of the 1780s see P.P. 1816, V, p. 145.

[36]William Paley, *Principles of Moral and Political Philosophy*, 1811 ed., p. 436.

[37]Barnard Turner and Thomas Skinner, *Account of the Alterations and Amendments in the Office of Sheriff*, 1784, p. 23.

[38]Colquhoun, *Treatise on Police*; also House of Commons Select Committee Report on Finance, 28, 1798, Police and Convict Establishment, pp. 45–51; Radzinowicz, *History of Criminal Law*, III, pp. 270–71.

[39]G. O. Paul, *Address to the Justices of Gloucester*, 1789, pp. v–vi.

[40]See also, Howard, *Lazarettos*, p. 221.

[41]19 Geo. III, cap. 74.

[42]P.P. 1819, VIII, Appendix, Criminal Law Committee.

[43]*Loc. cit.*

[44]H.O. 42/6 2nd Rep. Committee on Transportation, 1785; *Hansard*, XXV, March 16, 1785, col. 391; J.H.C., 1779, XXXVII, cols. 306–14; for Howard's view of the Botany Bay scheme see Waldegrave Mss., Howard to Whitbread, May 25, 1788, January 18, 1787.

[45]H.O. 43/1, August 24, 1782, Wright to Secretary of State.

[46]*Proceedings*, Old Bailey, 1789, VI, IV.

[47]H.O. 42/6.

[48]See Table 1.

[49]Harrowby Mss., Westbrook-Hay Papers, XCIV; Jeremy Bentham, *A View of the Hard Labour Bill*, 1778; Bentham Mss., 116 (a); 19 Geo. III, cap. 74.

[50]John Howard, *The State of the Prisons in England and Wales* ..., 1777, pp. 40–44.

[51]William Blackstone, *Commentaries on the Laws of England* (1769), 1813 ed., IV, p. 437.

[52]Harrowby Mss., Westbrook-Hay Papers, XCIV, f. 38.

[53]*Ibid.*, July 1, 1781, Thomas Bowdler to unnamed correspondent.

[54]H.O. 42/6, January 14, 1785, T. B. Bayley to Secretary Of State.

[55]James Neild, *The State of the Prisons*, 1812, appendix 1.

[56]W. Sussex R.O. QAP/4/WE 1.

[57]*Loc. cit.*

[58]Sidney Webb and Beatrice Webb, *English Prisons Under Local Government*, 1927, pp. 54–55; West Sussex, R.O. QAP/4/2; QAP/5/W 1–7; QAP/5/W 15.

[59]Middlesex R.O. MA/G/GEN, 1790–95.

[60]William Morton Pitt, *A Plan for the Improvement of the Internal Police of Prisons*, 1804.

[61]Thomas Beevor, "Account of the Origins . . . of the Penitentiary at Wymondham in Norfolk," *Annual Register*, 1786, pp. 87–94.

[62]Thomas Percival, *Biographical Memoirs of the late T. B. Bayley*, 1802; H.O. 42/8, January 22, 1786; H.O. 42/4, January 26, 1784.

[63]John Aikin, *Description of the Country from 30 to 40 Miles Round Manchester*, 1795, pp. 201, 285.

[64]*Ibid.*, p. 285.

[65]Bristol R.O. Bright Mss., Papers Relating to the Rebuilding of Newgate, 1788–1795, 11168 (70); Anon., *Address to the Citizens of Bristol Concerning the Repeal of the Obnoxious Jail Bill*, 1792; Anon., *Reply to the Delegates of the Several Parishes*, 1792; for similar dispute in Gloucester see Anon., *Some Observations on the Bill . . . Erecting a Gaol in . . . Gloucester*, 1780. This was the municipal jail, not the county jail erected by Paul.

[66]E. A. L. Moir, "Sir George Onesiphorus Paul," in H. P. R. Finberg, ed., *Gloucestershire Studies*, 1957; Gloucs. R.O. Paul Mss., Sotheron Estcourt Mss.

[67]P.P. 1807, I; P.P. 1813–14, IV, p. 88.

[68]Howard, *State of the Prisons*, "Gloucester."

[69]H.O. 42/3, 20 November 1783; H.O. 42/5, July 25, 1784.

[70]Paul, *Considerations*.

[71]Gloucs. R.O., R.O.L. C/5.

[72]J. R. S. Whiting, "Prison Reforms in Gloucestershire, 1776–1820," unpublished Ph.D. thesis, Bristol University, 1974.

[73]Paul, *Considerations*, p. 8.

[74]P.P. 1810–11, III, p. 44.

[75]G. O. Paul, *An Address to His Majesty's Justices of the Peace* . . . , 1809, p. 80.

[76]Whiting, "Prison Reforms in Gloucestershire," pp. 100–164.

[77]Gloucs. R.O., QAG/2–7.

[78]Howard, *Lazarettos*, p. 169.

[79]Berks, R.O. QAG 3/1; QSO/6–8.

[80]Gloucs. R.O. QGC/11, 1818.

[81]Moir, "G. O. Paul," pp. 212–13.

[82]Gloucs. R.O. QGC/11, 1815.

[83]Paul, *Address* ... (1809), p. 48.

[84]*Ibid.*, p. 53.

[85]Paul, *Considerations,* p. 54.

[86]P.P. 1819, VII, p. 388.

[87]Gloucestershire *General Regulations for the Inspection and Controul of Prisons,* 1790, p. 25.

[88]Gloucs. R.O. QGC/1, 1791.

[89]*General Regulations,* p. 26; also Webb and Webb, *English Prisons,* p. 103, quoting Chester Gaol regulations.

[90]Gloucs. R.O. QAG/11, 1792.

[91]Gloucs. R.O. QAG/12, 1792; QAG/11, 1793, 1794.

[92]Harrowby Mss., XXXIV, Papers Relating to Stafford Gaol, 1793; see J. T. Becher, *A Report on Southwell House of Correction,* 1806, p. 7, for staffing difficulties.

[93]Oxfordshire R.O. QSB 1786, Michaelmas Session.

[94]Robert Owen, *Life of Robert Owen written by himself,* 1857.

[95]Neil McKendrick, "Josiah Wedgwood and Factory Discipline," *The Historical Journal* 4, no. 1, 1961, p. 39.

[96]Gloucs. R.O. QAG/12, 1792.

[97]P.P. 1819, VIII, pp. 386–89; P.P. 1810–11, III, p. 30.

[98]P.P. 1837–38, XXX, 3d. Rep. (Home D.), p. 42.

[99]Paul, *Address to the Justices of Gloucester,* 1789, p. 49.

[100]Paul, *Address* ... (1809), endpaper.

[101]K. G. Ponting, *A History of the West of England Cloth Industry,* 1957, p. 118; Ephraim Lipson, *History of the Woollen and Worsted Industries,* 1921, p. 253; P.P. 1802–03, V, p. 15; P.P. 1806, III, p. 100.

[102]Paul, *Address* ... (1809), pp. 45–46.

[103]*Victoria County History of Gloucester,* 1909, p. 175.

[104]Paul, *Address* ... (1809), p. 129.

[105]Gertrude Himmelfarb, "The Haunted House of Jeremy Bentham," in her *Victorian Minds,* 1968.

[106]Bentham, *Panopticon,* p. 56.

[107]22 Geo. III, cap. 83.

[108]Bentham, *A View,* p. 25.

[109]Bentham, *Panopticon,* p. 1.

[110]P.P. 1810–11, III, pp. 12–15.

CHAPTER FIVE. **Whigs, Jacobins, and the Bastilles: The Penitentiary Under Attack**

[1]Thomas Percival, *Observations on the State of Population in Manchester,* 1789, p. 19.

[2]The Society for Bettering the Condition of the Poor, *Reports,* II, appendix, p. 79.

[3]Elizabeth L. Hutchins and Amy Harrison, *A History of Factory Legislation*, 1911, p. vii; 42 Geo. III, c. 73.

[4]A. W. Coats, "Economic Thought and Poor Law Policy in the Eighteenth Century," *Economic History Review* 13, no. 1, 1960.

[5]F. M. Eden, *The State of the Poor*, 1795, II, pp. 463–71; Arthur Young, *A General View of the Agriculture of Suffolk*, 1794, appendix by Thomas Ruggles.

[6]John Howard, *An Account of the Principal Lazarettos of Europe*, 1789, p. 210.

[7]Joseph Townshend, *A Dissertation on the Poor Laws*, 1786.

[8]Joseph Priestley, *An Essay on the First Principles of Government*, 1768, pp. 65–81.

[9]John Locke, *The Second Treatise of Government* (1698), Laslett ed., 1968, II, 8; IV, 23.

[10]William Godwin, *Enquiry Concerning Political Justice*, ed. by K. C. Carter, 1971, p. 247.

[11]*Ibid.*, p. 247.

[12]*Ibid.*, p. 271.

[13]32 Geo. III. cap. 53; Leon Radzinowicz, *A History of English Criminal Law*, 1947–1956, III, pp. 67–71.

[14]*Hansard*, XXIX, May 23, 1792, cols. 1464–75.

[15]Samuel Romilly, *Observations on a Late Publication* . . . , 1786, p. 102.

[16]Samuel Romilly, *Letters Containing an Account of the Late Revolution in France*, 1792.

[17]D. E. Swift, *J. J. Gurney*, 1962, p. 9.

[18]Gloucs. R.O., Paul Mss., D 589, Paul to Sir W. Guise, April 30, 1809.

[19]Anon., *Gloucester Bastile!!! Pathetic Particulars of a Poor Boy Sentenced to Suffer Seven Years in Solitary Confinement in Gloucester Gaol*, 1792.

[20]G. O. Paul, *An Address* . . . , 1809, appendix 1; Court of King's Bench June 20, 1803, R. vs. Ridgway; for 1808 libel see Gloucs. R.O., Sotheron-Estcourt Mss., D 1571, Paul to Thos. Estcourt, undated.

[21]Simon Maccoby, *English Radicalism, 1786–1832*, 1955, pp. 73–147. For Romilly's trial work see Anon., *The Trial of John Binns . . . for Sedition*, 1797; also E. P. Thompson, *The Making of the English Working Class*, 1963, pp. 80–82.

[22]R. B. Sheridan, *Speeches*, 1842, III, p. 366.

[23]John Binns, *Recollections of the Life of John Binns*, 1854, p. 163.

[24]William Eden, *Principles of Penal Law*, 1771, p. 133; George Rudé, *Hanoverian London*, 1971.

[25]George Rudé, *Wilkes and Liberty*, 1962, p. 52; J. C. Lettsom, *Hints Respecting the Prison of Newgate*, 1794, p. 2, for Lord George Gordon.

[26]Gloucs. R.O. D 2454/1/9; J. R. S. Whiting, "Prison Reforms in Gloucestershire: 1776–1820," Ph.D. thesis, University of Bristol, 1974, p. 19; Thompson, *Making of the English Working Class*, p. 175.

[27]H.O. 43/11, f. 151, 459, 491; Gloucs. R.O. QAG/11, 1801. Binns, *Recollections*, pp. 153–55.

[28]"Gilbert Wakefield," D.N.B.

[29]Wakefield, *Memoirs of the Life of Gilbert Wakefield*, 1804, II, pp. 270–71.

[30]*Ibid.*, p. 274; Dorset R.O. D/60X 49; William Morton Pitt, *A Plan for the Improvement of the Internal Police of Prisons*, 1804; M. B. Weinstock, "Dorchester Model Prison, 1791–1816," in Dorset Natural History and Archaeological Society *Proceedings* 78, 1956.

[31]For Despard see Francis Place, *Autobiography*, ed. by Mary Thale, 1972, p. 142; J.H.C. LIV, 441–67, April 1, 1799; Marianne Elliott, "The Despard Conspiracy Reconsidered," *Past and Present* 75, May 1977, pp. 46–62.

[32]Samuel Glasse, *The Sinner Encouraged to Repentance* ..., 1794, p. 8.

[33]*Ibid.*, p. 16.

[34]H.O. 42/45, October 26, 1798; Anon., *An Impartial Statement of the Cruelties Discovered in Coldbath Fields Prison*, 1800, p. 14.

[35]James Neild, *The State of the Prisons*, 1812, p. 600; P.P. 1814–15, XI, Papers Relating to Gloucester Gaol; Gloucs. R.O. QGC/11, 1809–1818.

[36]London Corresponding Society, *Moral and Political Magazine*, II, January 1797, pp. 26–29, Beinecke Library Coll., Yale Univ. I wish to thank Mr. Edward Thompson for this reference.

[37]J.H.C. LIV, pp. 441–67, April 19, 1799; Middlesex R.O. MJ/SP, 1798, Ap. 130–33.

[38]J.H.C. LIV, pp. 441–67, 1799.

[39]Frank O'Gorman, *The Whig Party and the French Revolution*, 1967; Charles James Fox, *Speeches*, 1815, V, p. 277.

[40]*Hansard*, XXXV, July 22, 1800, cols. 463–67.

[41]Reports from the Committee of Secrecy, 1798–1801, appendix 8, in Reports of the Committees of the House of Commons, 1798.

[42]Middlesex R.O. MA/G/GEN/450, December 1798.

[43]*Morning Chronicle*, December 22, 1798; Anon., *The Secrets of the English Bastille*, 1799, p. 7.

[44]Robert Isaac Wilberforce and Samuel Wilberforce, *The Life of William Wilberforce: By His Sons*, 1839, II, p. 321; Burdett-Coutts Mss., Bodleian Misc. Eng. Hist. Mss., c. 295.

[45]Bodleian Misc. Eng. Hist. Mss. c. 296.

[46]Thomas Hardy, *Memoir*, 1832, p. 15.

[47]"Jacob Bryant," D.N.B.; David E. Owen, *English Philanthropy, 1660–1960*, 1964, p. 93.

[48]J.H.C. LIV, 441–67, April 1799.

[49]"An Impartial Statement"; *The Times*, July 12, 1800.

[50]*The Times*, August 11, 1800; *Morning Chronicle*, August 16, 1800.

[51]Annual Register, XLIV, 1800, pp. 26–27; *Cambridge Intelligencer*, 23 August 1800; *London Observer*, August 17, 1800; *The Times*, August 16, 1800; H.O. 42/50, R. Baker to Secretary of State, August 15, 1800. I wish to thank John Bohstedt for sharing his sources with me.

[52]*The Times*, December 26, 1800.

[53]*The Times*, July 13, 1802.

[54]*Morning Chronicle*, July 20, 1802.

[55]*The Times*, July 14, 1802.

[56]Society for Preserving Liberty and Property Against Republicans and Levellers, *Association Papers*, I, 1793, p. 16.

[57]Hannah More, *Village Politics*, 2nd ed., 1792, p. 5.

[58]Anon., *Considerations on the Late Elections*, 1802, p. 43.

[59]H.O. 42/65, July 18, 1802; *The Times*, July 20, 1802.

[60]*The Times*, July 16, 1802.

[61]M. W. Patterson, *Sir Francis Burdett and His Times*, 1931, I, pp. 55–58.

[62] *The Times,* July 30, 1802; *Annual Register,* XLIV, 1802, pp. 184–86 *Morning Chronicle,* July 30, 1802.

[63]"Alexander Stephens," D.N.B.; Alexander Stephens, *Memoirs of Horne Tooke,* 2 vols., 1805.

[64] *Hansard,* X, Feb. 18, 1808, cols. 662–65; P.P. 1808, IX, Papers Relating to Coldbath Fields.

[65] P.P. 1808, IX; H.O. 42/217.

[66] *Hansard,* X, March 17, 1808.

[67] P.P. 1809, IV: Commission on Coldbath Fields; also H.O. 42/217.

[68] *1811 Dictionary of the Vulgar Tongue,* 1971 ed.

[69] P.P. 1818, VIII, p. 184; G. L. Chesterton, *Revelations of Prison Life,* I, 1856, p. 22.

[70] Henry Mayhew, *Criminal Prisons of London,* 1861, p. 302.

[71]"Paupers' Palace," in *The Penny Satirist,* May 1842.

[72] Quoted in Richard Phillips, *A Letter to the Livery of London,* 1808, p. 253.

[73] P.P. 1816, XVIII, Papers Relating to Petworth. The solitary confinement regime was discredited by the disclosure by H. G. Bennet that a woman had been confined for three years in Petworth and had lost her reason; also *Hansard,* 2nd ser., XXXIV, May 13, 1816.

CHAPTER SIX. **The Politics of Prison Reform in the Peterloo Era**

[1] Frances Cresswell, *A Memoir of Elizabeth Fry,* 1868, pp. 69–70, quoting from a letter of Fry's co-adjutor, Mary Sanderson, to T. F. Buxton.

[2] Elizabeth Fry, *Observations on the Visiting, Superintendence and Government of Female Prisoners,* 1827, p. 61.

[3] James Williams, *An Hour in His Majesty's Gaol of Newgate,* 1820, pp. 20–21; Joseph Lancaster, *Improvements in Education as It Respects the Industrial Classes of the Community,* 3d ed., 1805 (reprint ed., 1973), p. 8.

[4] Cresswell, *Fry,* pp. 86–87; P.P. 1818, VIII, p. 171.

[5] T. F. Buxton, *An Inquiry Whether Crime and Misery Are Produced or Prevented by Our Present System of Prison Discipline,* 1818, p. 127.

[6] Cresswell, *Fry,* pp. 84–85.

[7] Williams, *An Hour,* p. 7.

[8] Gurney Mss., 1/203, E. Fry to J. J. Gurney, 14 November 1818, Friends House London.

[9] Robert Owen, *A New View of Society,* 1813, p. 99.

[10] *Ibid.,* p. 39.

[11] William Allen, *Life,* 3 vols., 1846.

[12] Sarah Hoare, *Memoirs of Samuel Hoare,* 1911.

[13] Alexander Bain, *James Mill,* 1882, p. 147.

[14] Allen, *Life,* I, p. 348.

[15] *Ibid.,* III, p. 199.

[16] E. M. Howse, *Saints in Politics,* 1952; David E. Owen, *English Philanthropy, 1660–1960,* 1964, p. 94.

[17] William Wilberforce, *A Practical View of the Prevailing Religious System of Professed Christians,* 1797, p. 12.

[18] *Ibid.,* p. 196.

[19]Victor Kiernan, "Evangelicalism and the French Revolution," *Past and Present* 1, February 1952.

[20]Wilberforce, *Practical View*, p. 12.

[21]Noel Annan, *Leslie Stephen*, 1951, p. 116.

[22]Elizabeth Isichei, *Victorian Quakers*, 1970, introduction; E. D. Bebb, *Nonconformity and Social and Economic Life, 1660–1800*, 1935.

[23]D. E. Swift, *J. J. Gurney*, 1962, p. 80.

[24]*Ibid.*, pp. 6–7.

[25]*Ibid.*, p. 9.

[26]John Kent, *Elizabeth Fry*, 1962, pp. 17–19.

[27]Elizabeth Fry, *Memoirs*, 2 vols., 1847, I, p. 46.

[28]Swift, *Gurney*, p. 37.

[29]*Ibid.*, p. 87.

[30]Buxton, *Memoirs of Thomas Fowell Buxton*, ed. by C. Buxton, 1866, p. 55.

[31]Buxton, *Memoirs*, p. 43.

[32]Fry, *Memoirs*, I, p. 127.

[33]*Ibid.*, I, February 25, 1799.

[34]*Ibid.*, I, p. 31.

[35]J. J. Gurney, *Notes on a Visit Made to Some of the Prisons in Scotland and the North of England*, 1819, p. 129.

[36]P.P. 1826, XXI, Poor Law Returns.

[37]P.P. 1819, VIII, App. 1; P.P. 1831–32, XXXIII (Criminal Offences).

[38]V. A. C. Gatrell and T. B. Hadden, "Criminal Statistics and their Interpretation," in E. A. Wrigley, ed., *Nineteenth Century Society*, 1972, p. 373.

[39]C.L.R.O., Gaol Committee, Newgate, 1815.

[40]P.P. 1813–14, IV, p. 64.

[41]Buxton, *Inquiry*, p. 30.

[42]*Ibid.*, p. 28.

[43]C.L.R.O., Gaol Committee, Coroners' Returns, Newgate, 1800–1829.

[44]Prison Discipline Society, *Reports*, I, p. vii; also P.P. 1818, XVI (Criminal Tables).

[45]P.P. 1819, VII, p. 320.

[46]P.P. 1813–14, IV, p. 138.

[47]Gurney, *Notes*, pp. 81–82.

[48]London Committee for Investigating the Causes of the Increase in Juvenile Delinquency, *Report*, 1816, p. 12.

[49]Basil Montague, *The Case of Dennis Shiel Condemned to Die and Now Sentenced to be Transported for Life to Botany Bay*, 1810; for the invention of the letter see William Tallack, *Peter Bedford*, 1865, p. 17.

[50]W. L. Bowles, *Thoughts on the Increase of Crimes ...*, 1819, p. 38.

[51]George Holford, *Thoughts on the Criminal Prisons of this Country*, 1821, p. 173.

[52]Basil Montague, *Some Thoughts upon Liberty and the Rights of Englishmen*, 1819, p. 1.

[53]E. P. Thompson, The *Making of the English Working Class*, 1963, pp. 659–69, 681–91.

[54]J. M. Cobbett and J. P. Cobbett, eds., *Selections from Cobbett's Political Works*, 1842, V, p. 43.

[55] *The Black Dwarf,* May 31, 1820.

[56] *The Black Dwarf,* March 24, 1819.

[57] George Pellew, *Life and Correspondence of Viscount Sidmouth,* 1847, III, ch. 32; Thompson, *Making of the English Working Class,* ch. 15; Samuel Bamford, *An Account of the Arrest and Imprisonment of Samuel Bamford,* 1817.

[58] Hansard, XXXVII, January–February 1818.

[59] *The Black Dwarf,* IV, May 17, 1820.

[60] *Hansard,* XXXVI, June 20, 1817.

[61] Henry Hunt, *Investigation at Ilchester Gaol . . . ,* 1821; Hunt, *Peep into a Prison or Inside of Ilchester Bastille,* 1821.

[62] Hunt, *Peep into a Prison,* p. 21; T. F. Buxton, *Appendix to the First Edition of an Inquiry . . . Containing an Account of the Prisons at Ilchester and Bristol,* 1818.

[63] P.P. 1822, XI, p. 8.

[64] P.P. 1817, IV, p. 5.

[65] H.O. 40/3 pt. 3, f. 36.

[66] H.O. 40/9 f. 463–65.

[67] Buxton, *Memoirs,* p. 95.

[68] Donald Read, *Peterloo,* 1958, ch. 13; *Hansard,* XXXVI, June 3, 1817, cols. 87–134.

[69] Quoted in Read, *Peterloo,* pp. 167–68; see also C.L.R.O., Gaol Committee, Petition of Lord Mayor and Aldermen of London to the Secretary of State, 1819.

[70] *The Philanthropist,* V, 1815, p. 224.

[71] Buxton, *Inquiry,* p. 70.

[72] *The Philanthropist,* II, 1812, p. 3.

[73] Allen, *Life,* I, p. 147; Tallack, *Bedford,* pp. 11–31; Buxton, *Memoirs,* pp. 60–61.

[74] Buxton, *Memoirs,* p. 64; T. F. Buxton, *Speech . . . on the Subject of Distress in Spitalfields,* 1816.

[75] H.O. 40/3/pt. 3, f. 32; H.O. 40/9/ f. 71. Cobbett's Letter to the Lord Mayor of London, *Cobbett's Register,* December 7, 1816.

[76] Prison Discipline Society, *Reports,* IV, p. 16.

[77] *The Times,* September 21, 1818; C.L.R.O. Newgate Gaol Committee, 1818.

[78] Holford, *Thoughts,* p. 173.

[79] J. R. Poynter, *Society and Pauperism,* 1969; O. J. Dunlop, *English Apprenticeship and Child Labour: A History,* 1912; Karl Polanyi, *The Great Transformation,* 1944.

[80] Prison Discipline Society, *Rules,* 1820, p. iii.

[81] *The Philanthropist,* II, 1812, p. 2.

[82] Prison Discipline Society, *Reports,* II, p. 30.

[83] 4 Geo. IV cap. 64.

[84] P.P. 1819, VII, p. 6.

[85] *Hansard,* XXXIX, March 2, 1819, col. 812.

[86] P.P. 1819, VII, p. 9.

[87] Samuel Romilly, *Memoirs of the Life of Sir Samuel Romilly Written By Himself . . . ,* 1840, II, p. 486; P.P. 1818, VIII, p. 178.

[88] *Hansard,* XIX, March 29, 1811, cols. 637–38.

[89] Samuel Romilly, *Observations on the Criminal Law of England,* 1810, p. 15.

[90] *Hansard,* XVI, May 1, 1810, cols. 163–79.

[91] P.P. 1810–11, III; Harrowby Mss., Westbrook-Hay Papers, XCV–XCVIII.

[92] *Hansard,* XVI, May 9, 1810, col. 943; Harrowby Mss., XCVIII, f. 209.

⁹³P.P. 1819, VIII, p. 109; P.P. 1818, VIII, p. 171.

⁹⁴K. K. McNab, "Aspects of the History of Crime in England and Wales, 1805–1860," Ph.D. thesis, University of Sussex, 1965, p. 94.

⁹⁵George Holford, *A Short Vindication of the General Penitentiary at Millbank,* 1822.

⁹⁶Arthur Griffiths, *Memorials of Millbank,* 1884, p. 27.

⁹⁷P.P. 1817, XVI, p. 14.

⁹⁸Griffiths, *Millbank,* pp. 49, 106.

⁹⁹*Ibid.,* p. 151.

¹⁰⁰H.O. 20/3, March 3, 1835, Whitworth Russell to Home Secretary.

¹⁰¹P.P. 1828, XX; 7 and 8 Geo. IV, cap. 33; P.P. 1831–32, XXXIII, p. 19 (Corporal Punishment).

¹⁰²Griffiths, *Millbank,* p. 47.

CHAPTER SEVEN. **Prisons, the State, and the Labor Market, 1820–1842**

¹E. P. Thompson, The *Making of the English Working Class,* 1963, p. 700.

²Diary of William Dyott, of Freeford near Litchfield, July 5, October 4, 1828, Staffordshire R.O.; for similar attitudes to Fry see Duke of Richmond Papers, Goodwood Mss., West Sussex R.O. 1579/447, Richmond to Lord Stanley, 1835, no date.

³C. C. Western, *Remarks Upon Prison Discipline,* 1821, p. 54.

⁴P.P. 1828, VI (Commitments and Convictions), p. 15.

⁵P.P. 1831, VII, p. 40.

⁶Dyott Diary, Staffs. R.O.

⁷P.P. 1823, V, p. 114.

⁸P.P. 1823, V. p. 125.

⁹P.P. 1823, V, p. 125.

¹⁰P.P. 1822, XXII (Millbank Committee).

¹¹P.P. 1823, V, p. 130.

¹²*The Times,* July 11, July 19, 1823.

¹³P.P. 1823, V, p. 56.

¹⁴P.P. 1824, IV, p. 44.

¹⁵H.O. 158/1, January 27, 1843, Home Office Circular.

¹⁶*Reports* of the Society for the Improvement of Prison Discipline, 1818.

¹⁷Sydney Smith, "Prisons," in *Works,* 1854, II, p. 259.

¹⁸P.P. 1835, XII, 3d Report, p. 282.

¹⁹P.P. 1824, XIX, Statements Relating to Treadwheels.

²⁰H.O. 44/14, f. 30, f. 33, f. 7, f. 35; J. I. Briscoe, *A Letter on the Nature and Effects of the Treadwheel,* 1824; John Cox Hippisley, *Prison Labour,* 1823; P.P. 1825, XXIII (570), p. 3; J. M. Good, "Letter to Sir John Cox Hippisley on the Mischiefs Incidental to the Treadwheel," *The Pamphleteer,* XXIII, 1824.

²¹P.P. 1825, XXIII, p. 8.

²²4 Geo. IV, cap. 64.

²³P.P. 1835, XI, p. 445.

²⁴P.P. 1835, XI, p. 448.

²⁵Henry Mayhew, *The Criminal Prisons of London,* 1861, pp. 280–87; P.P. 1825, XXIII, Schedule B, p. 168; P.P. 1835, XLIV, pp. 153–55.

²⁶P.P. 1825, XXIII, Schedule B, p. 168; P.P. 1835, XLIV, pp. 153–155.

[27]Mayhew, *Criminal Prisons*, p. 163; Anon., *Five Years' Penal Servitude by One Who Has Endured It*, 1878, p. 180.

[28]P.P. 1835, 2nd Rep., p. 339.

[29]V. A. C. Gatrell and T. B. Hadden, "Criminal Statistics and their Interpretation," in E. A. Wrigley, ed., *Nineteenth Century Society*, 1972, p. 373.

[30]P.P. 1831–32, XXXIII, p. 5 (Criminal Returns, London and Middlesex).

[31]P.P. 1834, XLVI, Appendix 1 (Crawford's Report).

[32]P.P. 1819, VIII, Appendix to Report from Select Committee on Criminal Laws; P.P. 1826–27, XIX, P.P. 1831–32, XXXIII, Criminal Returns; P.P. 1839, XXI, 4th Rep. (Prison Insp.), Appendix.

[33]P.P. 1824, VI, p. 31; G. E. Mingay, "The Agricultural Revolution in English History: A Reconsideration," in W. E. Minchinton, ed., *Essays in Agrarian History*, 1968, II; E. J. Hobsbawm and George Rudé, *Captain Swing*, 1969, p. 43; P.P. 1828, VI, p. 23; P.P. 1826–27, VI, p. 10.

[34]P.P. 1828, VI, p. 8 (Commitments and Convictions).

[35]P.P. 1824, VI, p. 31.

[36]P.P. 1831–32, XXXIII (Gaol Act Returns), "Winchester."

[37]P.P. 1824, VI, p. 57.

[38]P.P. 1834, XXVII, pp. 40–41.

[39]P.P. 1834, XXVII, p. 23.

[40]P.P. 1824, VI, p. 35.

[41]P.P. 1824, VI, p. 3.

[42]P.P. 1824, VI, p. 4.

[43]P.P. 1828, VI, p. 3 (Criminal Commitments); also J. E. Wilmot, *A Letter to the Magistrates of England on the Increase of Crime*, 1827.

[44]P.P. 1826–27, V (Emigration), p. 3; P.P. 1828, VI, p. 8.

[45]P.P. 1828, VI, p. 48 (Metropolitan Police); P.P. 1816, V, p. 143; P.P. 1817, VII, pp. 362, 425–31.

[46]G. Stedman Jones, *Outcast London*, 1971. The best contemporary account of the London casual labor market, but for the period around 1850, is of course Mayhew's *London Labour and the London Poor*, 1851, II, pp. 297–335.

[47]Hobsbawm and Rudé, *Captain Swing*, p. 47.

[48]7 and 8 Geo. IV, cap. 29; 1 and 2 Wm. IV, cap. 32; 9 Geo. IV, cap. 31; 1 Geo. IV, cap. 56.

[49]P.P. 1828, VI, p. 4 (Commitments and Convictions); P.P. 1826–27, VI, p. 8; P.P. 1828, VI, p. 13 (Commitments and Convictions); P.P. 1835, XI, 2nd, p. 18; P.P. 1837–38, XXX, 3d Rep., p. 103; P.P. 1828, VI, p. 16 (Commitments and Convictions); *Morning Chronicle*, June 2, 1824, in Place Mss. Newspaper Cuttings, B. M. Add. Mss. 27826, f. 207.

[50]P.P. 1816, V, p. 9.

[51]P.P. 1837–38, XLVII (Statement of Crime in the Metropolis).

[52]K. K. McNab, "Aspects of the History of Crime in England and Wales, 1805–1860," Ph.D. thesis, University of Sussex, 1965, pp. 237, 291; Chadwick Mss., Univ. of London, Box 1, 1831, Memo on the New Police; P.P. 1838, XLIII (Criminal Statistics).

[53]P.P. 1834, XLVI, App., p. 192.

[54]P.P. 1826, XXIV, Schedule B, p. 156; P.P. 1833, XXVIII, Schedule B, p. 157.

[55]Mayhew, *Criminal Prisons*, p. 341.

[56] *Ibid.*, p. 342.

[57] Mepol 4/6 (Complaints against the Police); H.O. 45/6594 and 4837; H.O. 45/1892; H.O. 45/5694; W. L. Burn, *The Age of Equipoise*, 1964, p. 153.

[58] P.P. 1836–37, VI, p. 5; see also P.P. 1839, XXI, 4th, Home Dist., p. ii.

[59] Sergeant Adams, *A Letter to Benjamin Hawes*, 1838, p. 36.

[60] *Report*, Prison Discipline Society, 1827, pp. 14–28; P.P. 1831–32, VII, pp. 7, 115; Great Britain, *First Report of the Constabulary Commissioners*, 1839, p. 331; P.P. 1835, XI, p. 15.

[61] P.P. 1841, Sess. 2, IV, 6th Rep., p. 285.

[62] P.P. 1836, XXV, p. 86; pp. 50–68 (Northern Dist.); P.P. 1841, Ses. 2, IV, 6th (Home District), p. 62; P.P. 1837, XXXII, 2nd Rep. (Home District), p. 181.

[63] H.O. 20/3, June 9, 1836; H.O. 20/4, June 12, 1837; H.O. 20/5, August 15, 1837.

[64] G. L. Chesterton, *Revelations of Prison Life*, 1856, I, p. 22.

[65] S. H. Palmer, "Police and Protest in England and Ireland, 1780–1850; The Origins of the Modern Police Forces," Ph.D. thesis, Harvard University, 1973, p. 621; Norman Gash, *Mr. Secretary Peel*, 1961, pp. 312–13, 495–97.

[66] Arthur Griffiths, *Memorials of Millbank*, 1884, p. 154.

[67] W. L. Clay, *The Prison Chaplain: Memoirs of the Reverend John Clay*, 1867, p. 113.

[68] Robert Southey, *Letters from England*, 1807, p. 106; see usage at Millbank, P.P. 1817, XVI.

[69] John Howard, *The State of the Prisons in England and Wales* ..., 1777, p. 40; also E. Melling, ed., *Kentish Sources*, 1959, IV, p. 97.

[70] John Jebb, *Thoughts on the Construction and Polity of Prisons*, 1785, p. 6.

[71] P.P. 1837, XXXII, 2nd Rep. (Northern and Eastern District), p. 4.

[72] Chesterton, *Revelations of Prison Life*, pp. 56–57.

[73] *Ibid.*, pp. 86–88; P.P. 1831, VII, pp. 32–39; P.P. 1835, XI, pp. 245–47.

[74] Middlesex R.O. MA/G/GEN, 1243, 1842, f. 34.

[75] Goodwood Mss., West Sussex R.O., 1572, April 17, 1835.

[76] H.O. 45/6099; P.P. 1834, XVI, p. 10.

[77] P.P. 1834, XVI, p. 7.

[78] *Morning Chronicle*, November 4, 1830, in Place Mss. Newspaper Clippings, vol. 31, B.M., November 1830; P.P. 1833, XIII (Coldbath Fields Meeting).

[79] H.O. 20/2, March 1835.

[80] David Rothman, *The Discovery of the Asylum*, 1971, ch. 4; Boston Prison Discipline Society *Seventh Annual Report*, 1832, p. 68. H.O. 20/8, January 30, 1839, Jebb to Home Secretary.

[81] Basil Hall, *Travels in North America*, 1829, II, pp. 58, p. 352.

[82] P.P. 1834, XLVI, pp. 19, 39.

[83] P.P. 1835, XI, 1st Rep., p. 12.

[84] P.P. 1837–38, XXX, 3d Rep. (Home District), p. 42.

[85] H.O. 20/2, March 1835, Whitworth Russell to Home Secretary.

[86] P.P. 1831–32, VII, pp. 47–48.

[87] P.P. 1843, XXIX, p. 3.

[88] Peter Laurie, *Prison Discipline and Secondary Punishments* ..., 1837, p. 2.

[89] Charles Dickens, *American Notes for General Circulation*, 1850, ch. 7, p. 68.

[90]P.P. 1837–38, XXI, 3d Rep. (Southern and Western District), p. 3; P.P. 1837–38, XXI, 3d Rep. (Northern and Eastern District), pp. 4–5.

[91]P.P. 1839, XXII, 4th Rep. (Northern and Eastern District), p. ix.

[92]H.O. 45/1585.

[93]Clay, *Prison Chaplain*, p. 386.

[94]P.P. 1851, XXVIII, p. 24; George Holford, *Thoughts on the Criminal Prisons of this Country*, 1821, p. 171.

[95]Mayhew, *Criminal Prisons*, p. 139.

[96]*Ibid.*, pp. 280–87.

[97]Jebb Papers (London School of Economics), Box 2, September 23, 1856, Earl of Chichester to Home Secretary.

[98]P/COM/2/85, f. 31.

[99]P/COM/2/85, 635; P/COM/2/87, f. 1364; P/COM/2/86, f. 163.

[100]Goodwood Mss., 1662/1846.

[101]H.O. 21/4, January 20, 1848; U. R. Q. Henriques, "The Rise and Decline of the Separate System of Prison Discipline," *Past and Present* 54, 1972, p. 86.

[102]P/COM/2/89, November 27, 1859.

[103]Joseph Kingsmill, *Chapters on Prisons and Prisoners*, 1854.

[104]Charles Dickens, *David Copperfield*, ch. 61.

[105]P.P. 1859, XXVI, p. xix.

[106]*Hansard*, 3d ser., XXVII, March 23, 1837, col. 728; P.P. 1856, XVII, p. 106.

[107]H.O. 12/4/362; H.O. 12/3015; P.P. 1854–55, XXV, pp. 15–16.

[108]P.P. 1862, XXV, pp. 12–14; P.P. 1857–58, XXIX, p. 83.

[109]*The Times*, April 17, 1850, October 20, 1853; Mary Carpenter, *Our Convicts*, 1864, I, p. 3; C. B. Adderly, *Transportation Not Necessary*, 1851; P.P. 1857–58, LVII, p. xvii; *Hansard*, 3d ser., CXXVII, May 10, 1853, col. 14.

[110]*Morning Chronicle*, March 14, 1856, January 28, 1857; *The Times*, January 28, 1857.

[111]*Morning Chronicle*, January 28, 1857.

[112]P.P. 1854–55, XXV; H.O. 12/108/24628; H.O. 12/99/18903; H.O. 12/100/19512; 14 and 15 Vic., cap. 19; 16 and 17 Vic., cap. 99; 18 and 19 Vic., cap. 126.

[113]P.P. 1854, XXXIII, p. 87; P.P. 1854–55, XXV, p. 37; H.O. 12/4/362.

[114]P.P. 1856, XXXV, p. 79; Mayhew, *Criminal Prisons*, pp. 180–82; P.P. 1860, XXV, pp. 58, 258; P.P. 1861, XXX, p. 71; P.P. 1863, IX, p. 369.

[115]P.P. 1859, XIII, p. 306.

[116]P.P. 1859, XIII, p. 308.

[117]20 and 21 Vic., cap. 3.

[118]*The Times*, January 19, February 13, March 26, 1861; P.P. 1862, XXV, pp. 12, 18.

[119]P.P. 1863, XXI, vol. 2, p. 130; P.P. 1865, XXV, pp. 6–7, 88.

[120]Mepol 2/172; Mepol 2/186; H.O. 45/9509/16260; H.O. 45/9568/84847.

[121]P.P. 1893–94, LXXII (Interdepartmental Committee on Criminal Identification); H.O. 12/184/85459; H.O. 12/190/90611.

[122]P.P. 1863, XXI, vol. 1, p. 88.

[123]Home Office, Prison Department, People in Prison, London: H.M.S.O., Cmnd. 4214, 1969.

CONCLUSION

[1] P.P. 1854, XXX, p. x; P.P. 1854, XXXIV, p. v; P.P. 1850, XVI, pp. 233–36.

[2] Gustave de Beaumont and Alexis de Tocqueville, *On the Penitentiary System in the United States and Its Application in France* (1835), 1964 ed., p. 79; see also Christopher Lasch, "The Discovery of the Asylum," in his *The World of Nations*, 1973, p. 17.

[3] David Rothman, *The Discovery of the Asylum*, 1971, introduction.

[4] Andrew Scull, *Decarceration: Community Treatment and the Deviant, A Radical View*, 1977, pp. 46, 68.

[5] Norval Morris, *The Future of Imprisonment*, 1974, ch. 4.

[6] Scull, *Decarceration*, ch. 4; the phrase "carceral archipelago" is Michel Foucault's. See his *Discipline and Punish: The Origins of the Prison*, 1978, pp. 293–308.

[7] Christopher Lasch, "Review of Gail Sheehy's *Passages*," *New York Review of Books*, October 28, 1976.

Bibliography of Manuscript Sources

A. Private Papers

Bentham Mss.
  University College, London
  Panopticon Papers, Boxes 107–21.

Bright Mss.
  Bristol Record Office, Bristol
  Papers Relating to the Rebuilding of Newgate, 1788–1795.

Burdett Mss.
  Bodleian Library, Oxford
  Misc. Eng. Hist. Mss., c. 295–96, Papers Relating to Coldbath Fields Prison.

Chadwick Mss.
  University College, London
  Boxes 1–4, 11–13, 16, 17. Notes, Memoranda, and Clippings on Police, Crime and the Constabulary Commissioners.

Goodwood Mss.
  West Sussex Record Office, Chichester
  Correspondence of the 5th Duke of Richmond, 1835–1842.
  Mss. 618, 1571–89; 1649; 1662.

Gurney Mss.
  Library of the Religious Society of Friends, London
  Correspondence of J. J. Gurney and Elizabeth Fry,
  1817–1838; 1/203–3/835.

Harrowby Mss.
In the possession of the Earl of Harrowby, Sandon Hall, Staffordshire
Westbrook-Hay Papers, vols. 94–101; vol. 34, Papers on Stafford Gaol, 1793–94.

Howard Mss.
Bodleian Library, Oxford
Misc. Eng. Hist. Mss., c. 332, 399, 400–1; Notes and Correspondence of John
Howard, 1770–1789.

Jebb Mss.
London School of Economics, London
Papers and Correspondence of Joshua Jebb, 1842–1862.
Boxes 1–11.

Paul Mss.
Gloucestershire Record Office, Gloucester
Papers of Sir G. O. Paul, 1777–1818.

Place Mss.
British Museum, London
B. M. Add. Mss. 27826. Papers of Francis Place on Crime and the London
Working Class.

Waldegrave Mss.
In the possession of Earl Waldegrave, Chewton House, Chewton Mendip,
Somerset
Whitbread-Howard Correspondence, 1787–1789.

Whitbread Mss.
Bedfordshire Record Office, Bedford
Correspondence of Samuel Whitbread and John Howard, 1785–1789.

Wilberforce Mss.
Bodleian Library, Oxford
Misc. Eng. Hist. Mss., d. 13–17; c 3.

B. Quarter Sessions Records

Bedfordshire Record Office, Bedford:
QGE/1; QGR/1–5; QSR, 1819, 1827, 1834; W/1 4962–5008; QSS, QSM, 1780–1820.

Berkshire Record Office, Reading:
QAG/3/1; QSO/2–8; D/EX/343/1–5.

City of London Record Office, London:
Gaol Committee Papers, 1813–1819; Gaol Committee Rough Minutes, 1790–1791; Misc. Mss. 185.2: Newgate Gaol Committee, 1755–1762; Misc. Mss. 54.8; 249.12; 183.3; 185.6.

Dorset Record Office, Dorchester:
D 60 X 49: Papers Relating to a Complaint Against the Gaoler, 1804.

Gloucestershire Record Office, Gloucester:
QAG/1–11; 30; 34; Sotheron Estcourt Mss., D 1571; R.O.L. C/5; QGC/1; QSG, 1770–1795.

Lancashire Record Office, Preston:
QGV 2/2, 1793.

Middlesex Record Office, London:
MA/G/GEN/441, 450, 750–56; 1187 a–b; 1243; 1269; MA/G/CBF/201 a–d;
MSP/1798/Ap 131 a; MJ/OC 24–26.

Oxfordshire Record Office, Oxford:
QSM 1773–1784; QSB 1784–1786.

Staffordshire Record Office, Stafford:
QSB 1785–1787.

Surrey Record Office, Kingston:
QS/2/1/24–26; QS/5/1.

West Sussex Record Office, Chichester:
QAP/4–5.

C. Public Record Office

1. State Papers, Domestic: 1761–1786

S.P. 37/11–15; 23–7	Letters and Papers, 1775–1784
S.P. 44/91–96	Criminal Papers, 1770–1782
S.P. 44/143	Letter Book, 1775–1782
S.P. 44/144	Entry Book, 1761–1786

2. Home Office Papers

H.O. 12	Criminal Papers, 1849–1871
H.O. 14/1–37	Criminal Papers, Register, 1849–1871
H.O. 17/1	Criminal: Misc. Petitions, 1819–1825
H.O. 18/378–81	Criminal: Misc. Petitions, 1853–1854
H.O. 20/1–12	Prison Inspectors, Correspondence and Papers, 1835–1847
H.O. 21/1–13	Criminal Entry Books, Convict Prisons, 1847–1849
H.O. 22/1–17	Criminal: Prisons, Entry Books, Ser. II, 1849–1871
H.O. 25/13	Criminal: Letter Book, 1870–1871
H.O. 42/1–17; 42-5; 92–104; 158–72	Domestic, Disturbances: Letters and Papers, 1782–1817
H.O. 43/1,2,9,10,16,26	Domestic Entry Book, 1782–1817
H.O. 44/40–46	Misc. Unclass. Papers, 1782–1813
H.O. 45	Registered Papers, Domestic, 1841–1886
H.O. 59/8	Police Courts and Magistrates Correspondence, 1838
H.O. 62/1	Daily Police Reports, 1828
H.O. 65/9	Police Entry Book, 1870–1871
H.O. 73/16	Lords' Committee on the Gaols, 1835–1837; Papers of W. A. Miles
H.O. 144	Restricted Papers, New Series, 1870–1890
H.O. 158/1–3	Home Office Circulars, 1835–1875

3. Prison Commission Records

P/COM/2/84–89	Pentonville Minute Books, 1842–1850
P/COM/2/90	Pentonville Commissioners' Books, 1843–1854
P/COM/2/91–92	Pentonville Directors' Books, 1854–1885
P/COM/2/93	Visitors' Book, 1862–1863
P/COM/2/94	Visitors' Minute Book, 1842–1849
P/COM/2/96–97	Visitors' Order Book, 1842–1850
P/COM/2/164	Millbank Suggestion Book, 1855–1863
P/COM/2/290	Wandsworth Prisoners' Register, 1870
P/COM/2/353	Chaplain's Journal, 1846–1851

ABOUT THE AUTHOR

Michael Ignatieff has taught history at
the University of British Columbia, and
is currently a senior research fellow at
King's College, Cambridge.

Index